Culturally Responsive Teaching for Multilingual Learners

We dedicate this book to all the educators who work tirelessly for equitable and socially just education for their students and to the teachers, administrators, and educational support staff who faced the unexpected challenge of distance learning with tenacity, creativity, and empathy. Thank you for all you do.

Culturally Responsive Teaching for Multilingual Learners

Tools for Equity

Sydney Snyder and Diane Staehr Fenner

Foreword by Ayanna Cooper
Sketchnotes by Kate Monick

FOR INFORMATION:

Corwin

A SAGE Company

2455 Teller Road

Thousand Oaks, California 91320

(800) 233-9936

www.corwin.com

SAGE Publications Ltd.

1 Oliver's Yard

55 City Road

London EC1Y 1SP

United Kingdom

SAGE Publications India Pvt. Ltd.

B 1/I 1 Mohan Cooperative Industrial Area

Mathura Road, New Delhi 110 044

India

SAGE Publications Asia-Pacific Pte. Ltd.

18 Cross Street #10-10/11/12

China Square Central

Singapore 048423

Program Director and Publisher: Dan Alpert

Senior Content
   Development Editor: Lucas Schleicher

Associate Content
   Development Editor: Mia Rodriguez

Production Editor: Tori Mirsadjadi

Copy Editor: Amy Hanquist Harris

Typesetter: C&M Digitals (P) Ltd.

Proofreader: Dennis Webb

Indexer: Integra

Cover Designer: Gail Buschman

Marketing Managers: Sharon Pendergast
                     and Maura Sullivan

Copyright © 2021 by Corwin Press, Inc.

All rights reserved. Except as permitted by U.S. copyright law, no part of this work may be reproduced or distributed in any form or by any means, or stored in a database or retrieval system, without permission in writing from the publisher.

When forms and sample documents appearing in this work are intended for reproduction, they will be marked as such. Reproduction of their use is authorized for educational use by educators, local school sites, and/or noncommercial or nonprofit entities that have purchased the book.

All third-party trademarks referenced or depicted herein are included solely for the purpose of illustration and are the property of their respective owners. Reference to these trademarks in no way indicates any relationship with, or endorsement by, the trademark owner.

Printed in the United States of America

Library of Congress Cataloging-in-Publication Data

Names: Snyder, Sydney, author. | Fenner, Diane Staehr, author.

Title: Culturally responsive teaching for multilingual learners : tools for equity / Sydney Cail Snyder and Diane Staehr Fenner.

Description: Thousand Oaks, California : Corwin, 2021. | Includes bibliographical references and index.

Identifiers: LCCN 2020045740 | ISBN 9781544390253 (paperback) | ISBN 9781071817223 (epub) | ISBN 9781071817247 (epub) | ISBN 9781071817254 (pdf)

Subjects: LCSH: Culturally relevant pedagogy—United States. | English language—Study and teaching—Foreign speakers—Social aspects. | Multilingualism—United States.

Classification: LCC LC1099.3 .S626 2021 | DDC 370.1170973—dc23

LC record available at https://lccn.loc.gov/2020045740

This book is printed on acid-free paper.

21 22 23 24 25 10 9 8 7 6 5

DISCLAIMER: This book may direct you to access third-party content via web links, QR codes, or other scannable technologies, which are provided for your reference by the author(s). Corwin makes no guarantee that such third-party content will be available for your use and encourages you to review the terms and conditions of such third-party content. Corwin takes no responsibility and assumes no liability for your use of any third-party content, nor does Corwin approve, sponsor, endorse, verify, or certify such third-party content.

Contents

Note From the Publisher: The authors have provided video and web content throughout the book that is available to you through QR (quick response) codes. To read a QR code, you must have a smartphone or tablet with a camera. We recommend that you download a QR code reader app that is made specifically for your phone or tablet brand.

Videos may also be accessed at **https://resources.corwin.com/ CulturallyResponsiveTeaching**

Use this hashtag for book discussions on Twitter: #CRTforMLs

Foreword

by Ayanna Cooper

Culture—what is it, exactly? What is equity? How do we define them? How similar or different are our definitions? More important than how we define them is what we do with them: how we preserve and respect them. How are culture and equity related to culturally responsive teaching? These are some of the questions posed in this book, along with answers that help move readers from understanding to unpacking the work that needs to be done.

Recent events have led us to reexamine our lives, our morals, and our identities as part of society. Between a global pandemic and the revitalization of the Black Lives Matter movement, access, equity, and compassion have weighed heavily on the hearts and minds of people who want to contribute positively to where we, as a people, are now and where we hope to be in the future. In striving to make positive contributions, it is important for educators of all students, but especially those who are from linguistically diverse backgrounds, to engage in continued learning. The exploration of culture and how it defines us is a never-ending journey that enriches who we are and how we engage with the world. Sydney Snyder and Diane Staehr Fenner provide this book to aid educators in critical reflection while equipping them with tools that will help them shape themselves and their learning communities to be more diverse, inclusive, and equitable.

GETTING COMFORTABLE WITH BEING UNCOMFORTABLE

Years ago, I had the opportunity to teach an undergraduate Diversity in Education course. I remember being excited for the semester to start and to meet my students. I also remember a department chair warning me that this particular course was difficult to teach and that students could be resistant. With that warning in mind, I wanted to be prepared for a potentially unreceptive environment; I wanted to find a fun and relevant way to facilitate an ice breaker.

The ice breaker started off with me having everyone, myself included, take off their shoes and put them on the opposite foot. My students' footwear included high heels, flip flops, cowboy boots, and tennis shoes. I asked them to do a couple of stomps, as if marching in place; balance on one foot, then the other; spin around to the left and then to the right; and then stop, face forward. I then asked my students, "How do you feel?" They said they felt awkward, silly, confused, pained, annoyed, and, most important, curious why we were doing this activity. I said, "Welcome to diversity in education!" I explained that throughout the semester, we'd embark on a number of topics and, at some point, they would probably experience these same uncomfortable feelings. I assured them that this was part of the discovery process and that they needed to hang in there and be open to learning. I wrote the list of their feelings on the board and kept it for the entire semester, referring to it every time we needed a reminder.

THE ICEBERG ANALOGY

That same advice is appropriate for this book. Snyder and Staehr Fenner invite educators to learn about culture—not only the culture of multilingual learners but also one's own culture. They help readers define and sharpen their understanding of equity and what it means to provide access. They also pose the notion that school communities have their own cultures in which we, as participants, interact while still owning our own cultures.

What happens when multiple cultures are merged, even temporarily? Picture culture as an iceberg; we can only see the small portion above the water and not what is beneath. Now picture three icebergs—one that represents a multilingual learner, another representing a teacher, and the other a school.

We only see the tops of those icebergs, so we don't see how deep or wide they truly are, and we don't know whether they are connected to one another. When pieces of icebergs break off or crash into each other, what happens to the remnants? We do know that icebergs can coexist, stay frozen, melt, or merge, depending on the environment. What kind of environment is needed for the best outcomes? This book affirms that we can, like icebergs, successfully coexist while maintaining our own forms.

DISPELLING THE MYTH: THE ILLUSION OF INCLUSION

Learning communities have been working toward being more welcoming of diversity for decades. With the push for more multicultural books, resources, curriculum, and pedagogical practices, the field of education has evolved, and we've seen it: welcome signs in multiple languages, potlucks in which you bring a dish from your culture, and vision and mission statements that profess antiracism. But it must go further. Our embrace of diversity should be exemplified in our daily practices and actions. We can't allow ourselves to believe that once we do something, anything that promotes diversity, that it is enough. We can avoid the *illusion of inclusion* by getting to the core of our beliefs and acting upon it. Snyder and Staehr Fenner do this by helping us understand why culturally responsive teaching matters and how to build our capacity to become more culturally competent practitioners.

When we see and hear things that make us or our colleagues uncomfortable, such as microaggressions, how and when do we address them? For example, what should we do when we see educators change the names of multilingual learners to more American-sounding names or when derogatory assumptions are made about where multilingual learners are coming from and why they are here in the United States? Truly embracing diversity means welcoming all of our multilingual learners and their families. An example of this was when an elementary school at which I taught changed its annual Cinco de Mayo celebration to a more inclusive celebration of all the cultures represented by its teachers, students, and families. Positive and intentional changes are made when we evaluate and dismantle barriers that exist in our schools, such as deficit mindsets and low expectations, in order to assure access for all students. This book helps to create school communities that celebrate, elevate, and validate the lives and experiences of multilingual learners—this will take time and energy, but it will yield results beyond our expectations.

It is my hope that this book helps you get uncomfortable. How uncomfortable? That depends. Not so uncomfortable that you'll be immobilized (just stomp, balance, and spin), but enough for you to keep moving forward while also reflecting on what made you uncomfortable in the first place. Only you will know to what extent to engage and how far you'll go. What matters most is that this book helps educators to take steps, either individually or collectively, to create learning communities that are diverse, inclusive, and empowering for all.

Why We Wrote This Book

We work with school districts across North America to help teachers and administrators better support their English learners (ELs) and multilingual learners (MLs). One of our many services to districts is providing professional development (PD). Quite often, PD participants would like an assortment of fun activities and strategies to use with MLs in instruction. Some administrators request a one-day or half-day professional development session that will give teachers something to use in class the next day. We completely understand that approach, as we were once classroom teachers ourselves. We are firm believers that a little professional development is better than no professional development, even though we know that a few hours of strategies realistically won't move the needle significantly in terms of making positive changes to support MLs' equity and achievement.

While we recognize the need for effective instructional strategies that are engaging for students, we have also seen the urgent need to examine educators' beliefs about and expectations for MLs. We define MLs as students who speak or are exposed to a language in addition to English and students who may come from cultures that are different from the educators' own. We believe that we—and the educators we collaborate with—must focus on what is happening in the classroom context in which teaching is taking place, as well as expand our lenses to be aware of the larger contexts of school, district, state, and nation. Instructional strategies in and of themselves aren't the magic bullet to ensure MLs receive an equitable education. Through this book, we will take a deeper look at the practice of culturally responsive teaching (CRT) as a framework for changing educational outcomes for MLs and the steps needed to develop a culturally responsive climate in which all students' backgrounds, experiences, and cultures are honored and appreciated and diversity is commonly understood to make a school community stronger. It takes a more holistic, sustained approach that includes focusing on the culturally responsive component to change practices in working with students and their families.

Prior to the publication of this book, our most recent book together was *Unlocking English Learners' Potential: Strategies for Making Content Accessible* (Staehr Fenner & Snyder, 2017). When we sent in the prospectus for that book, our wise editor Dan Alpert read it thoroughly and suggested we add a chapter on culture. In writing that chapter, we recognized that its inclusion was crucial in situating research-based strategies and academic language for ELs within the larger sociocultural context. As we worked with districts across North America in bringing the research and strategies of that book to life, we began noticing that culture was often left out of the equation when it came to teachers, administrators, schools, and districts who voiced a desire to improve equity for MLs. In our work, we would sometimes hear PD participants espouse a deficit perspective of multilingual learners while at the same time expressing the desire to start with a strengths- or assets-based perspective of their MLs. We knew we were ready to write our next book, and when deciding on the topic for this book, the one you're holding right now, we decided there was so much to unpack in that original culture chapter that it warranted its own focus.

With a teacher workforce that is primarily monolingual, female, and white, many MLs do not experience the benefit of teachers who understand and connect to their linguistic and cultural backgrounds. This book seeks to help bridge that gap by providing educators who may not share the linguistic, cultural, ethnic, or racial makeup of their students an opportunity to reflect on the importance of MLs' culture in teaching and learning. To do so, we guide teachers through recognizing their own culture and its impact on their teaching and interactions with MLs. We are aware that readers of this book will be at various stages in their work for more culturally responsive and equitable schools, and we have written the book with multiple audiences in mind. No matter where you are in your journey, we encourage you to be ready to listen, to take risks, and to sit with the discomfort that this work may bring. The work is ongoing, and there is always more that we can learn.

As two white educators, we know that we also still have much to learn about how to advocate for and improve education for students of color, multilingual learners, and other marginalized student populations that are not receiving equitable education in our nation's schools. In writing this book, we have sought out the perspectives of academics and educators of color to better understand the work that needs to be done yet are keenly aware that we may never fully understand. At the same time, we recognize the scholarship that people of color have contributed to the field all along and honor their work. We look forward to discussing the ideas in this book with other educators, and we know that we will learn much from these future discussions.

We began writing the book in a time in which anti-immigrant sentiment was no longer hidden from view and even became acceptable, embraced, and endorsed in some circles. As we were putting together the final chapters, the world as we knew it seemed to spin further out of control. The COVID-19 pandemic first struck in spring 2020, and the nation's school districts moved to a remote teaching model, in many cases overnight. During this time, we saw existing inequities become more exposed and impact education in ways they had not before. Factors such as families' access to technology and the internet now determined if students could take part in teaching that was suddenly happening online. Due to these inequities, many students were unaccounted for. School districts also faced challenges in effectively shifting to remote learning, resulting in a patchwork quilt of approaches to educating students with varying results. During the same time period, the United States experienced the largest protest movement that our country has witnessed in response to the brutal murder of George Floyd at the hands of a white Minneapolis police officer. The death of George Floyd in May 2020 marked a tipping point in a long list of police violence against Black Americans, including Breonna Taylor, Atatiana Jefferson, Trayvon Martin, Stephon Clark, Philando Castile, Tony McDade, and numerous others.

The inhumane federal anti-immigrant policies that have been enforced in recent years, the inequitable access to learning opportunities that were brought to the surface during distance learning, and the protests against systemic racism in our country have led to renewed attention to issues of equity. More educators are joining in conversations about what it means to teach and advocate for social justice, anti-racism, and equity. We acknowledge the work that has been done on these issues for many years and are cautiously optimistic that the events that took place in spring 2020 are ripping off the Band-Aid and inviting even more voices into these conversations. It can be challenging to understand what these theoretical concepts look like in practice in schools and classrooms. Keeping in mind the work that has been done in the past, with this book we have attempted to make these abstract ideas even more concrete, actionable, and relevant to our current reality. However, we recognize that there may be some who say we haven't gone far enough. We agree this is only a first step as we add to the body of work, and this book does not contain all the answers. However, we are committed to learning more about how to better support MLs with your help. In order to start our work, we need to allow ourselves to be vulnerable and begin with humility.

As educators, we can no longer deny the responsibility that we have in engaging in equity and anti-racism work. At the same time, it can be valuable to recognize the joys that come with this challenging task. Your teaching will be enriched when you begin from a strengths- or assets-based perspective of MLs and create a space for the multifaceted experiences of language, culture, and life that they bring with them. As you develop your advocacy and allyship, you will notice your ability to spot inequities, and your strength to speak out against these inequities will grow. Last but certainly not least, your students will thrive when your local classrooms, schools, families, and communities collaborate to recognize MLs' academic and social-emotional learning strengths and meet their needs.

Acknowledgments

Just as a classroom is made richer when there is ample opportunity for diverse voices to be shared, heard, and celebrated, the same is true for this book. We could not have written this book without the collaboration and support of many.

We would like to express our deep gratitude to Corwin Program Director and Publisher Dan Alpert, who first inspired us to add a chapter about the role of culture in teaching multilingual learners in our previous book and who has encouraged us at every step of this journey. We deeply appreciate his quiet, calming effect on our writing as well as on our lives, especially when our worlds turned upside down. We'd also like to thank Senior Content Development Editor Lucas Schleicher for his attention to detail during the filming of video through the publication of the book. We would like to say a heartfelt thank you to Director of Marketing Strategy Maura Sullivan for her wise guidance in the promotion of this publication and to our project editor Tori Mirsadjadi and copyeditor Amy Hanquist Harris for their support in guiding this project over the finish line. A big thank you also to Davis Lester for his keen eye throughout the filming and production of the videos that bring the strategies in this book to life. We would also like to thank Dave Bartlett and Kelley Hildmeyer for the support they provided during the filming.

We'd like to give a huge shoutout to our colleagues who contributed so much to the production of this book. We conceptualized the idea of integrating sketchnotes and custom-made graphics together with our colleague Kate Monick. Kate worked tirelessly, drawing from her vast creativity, style, and uncanny ability to "snazzify" to develop the sketchnotes and graphics that visually represent our ideas. We are grateful to our longtime colleague Ayanna Cooper, who is always willing to offer us her thoughtful feedback that pushes us to think about our content in different and important ways—not to mention her foreword, which captures the essence of today's complex context. Additionally, we would like to express our gratitude to Margarita Calderón for her thoughtful review and recommendations on our writing. Thank you also to Joanna Duggan, Eleni Pappamihiel, Teddi Predaris, and Marley Zeno for always being willing to provide an example, answer a question, and review our writing at a moment's notice. Also, many thanks to Shannon Webb for her support with research, edits, and suggestions to improve our writing.

We would like to give thanks to the many educators, students, and families of the Syracuse City School District (SCSD) who opened their schools, classrooms, and communities to us and agreed to share their experience and expertise through the many videos that accompany this book. While we can't name everyone who helped us out, we would like to thank Pedro Abreu, Abdulilah Al-Dubai, Megan Brown, Susan Centore, Sangita Chadha, Perry Crain, Nicole Heath, Stephanie Horton-Centore, Gloria Kimmich, Leana Landrian, Angela Matarazzo, Brittany Mazzaferro, Sandra McKenney, Ei Mi, Taryn Michael, James Nieves, Jesus Ortiz, Jaime Perez, Razan Shalash, Si, and Lillian Zayas. We'd also like to offer a very special thank you to Jacqueline LeRoy, Kristina Crehan, Erica Daniels, and Meredith Green at SCSD for all they did to help coordinate the filming. We couldn't have included videos in this book without their help. We are excited to showcase SCSD's relentless focus on equity for multilingual learners through these videos.

We'd also like to extend our deep appreciation to educators who are working to develop and support culturally responsive communities of practice in their schools and districts and who took the time to share their work with us. Thank you to Aimee Ackley, Caroline Espinoza-Navarrete, Emily Francis, George Guy, Susan Hafler, Tu Phillips, and Stephanie Reyes. We'd like to acknowledge the input on community walks from Lauren Markham, Community School Manager at Oakland International High School in California. This book is made richer by all their contributions.

Finally, we offer our thanks to our families. Without their support, we would not be able to do the work that we do. Thank you to Gus, Sylvia, and Iris Fahey; Tom and Lynne Snyder; and Paul and Rosemarie Fahey, as well as David, Zoe, Maya, and Carson Fenner; August and Jean Staehr; and James and Mary Fenner (in spirit).

PUBLISHER'S ACKNOWLEDGMENTS

Corwin gratefully acknowledges the contributions of the following reviewers:

Margarita Calderón
Professor Emerita and
    Senior Research Scientist
Johns Hopkins University
Baltimore, MD

Gail Cappaert
Teacher
District 428
Dekalb, IL

Ayanna Cooper
English Language Specialist
A. Cooper Consulting
Dallas, GA

David Freeman
Professor Emeritus
University of Texas at
    Brownsville
San Diego, CA

Yvonne Freeman
Professor Emerita
University of Texas at
    Brownsville
San Diego, CA

John F. Mahoney
Lecturer in Mathematics
Montgomery College
Rockville, MD

Melissa Miller
Science Instructor
Farmington Middle School
Farmington, AR

Tricia Peña
Professor, Department of
    Educational Leadership,
    College of Education
Northern Arizona University
Flagstaff, AZ

About the Authors

Sydney Snyder, PhD, is a principal associate at SupportEd. In this role, Sydney develops and conducts interactive professional development for teachers of multilingual learners. She also works with the SupportEd team to offer technical assistance to school districts and educational organizations. Sydney has extensive instructional experience, having taught ESOL/EFL for over 15 years. She started her teaching career as a Peace Corps Volunteer in Guinea, West Africa. This experience ignited her passion for both teaching English and culturally responsive instruction. Sydney is coauthor of *Unlocking English Learners' Potential: Strategies for Making Content Accessible.* She served as an English Teaching Fellow at Gadja Mada University in Yogyakarta, Indonesia. She earned her PhD in multilingual/multicultural education at George Mason University and her MAT in TESOL at the School for International Training. You can connect with her on email at Sydney@GetSupportEd.net or on Twitter at @SydneySupportEd.

Diane Staehr Fenner, PhD, is the president of SupportEd (www.Get SupportEd.net), a woman-owned small business located in Washington, DC, that is dedicated to empowering multilingual learners and their educators. She collaborates with her team to provide ML professional development, technical assistance, and curriculum and assessment support to school districts, states, organizations, and the US Department of Education. Prior to forming SupportEd, Diane was an ESOL teacher, dual language assessment teacher, and ESOL assessment specialist in Fairfax County Public Schools, VA. She has also taught in Berlin, Germany, and Veracruz, Mexico, and speaks German as well as Spanish. Diane grew up on a dairy farm in central New York and is a first-generation college graduate. She has written several books on EL education, including coauthoring *Unlocking English Learners' Potential: Strategies for Making Content Accessible* and authoring *Advocating for English Learners: A Guide for Educators*. She is a frequent keynote speaker on ML education at conferences across North America. You can connect with her by email at Diane@GetSupportEd.net or on Twitter at @DStaehrFenner.

How to Approach This Book

HOW WE TOOK YOU INTO CONSIDERATION WHILE WRITING THIS BOOK

We have purposefully written this book so that different types of readers can see themselves reflected in it. We would like to be sure we offer multiple entry points for people in different roles. When we work with teachers through professional development, we always ask what their roles are to tailor our content and application activities to their specific content, grade level(s), and students. Similarly, we also offer different options for administrators, instructional coaches, and other educators not in the classroom to apply the content we're sharing to their contexts. For example, instead of asking administrators to create a lesson plan, we might have them collaborate with teachers to plan a mini–professional development on a given topic.

Reading this book could be a journey you're taking as an individual or with a professional learning community (PLC) as a book study in a school or in a district. Your journey could very well be at the university level. We've made sure to differentiate and/or include considerations for these settings so you can choose your own path. Table A details different types of readers who may be interacting with this book.

Table A   Types of Readers Interacting With This Book

Type of Reader	Description	How the Book Is Tailored to You
Preservice educator	Student working toward certification in a teacher licensure program	We ensure that our application activities and reflective questions allow you entry points to our content without a current classroom of K–12 students.
Inservice teacher	Teacher in a K–12 setting (classroom teacher and specialists)	We provide you ample opportunities to ensure your learning is practical and involves your students through application activities and reflective questions.
Administrator	Assistant principal, principal, district or state administrator	We tailor our application activities to you so that you can share your learning with teachers and other administrators you collaborate with and support.
Other educators not in the classroom	School psychologists, guidance counselors, school librarians, instructional coaches, etc.	We make sure the application activities can be customized to your unique context and adapted for your setting.

HOW EACH CHAPTER IS STRUCTURED

We have structured the chapters in a way that invites you, the reader, to reflect, connect, and apply the content to your own context in a safe space yet challenges your thinking and brings you out of your comfort zone. We recognize that in our own learning, we don't make any gains until we're feeling slightly out of our element. We aim to create the same conditions in this book, recognizing your expertise yet stretching your learning.

We encourage you to write in each chapter of this book, use sticky notes to mark what is important to you, and make it relevant to you personally. Each of our first two chapters presents the urgency for each topic and shares a digestible amount of research, broken up by reflection questions and opportunities for application. Beginning in Chapter 2, each chapter opens with a scenario about one of two MLs, either Manny or Lian. Following the scenarios, you will find some type of reflection activity to give you space to think about the scenario and connect it to your own context. Next, you'll find a chapter overview. Then, you'll read relevant research and background that illustrates and situates the importance of the chapter's theme and defines any key terms. You will also find look-fors that provide practical, observable actions (to see how the content looks in practice). We will then share specific activities or examples of resources to give you new ideas for your practice in enacting the chapter's culturally responsive principle. You'll find sketchnotes, tools, and notes about videos integrated throughout each chapter to bring it to life. After this section, we will share three steps that you can take to integrate this culturally responsive principle in your practice. The chapter then concludes with a bulleted summary, reflection questions for you to deepen your own thinking, and references.

OTHER UNIQUE RESOURCES IN THIS BOOK

Use #CRTforMLs to tag the book on Twitter.

We would like to highlight the additional resources that distinguish this book from others, bring this book to life, and also help ground it in reality. We often are asked what concepts, strategies, and tools "look like" in real life, and it can be challenging to describe. We prefer to *show* you how it can look, and we are able to do so through using authentic videos, student scenarios, sketchnotes, and practical tools.

- **Resource 1: Videos.** We were honored to partner with our longtime collaborator, Syracuse City School District in Syracuse, New York. Over the course of two days during the first snowstorm in November (!), we were fortunate to film classroom footage, interviews with educators, and an evening parent meet and greet. We weave in one or two video clips per chapter, which you will notice when you see a QR code, a URL, and a description. These video clips illustrate the concepts we are describing in each chapter to show you what they look like in action.

- **Resource 2: Student portraits.** We chose to create student portraits as ways to illustrate or apply content and also to model what the strategies we describe might look like in an actual classroom setting with real students. To do this, we created the portrait of Manny, a third grader, and Lian, a ninth grader. You will notice that we alternate between the two students in each chapter, and you will uncover new discoveries about each one as you progress through the book. We have included the student scenarios to provide a portrait of the types of experiences that MLs may have in schools. These scenarios and student portraits are not meant to be representative of the experiences of all MLs.

- **Resource 3: Sketchnotes.** Sketchnote graphics serve as eye-catching visual supplements to help reinforce key concepts and spotlight central themes within a body of text. Incorporating a unique graphic style helps differentiate content, adds a secondary layer of personality and memorability, and introduces a visual that reinforces information in a format that is easy for readers to digest and relate to. Stylistically, this form of graphic brings an additional layer of personality to our content while shedding greater light on pressing issues. All sketchnotes are hand-drawn, scanned, and imported into Photoshop to arrange layouts, edit sketches, and finalize the graphic. We are fortunate to have an incredibly talented in-house graphic designer, Kate Monick, who draws from our content to design sketchnotes. Using sketchnotes has helped our content gain a great degree of online traction through social media and helps tell a story. Sketchnotes that are framed around specific strategies can also be a useful resource to share with colleagues in your collaboration to build a culturally responsive school climate.

- **Resource 4: Appendices.** Our book contains six appendices, which are made up of several practical, printable tools to allow you to dig a little deeper on the topics we describe. We encourage you to print out these tools and use them as a catalyst to your own conversations around MLs' equity. In addition, our final appendix is a comprehensive list of supporting resources. While we cite all the references in each of our chapters, the final appendix provides additional materials, curated by topic, that you may wish to refer to on your journey to culturally responsive teaching MLs. Some topics include anti-racism and anti-bias resources, recommended booklists for K–12 students, and additional resources on social justice.

Chapter Overview

CHAPTER 1: WHY CULTURALLY RESPONSIVE TEACHING MATTERS

This chapter frames the content that you will encounter in the rest of the book. We define who we mean by multilingual learners, comparing them to other groups of students. We then examine the concepts of race, ethnicity, and culture as facets of MLs' identities. Next, we ask you to reflect on the relationship between culture and equity for MLs. In the subsequent part of the chapter, we share concepts of culturally responsive teaching (CRT) from three leading educators. The following portion of our chapter is devoted to framing our five guiding principles for CRT of MLs and presenting suggestions for a culturally responsive teaching cycle.

CHAPTER 2: BUILDING CULTURAL COMPETENCY

In Chapter 2, we discuss what it means to build cultural competency in today's context, weave in relevant research, and provide five elements of cultural competency, ranging from understanding your own culture to looking at the role of culture at an institutional level. You can then reflect on your own cultural beliefs and expectations and also explore potential personal bias that you might bring to your interactions with MLs. We conclude this chapter—and the next several chapters that follow—with three practical steps that you can use to continue your exploration of this topic at an individual and/or school level.

CHAPTER 3: OPERATING FROM AN ASSETS-BASED APPROACH

This chapter is framed around the following guiding principle "Culturally responsive teaching is assets-based." This chapter examines what an assets-based approach is for MLs and provides multiple strategies to help shift yourself and others to operate from a place of MLs' strengths. The chapter shares relevant research and contains many practical tools as well as three concrete steps in order to respond to and mitigate deficit-thinking related to multilingual students in your schools and districts. Case studies and reflection questions found in this chapter also guide your work in this area.

CHAPTER 4: SIMULTANEOUSLY SUPPORTING AND CHALLENGING STUDENTS

Chapter 4 is framed around the following guiding principle: "Culturally responsive teaching simultaneously challenges and supports students." In this chapter, we ask you to examine equitable education opportunities for MLs in your context and reflect on how you can support all learners on their academic journeys. We focus on three key areas supported by research: (1) MLs' access to content and programs, (2) ways to support MLs as they acquire language and content, and (3) how to challenge MLs to think critically and build cross-curricular connections. The chapter contains a wealth of strategies supporting MLs through scaffolded instruction, as well as using interdisciplinary, project-based learning and social justice units.

CHAPTER 5: PLACING STUDENTS AT THE CENTER OF THE LEARNING

This chapter is framed around the following guiding principle: "Culturally responsive teaching places students at the center of learning." We begin by defining what it means to put students at the center of learning and share research that supports student-centered pedagogy. You will benefit from specific strategies for learning about your students and their learning preferences and setting a collaborative tone in your classroom. Next, we explore strategies for engaging ML students and families in goal setting and involving MLs in taking part in self- and peer assessment. We also share strategies for fostering engaging, peer-to-peer interactions and ways to honor ML growth and achievement.

CHAPTER 6: LEVERAGING STUDENTS' LINGUISTIC AND CULTURAL BACKGROUNDS

Chapter 6 is framed around the following guiding principle: "Culturally responsive teaching leverages students' linguistic and cultural backgrounds." In this chapter, we share relevant research and the urgency around why leveraging MLs' linguistic and cultural backgrounds is essential to culturally responsive teaching and what it means to do so. We then take an in-depth look at strategies for leveraging MLs' cultural and linguistic backgrounds, tools for incorporating multicultural resources into the curriculum, and strategies for incorporating translanguaging and home language practices into your teaching.

CHAPTER 7: UNITING STUDENTS' SCHOOLS, FAMILIES, AND COMMUNITIES

This chapter is framed around our final guiding principle: "Culturally responsive teaching unites students' schools, families, and communities." In this chapter, we expand our lens to focus on the critical job of building partnerships with families and communities in support of MLs. We begin by exploring research on what family engagement is and why it is important for our work with MLs. Next, we share five strategies related to fostering ML family engagement and collaborating with ML communities. These five strategies are as follows: (1) create a welcoming environment for ML families, (2) build relationships with ML families, (3) communicate effectively with ML families, (4) overcome barriers to ML family engagement, and

(5) empower ML families. As with our other chapters, we provide examples and tools to support three practical steps you can take to unite MLs' schools, families, and communities.

CHAPTER 8: PUTTING IT ALL TOGETHER

In our final chapter, we share examples of practical ML advocacy tools and strategies that you can use as you work to implement the five principles in your context. We begin by introducing the National Education Association's (NEA) five-step framework for EL advocacy and reflect on how it can be applied to strengthening culturally responsive teaching for MLs and their families. We weave a specific case study throughout the chapter as a way to exemplify the ML advocacy steps. We then share several examples of innovative programs that are being used in various school districts that help to foster a districtwide climate that is supportive of MLs. We conclude the chapter by sharing some final thoughts on the urgent need for CRT work and highlighting key themes that are found throughout this book.

Why Culturally Responsive Teaching Matters

CHAPTER OVERVIEW

This chapter will frame the content that you will encounter in the rest of the book. We'll begin by defining who we mean by multilingual learners (MLs) and comparing them to English learners (ELs). We'll then take a look at what race and ethnicity are and how they may form one piece of multilingual learners' identities. Next, we'll ask you to reflect on what culture is, and then, we'll ask you to think about the relationship between culture and equity for MLs. After that, we'll share concepts of culturally responsive teaching (CRT) from three leading educators. The next component of the chapter will share the sense of urgency around CRT, focusing on three key reasons this topic is absolutely essential at this particular moment in time. Next, we'll share our five guiding principles for CRT of MLs and will end our chapter with suggestions for a culturally responsive teaching cycle. Before we get started with this chapter, we'd like you to know that this chapter will contain the most theory that you will encounter in the book.

We attempt to present it in a way that's engaging and allows you to reflect on what you're learning as you go.

DEFINING MULTILINGUAL LEARNERS

There are many different, often confusing, terms being used today for students who speak a language in addition to English (Sugarman, 2020). English learners (ELs) and emergent bilinguals are different names for the same students whose parent or guardian reports speaking one or more languages other than English in the home. These students are eligible for language support services. While EL is used by the federal government and most states to describe students who are exposed to a language in addition to English, some argue that the term "English learner" focuses more on students' deficits of learning a language while ignoring the strength of their home language (García, 2009b; Zacarian & Staehr Fenner, 2020). While we agree that we should always focus on students' assets (e.g., Zacarian & Staehr Fenner, 2020), we feel we still have a great deal of work to do in terms of agreeing on a name to call the students we strive to serve.

Although our previous work is in support of ELs (e.g., Staehr Fenner & Snyder, 2017), for this book we chose to widen our scope and focus on the larger group of students called multilingual learners. Educators sometimes use the terms "English learner" and "multilingual learner" interchangeably, but it is our understanding that ELs and MLs share some, but not all, characteristics. **We define multilingual learners as students whose parent or guardian reports speaking one or more languages other than English at home.** MLs may or may not qualify for English language support, depending on their level of English proficiency.

According to the Wisconsin Center for Education Research (WIDA, 2019), the term "multilingual learners" refers to "all children and youth who are, or have been, consistently exposed to multiple languages. It includes students known as English language learners (ELLs) or dual language

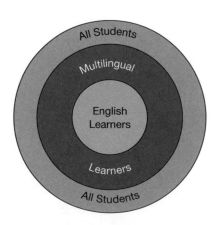

learners (DLLs); heritage language learners; and students who speak varieties of English or indigenous languages" (p. 1). Let's unpack some of these terms a bit more.

- The term **"dual language learner" is used in early childhood education to refer to children from homes where a language other than English is spoken.** However, these children, ranging from birth to prekindergarten, are too young to be formally designated as EL using the Department of Education's official definition. The term "dual language learner" is useful in that it highlights how young children are learning their home language from a more developmental perspective and are also learning English if they are being instructed in that language.

- **Heritage language learners are students who are studying a language that they have cultural proficiency in or a cultural connection to.** For example, this term would apply to a Mexican American student taking a Spanish heritage language class or Spanish for native speakers class.

- **Students who speak varieties of English include Caribbean English speakers, speakers of African American language, and speakers of Hawaiian American language, among others.** These students speak a "variety of English that is different in structure and form than academic English" (Los Angeles Unified School District, 2018, p. 22).

- **Students who speak indigenous languages speak a language native to a region.** For example, Quechua is an indigenous language spoken in Peru, and Aleut is an indigenous language spoken in Alaska.

The takeaway is that MLs aren't coming to school with the same shared knowledge. Intake forms used when students enroll in a school or district may not catch these differences either. For example, it may not be apparent that a student enrolling from Mexico speaks an indigenous language instead of Spanish as his or her home language.

Table 1.1 takes a deeper look at different students who speak a language in addition to English, sharing characteristics of their home language and eligibility for language support services.

Table I.I   Definitions of Different Types of Language Learners

Name of Learner	Home Language	Eligibility for English Language Services
Dual language learner	Student (birth to prekindergarten) whose parent or guardian reports speaking one or more languages other than English at home; student is acquiring home language proficiency while simultaneously learning English	May or may not qualify for English for Speakers of Other Languages (ESOL) services
English learner or emergent bilingual	Student whose parent or guardian reports speaking one or more languages other than English at home	Qualifies for ESOL services
Former EL	Student whose parent or guardian reports speaking one or more languages other than English at home	Qualified for and may have received ESOL services in the past and has since tested out of the need for services
Ever EL	Current ELs and Former ELs as a group	Qualified for and may or may not have received or be receiving ESOL services
Heritage language learner	Student who is studying a language that he or she has cultural proficiency in or a cultural connection to	May or may not have received or be receiving ESOL services
Multilingual learner	Student whose parent or guardian reports speaking one or more languages other than English at home	May or may not qualify for ESOL services
Never EL	Student who reports speaking one or more languages other than English at home	Did not qualify for ESOL services due to linguistic proficiency in English

Source: Adapted from Kieffer and Thompson, 2018.

We believe that all educators should have a sense of the national context (i.e., the big picture) and how it impacts their work in schools and districts. In the United States in 2016–2017, school-age ELs numbered approximately 4.86 million, making up nearly 10 percent of the school-age population (NCES, 2017; see Figure 1.1). Due to their level of English proficiency, ELs are eligible for language support services, such as English for speakers of other languages (ESOL). In contrast, MLs, as a group, encompass markedly more students than ELs, with close to 12 million or 22 percent of children ages 5 to 17 speaking a language other than English at home, according to U.S. census figures in 2017 (U.S. Census, 2017). Multilingual learners may or may not qualify for ESOL services.

Figure 1.1   Population of EL and ML School-Age Children in the United States

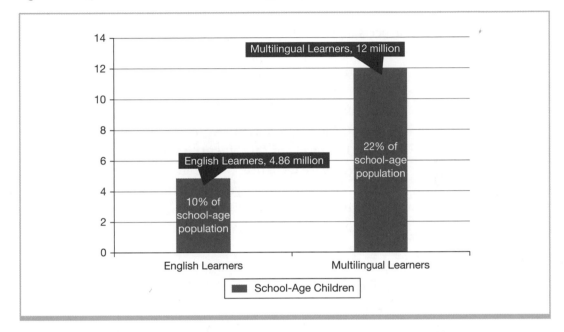

Source: U.S. Department of Education, National Center for Education Statistics, Common Core of Data (CCD), "Local Education Agency Universe Survey," 2000–01 through 2016–17. https://nces.ed.gov/programs/digest/d18/tables/dt18_204.20 .asp?current=yes

We recognize that states and districts may have different terms for language support programs, such as English language development (ELD), English as a second language (ESL), structured English immersion (SEI), and so on. For the purposes of simplicity, we will refer to the general term "English for speakers of other languages" (ESOL) from this point forward. We also wish to note that the ideal scenario for all students—both ML and non-ML—and one that is mandated in some locations is dual language instruction. In dual language settings, the student makeup is approximately half native English speakers and half target language speakers (e.g., Spanish, Korean, Arabic). Students receive content-rich instruction in both languages as they acquire proficiency in the two languages and also learn about both cultures.

THE INTERSECTION BETWEEN RACE AND ETHNICITY AND MLs

Now that we have defined who MLs are in the context of K–12 students, we also need to have a sense of what race and ethnicity are, as these constructs may have an impact on many aspects of MLs' lives, including the privilege they are granted (or not) and the ways in which their teachers may (or may not) connect with them. When we were in our teacher educator programs, we weren't provided any guidance beyond the imperative to "know our students' language and culture." We didn't have any potentially uncomfortable conversations about other facets of MLs' identities, including race and ethnicity. While we recognize the information we're sharing here is limited, we encourage you to learn more about the intersectionality between MLs' languages, cultures, races, ethnicities, and privilege in order to better prepare yourselves for CRT. We acknowledge that we cannot possibly do these topics much justice here, but we urge you to do more research to have a more informed sense of MLs' identities beyond their languages and cultures.

One definition of race is "a grouping of humans based on shared physical or social qualities into categories generally viewed as distinct by society" (Barnshaw, 2008, p. 1091). In the book *White Fragility*, DiAngelo (2018) tells us that, like gender, race is also a social construct with there being no true biological race. External, superficial characteristics that are commonly used to define race (e.g., hair texture, skin color) are actually not reliable indicators of genetic variation between people (Cooper et al., 2003). However, many tend to believe racial differences are biologic. Instead, DiAngelo (2018) imparts us to understand that society was organized along racial lines. She shares that the idea of racial inferiority in the United States was created as the US was being formed to justify unequal treatment of enslaved African people, Native Americans, and Mexicans, among other people.

***Merriam-Webster* (n.d.) defines ethnicity as "a particular ethnic affiliation or group" and ethnic as "of or relating to large groups of people classed according to common racial, national, tribal, religious, linguistic, or cultural origin or background."** In addition, Nagel (1994) states that ethnicity is made up of the two building blocks of identity and culture and is dynamic and constantly evolving. According to the U. S. Census Bureau, ethnicity has a limited definition, used to determine "whether a person is of Hispanic origin or not" (2017, p. 1), but DiAngelo (2018) notes some wider examples of ethnic groups, such as the Irish, Italians, and Polish European ethnic groups.

It's important for educators to have a sense of what race and ethnicity are due to our potential for subconscious racial biases as teachers of MLs.[1] While some MLs and their educators may share a common racial or ethnic identity, many do not. As white educators ourselves who have been granted many unearned privileges, we (the book authors) must become aware of and reflect on what these biases and privileges might mean for our practice as teachers. No matter what our racial identity and ethnicity, all of us need to approach this work with humility. We should place the focus on increasing equity for our students, not on making ourselves feel better, and part of this work is to identify how our culture and biases as educators influence who we are and how we interact with students. It takes educators collaborating, checking their biases, and speaking out against inequities to begin to truly support MLs.

ASPECTS OF CULTURE

Now that we have shed some light on who MLs are, let's turn our focus to examining culture. Let's begin by reflecting on the word "culture." How do you define culture?

---

[1]We will discuss this topic more in Chapter 2.

Application Activity 1a.
Defining Culture

Here are three aspects of culture. Choose the one that resonates the most with you. Why does it stand out to you?

1. Culture includes customs, values, norms, and ideas that are learned through socialization and participation in families and communities, including schools; there is great variability in terms of how the culture is manifested (Erickson, 2007).

2. Culture is "a way of life, especially as it relates to the socially transmitted habits, customs, traditions, and beliefs that characterize a particular group of people at a particular time. It includes the behaviors, actions, practices, attitudes, norms, values, communication styles, language, etiquette, spirituality, concepts of health and healing, beliefs, and institutions of racial, ethnic, religious, or social group. Culture is the lens through which we look at the word. It is the context within which we operate and make sense of the world. Culture influences how we process learning, solve problems, and teach" (Saifer et al., 2011, p. 9).

3. An analogy is often made between three levels of culture—surface, shallow, and deep—and an iceberg (Hall, 1976). The elements of culture that are visible (at the surface level), such as food, clothing, and language, are understood to carry a low emotional load. This surface-level culture means that people expect such differences, and these differences are less likely to cause conflict or misunderstandings between people or groups of people. However, the invisible elements of culture (the greater and more meaningful aspects of culture) that include both shallow and deep culture are much more likely to carry an emotional weight. Shallow culture, which consists of the beliefs we hold, include such aspects as our attitudes about concepts of time and nonverbal communication. Deep culture, which is made up of our values and thought patterns, includes aspects of cultures such as ideas about fairness and justice or expectations related to gender roles (Hall, 1976; Hammond, 2015).

And since many of us like to also represent concepts visually, look at these four images of culture. Which image best represents culture to you? Why?

1.

Photo by Mostafa Meraji on Unsplash: https://unsplash.com/photos/cHxgOIyHGvA

2.

Photo by Charles Postiaux on Unsplash: https://unsplash.com/photos/efkSRelxQAw

3.

Photo by Husniati Salma on Unsplash: https://unsplash.com/photos/ldkHWg5s3Ec

4.

Photo by Jimmy Salazar on Unsplash: https://unsplash.com/photos/_JYtfcL_jog

Reflection Questions

Why did you choose the aspect and/or image of culture that you did? Or like a lot of educators we collaborate with, did you choose a little bit of each definition and/or image to represent your own concept of culture? If so, why?

No matter how you define culture, it is important to remember that everyone is a member of various cultural groups and that even within cultural groups there can be great variability in terms of beliefs, expectations, and behaviors. For this reason, it is important that we don't put students on the spot and ask them to speak for an entire cultural group. Instead, we can ask them to share their experiences as a member of one or more cultural groups in a way that puts them at ease (e.g., with a partner, in a small group, in writing)—but only if they feel comfortable doing so.

THE RELATIONSHIP BETWEEN CULTURE AND EQUITY

Now that we have explored some concepts of culture, we'd like to dispel some misconceptions about culture and ask you to think about how you conceptualize the relationship between culture and equity. **When we think of culture, we run the risk of only scratching the surface level of culture (e.g., food and fiestas) and avoiding challenging conversations about equity for MLs.** Social justice educator Paul Gorski (2016) shares that culture is important as one piece of students' multilayered identities, noting that cultural sensitivity is an important facet when working toward educational equity as long as we recognize and embrace students' whole selves instead of assigning them to "cultural groups" based on one dimension of their identities. He states, "No amount of cultural knowledge can prepare me sufficiently to recognize and respond justly to the insidious and often implicit and intersectional inequities experienced by many students" (p. 224). Further, focusing on culture alone may serve as a euphemism for such deep equity concerns as race or socioeconomic status, putting privileged educators in a more comfortable position and diminishing their potential discomfort when addressing complex issues (Ladson-Billings, 2006; Park, 2005).

Although it may seem fun and informative, celebrating cultural diversity does not get to the hard work of educators advocating, serving as allies, and relentlessly striving for equity for MLs. We want to be sure our work with culturally responsive teaching does not get stuck in the safe space of celebrating cultural diversity but instead works toward ensuring MLs' equitable education, even if—especially if—that means breaking out of our comfort zones. Gorski (2016) argues educators' focus should shift from culture to equity, as the concept of culture itself remains contested by many, to the point that "nobody seems to know with any precision what it means" (p. 223). Educators are urged to ensure we distinguish between cultural initiatives and equity initiatives, beginning by dismantling a "culture fetish" that is reflected in initiatives such as cultural competence, cultural proficiency, multicultural education, and intercultural communication, which may minimize or entirely wipe out a focus on equity for marginalized students (Gorski & Swalwell, 2015). We agree that we will never make progress in terms of dismantling inequity for MLs until we enter into difficult, potentially emotionally charged conversations and take actions that go beyond the surface levels of our students' cultures. Our goal of CRT is to achieve equity for MLs. While this book does not hold the answers, it provides some entry points that dig in deeper beyond the fun, comfortable aspects of culture in order for educators to do the hard work toward the goal of equity and justice for MLs.

DEFINING CULTURALLY RESPONSIVE TEACHING

While there has been a growing body of research on the concept of culturally responsive teaching,[2] we will share a brief synthesis of three prominent educators who have contributed significantly to this field—Gloria Ladson-Billings, Geneva Gay, and Zaretta Hammond—while recognizing there are many others who are shaping CRT (e.g., Django Paris, Sonia Nieto, and Paul Gorski, among others). We expand on other theories of CRT in subsequent chapters of this book and also include an appendix with additional resources we don't directly cite in this book.

Gloria Ladson-Billings

Ladson-Billings coined the term "culturally relevant pedagogy" to describe what she calls a pedagogy of opposition (1992). **She explains that CRT empowers students intellectually, socially, emotionally, and politically, and she emphasizes the importance of including**

---

[2]Culturally relevant teaching is also known as culturally responsive teaching.

students' cultural references throughout all aspects of learning (Ladson-Billings, 1994). In her theory of culturally relevant teaching, Ladson-Billings (1995) outlines two key theoretical underpinnings that are critical to the development of culturally relevant pedagogy:

1. Sociocultural consciousness, which she generally refers to as conceptions of self and others

2. Caring for students, which expands beyond caring about students' academic well-being to a holistic focus on their overall needs, coupled with having high expectations of them

Ladson-Billings details her three central tenets of this type of constructivist equity pedagogy in Table 1.2.

Table 1.2   Central Tenets of CRT

Ladson-Billings' Central Tenet	Definition of What CRT Does Through This Tenet
1. High expectations	Emphasizes academic success for all students
2. Cultural competence	Assists students in the formation of a positive cultural identity
3. Critical consciousness	Guides students in developing a critical consciousness they can use to critique or interrupt current and historical social inequities

Source: Adapted from Ladson-Billings, 1995.

To Ladson-Billings, CRT goes beyond individual student empowerment, extending to collective empowerment. The goal is not to have students relinquish their culture to take on the dominant culture's norms but rather develop students' sense of a synergistic relationship between their home and community culture and the school culture. In addition, teachers must guide students in recognizing and addressing social inequities (Ladson-Billings, 1995). Within CRT, students achieve academic success, develop or maintain cultural competence, and develop a critical consciousness.

Reflection Question

What takeaways do you have about Gloria Ladson-Billings's scholarship on culturally relevant pedagogy?

Geneva Gay

Geneva Gay (2010) defines culturally responsive teaching as **"using the cultural knowledge, prior experiences, frames of reference, and performance styles of ethnically diverse students to make learning encounters more relevant to and effective for [students]"** (p. 31). Similarly, teachers who use a culturally responsive method in their teaching view culture as an asset, which can be used effectively to enhance academic and social achievement. The concept of culture as a student asset looks closely at what all students bring to their learning as opposed to what we might erroneously presume they don't. Gay (2002) contends that preparing for culturally responsive teaching requires understanding the cultural characteristics and contributions of different ethnic groups in order to make schooling more "interesting and stimulating for, representative of, and responsive to (MLs)" (p. 107). It also requires being able to analyze the strengths and weaknesses of curricula and instructional materials and make the changes necessary to improve their overall quality as needed.

According to Gay (2013), culturally responsive teaching is embodied in four practical actions. Culturally responsive teachers should focus on the following facets:

1. Restructuring attitudes and beliefs: replacing deficit perspectives with assets-based perspectives

2. Resisting resistance: understanding where resistance to CRT comes from and addressing opposition to ethnic, racial, and cultural diversity

3. Centering culture and difference: understanding how and why culture and difference are essential ideologies and foundations of CRT

4. Establishing pedagogical connections: shaping instructional practices by the sociocultural characteristics of students' and teachers' contexts

Reflection Question

What stands out for you from Geneva Gay's work on CRT?

Zaretta Hammond

Hammond defines CRT in the following way:

> **[CRT is] an educator's ability to recognize students' cultural displays of learning and meaning making and to respond positively and constructively with teaching moves that use cultural knowledge as a scaffold to connect what the student knows to new concepts and content in order to promote effective information processing. All the while, the educator understands the importance of being in relationship and having a social–emotional connection to the student in order to create a safe space for learning.** (2015, p. 15)

To embody CRT, educators must develop sociopolitical consciousness, understanding the racialized society in which we live that grants unearned privilege to some while others, including MLs, experience disadvantage due to their race, gender, class, or language.

Hammond (2015) describes the importance of culturally responsive teaching and what we know about the brain and learning, emphasizing the way in which the brain seeks to minimize social threats and maximize opportunities to connect. As educators, we may be unaware of language and behaviors that students might perceive as threats. We need to consciously work to make sure that all students feel included and valued. Such positive relationships will help keep our safety/threat detection system in check and allow for higher-order learning to take place. Some students may come from cultures with strong oral traditions, and teachers' use of stories, art, music, and movement will support learning. Hammond stresses that new information must be coupled with students' existing funds of knowledge (Moll et al., 1992). Students' background knowledge is especially crucial for MLs (Staehr Fenner & Snyder, 2017) and is an important facet of CRT. When all these conditions are in place, the brain will physically grow through challenge and stretch. Table 1.3 summarizes key information about CRT from Ladson-Billings, Gay, and Hammond.

Reflection Question

What resonates with you from Zaretta Hammond's definition of CRT?

Table 1.3   Comparison of Ladson-Billings, Gay, and Hammond's Views of CRT

Educator	CRT Goals	Teachers' Actions
Ladson-Billings	• Empower students intellectually, socially, emotionally, and politically. • Develop sociocultural consciousness and caring for students. • Foster students' sense of cultural competence and the relationship between home/community and school culture.	• Encourage academic success and cultural competence. • Help students to recognize, understand, and critique current social inequities.

(Continued)

Table 1.3 (Continued)

Educator	CRT Goals	Teachers' Actions
Gay	• Use the cultural knowledge, prior experiences, frames of reference, and performance styles of ethnically diverse students to make learning encounters more relevant and effective. • Look closely at what all students bring to their learning. • View culture as an asset, which can be used effectively to enhance academic and social achievement.	• Restructure attitudes and beliefs. • Understand resistance to CRT. • Center culture and difference. • Establish pedagogical connections.
Hammond	• Focus on the impact of CRT on the brain and learning; the brain seeks to minimize social threats and maximize opportunities to connect. • Couple all new information with existing funds of knowledge in order to be learned. • Ensure that cultural knowledge serves as a scaffold to connect what the student knows to new concepts and content in order to promote effective information processing.	• Use stories, music, and repetition to connect to students and build intellective capacity. • Consciously work to make sure that all students feel included and valued. • Develop a sociopolitical consciousness. • Create student–teacher relationships and social-emotional connections to students.

To learn how some Syracuse City School District (SCSD) educators define CRT and its importance to MLs, take a look at the video clip *Why Culturally Responsive Teaching Matters*.

Video 1.1

Why Culturally Responsive Teaching Matters

To read a QR code, you must have a smartphone or tablet with a camera. We recommend that you download a QR code reader app that is made specifically for your phone or tablet brand.

resources.corwin.com/CulturallyResponsiveTeaching

Reflection Question

What would you like to learn about CRT for MLs?

WHY CULTURALLY RESPONSIVE TEACHING IS CRITICAL FOR EQUITABLY EDUCATING MLs

Now that we have explored various definitions of culture and CRT, let's begin examining why culturally responsive instruction is a critical component of multilingual learners' education. Although we could look at many more reasons, we will touch upon three here: the mismatch between MLs, teachers, and families; microaggressions and the increased bullying of MLs; and the revised TESOL Pre-K–12 Professional Teaching Standards.

Mismatches Between MLs, Teachers, and Families

Figure 1.2   Student and Teacher Populations by Race

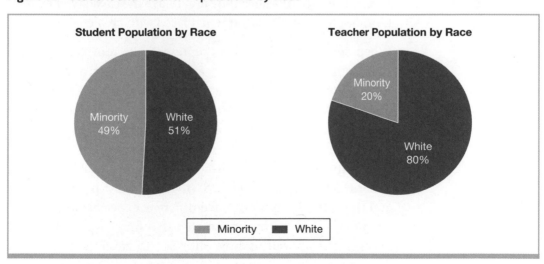

Source: Adapted from Ingersoll, R. M., Merrill, E., Stuckey, D., & Collins, G. (2018). *Seven trends: The transformation of the teaching force.* CPRE Research Reports.

One type of mismatch that exists is between teachers' and students' race and ethnicity (see Figure 1.2). Ingersoll et al. (2018), in their analysis of trends in the teacher workforce, explain that while the number of teachers of color is on the rise, there is still a significant gap between the percentage of teachers of color and the percentage of students of color nationally in the United States. Educators remain a primarily white, non-Hispanic workforce. White students make up 51 percent of the school-aged population while minority students make up 49 percent. However, 80 percent of teachers are white while 20 percent are minority. **This misalignment is significant because it means that many students of color in the nation's schools lack adult role models and contact with teachers who may more easily "get it"—those who understand their MLs' ethnic, racial, linguistic, and/or cultural backgrounds.** We should note that most parents or guardians of MLs help their children develop positive self-esteem and feel proud of their assets, including their language and culture. However, Hammond (2015) notes it is when they come to school that many MLs begin to experience the feelings of being marginalized, unseen, and silenced. These types of mismatches, which include educators' low expectations for students, can manifest themselves in MLs falling to a state of learned helplessness, in which students believe they have no control over their ability to improve as a learner. Because they then believe they don't have the capacity, they may learn not to exert any effort when faced with challenging work.

When students and teachers represent different cultures and backgrounds, it can result in a home–school mismatch on a more systemic level. The home–school mismatch is present when students have learning styles, discourse behaviors, or values of education that are different from their teachers, which can be detrimental to student learning and negatively impact the relationship between student and teacher (Delpit, 2006; Heath, 1983; Ogbu, 2003). When MLs' home cultures and the culture of school have different expectations, norms, or values, there can be a mismatch that may impact students' engagement as well as how they see themselves as learners (Cummins, 1986). Educators must have the deep understanding and skills to recognize and honor the home cultures of their students while teaching students the nuances of school culture (Calderón et al., 2011; Delpit, 1995; Saifer et al., 2011).

Microaggressions and School Bullying of MLs

One especially worrisome, growing trend we've been keenly aware of is the increasing number of microaggressions and school bullying instances that have been reported for MLs in recent years. This bullying has taken place from student–student and, even more sadly, teacher–student. Social media and mainstream media have also served to proliferate the ease with which MLs can be bullied. The concept of bullying includes the more covert behavior of microaggressions, which serves to maintain an imbalanced power structure (Rivera, 2011). **Microaggressions are the brief verbal, behavioral, or environmental indignities—whether intentional or unintentional—that communicate slights, snubs, or insults to people based solely to any group, but to culturally marginalized groups in particular** (Sue, 2010). While microaggressions may appear harmless to observers, they can be detrimental to those groups who endure them. Some examples of microaggressions include assuming people of color are from a different country (e.g., "So where are you *really* from?") or insisting that a person of color does not face any discrimination (Sue et al., 2007).

While microaggressions are a more covert form of bullying, more obvious bullying itself is also on the rise among school-aged children. An online survey of more than 10,000 kindergarten through 12th-grade educators by the Southern Poverty Law Center (2016) found that more than 2,500 students described specific incidents of bigotry and harassment, with the overwhelming majority of these incidents not making the news. Eight in 10 educators who responded reported heightened anxiety for marginalized students, including MLs, Muslims, and African American students. In addition, many educators reported white students telling students of color they would be deported, with nearly 1,000 educators sharing family separation or deportation as one of ML students' concerns. Some of the instances of bullying that were reported in *The Washington Post* (2020) include the following:

- A physical education teacher told a student that he would be deported.

- A substitute teacher promised a Lebanese American student, "You're getting kicked out of my country."
- A school employee flashed a coin bearing the word "ICE" at a Latino student.

Some schools have stepped up to be proactive in terms of addressing the bullying of MLs. For example, in California's Riverside Polytechnic High School, educators have expanded a student club focused on improving the school's culture and climate so that all students feel more welcomed. The school, which is 60 percent Latino, also offers three courses—African American, Chicano, and ethnic studies—that are designed to help students better understand one another. Another high school in Maryland has created an approach to mitigate bullying against MLs and other minority students in the diverse school. Educators there created a global community citizenship class in 2017, and the course eventually became mandatory for all freshmen in the district. Through the course, students first use self-exploration to understand how their culture has shaped their views, behaviors, and goals. Later, they explore traditions of people in their local and global communities, with the goals of "fostering values of acceptance and inclusion of all people" (Anne Arundel County Public Schools, n.d.).

The TESOL Standards and CRT

Many K–12 classroom teachers may not be familiar with the TESOL Pre-K–12 Professional Teaching Standards. These standards are used across the United States and also worldwide to provide the framework for national recognition by the Council for the Accreditation of Educator Programs (CAEP) for hundreds of ESOL teacher licensure programs. The TESOL standards were revised in 2019 and include a nuanced view of what the field feels is required for teachers to know about ML assets and culture. Beyond these standards' use for initial ESOL teacher licensure at the university level, it is suggested they be used as a rich resource to guide inservice teacher training for all teachers (Staehr Fenner & Kuhlman, 2012).

In terms of culturally responsive teaching and MLs, the TESOL standards (TESOL International Association, 2019) specify this:

(Teachers) demonstrate and apply knowledge of the impact of dynamic academic, personal, familial, cultural, social, and sociopolitical contexts on the education and language acquisition of ELLs[4] as supported by research and theories. (Teachers) investigate the academic and personal characteristics of each ELL, as well as family circumstances and literacy practices, to develop individualized, effective instructional and assessment practices for their ELLs. (Teachers) recognize how educator identity, role, culture, and biases impact the interpretation of ELLs' strengths and needs. (p. 8)

The K–12 educational landscape has shifted in a way that we have moved past compartmentalized job descriptions that lead to working in silos (Zacarian & Staehr Fenner, 2020). We are *all* teachers of MLs and must collaborate for their academic success and personal well-being. In addition, administrators must be committed to all students' success (Staehr Fenner, 2014; Staehr Fenner & Snyder, 2017).

Reflection Question

Do you think that there is an urgent need for implementation of CRT with MLs? Please explain your response.

OUR GUIDING PRINCIPLES FOR CULTURALLY RESPONSIVE TEACHING OF MLs

Given all the reasons why CRT for MLs is especially urgent, we present five guiding principles that frame our approach to supporting MLs in culturally responsive ways. These principles synthesize our beliefs about educating MLs and are grounded in research and practice. We created the first four guiding principles in one chapter of our book *Unlocking English Learners'*

---

[4]Please note the TESOL standards use the term English language learner (ELL).

Potential (Staehr Fenner & Snyder, 2017). Our thinking is constantly evolving, and for this book, we are revising some of the first four guiding principles and are adding a fifth. It is also critical to note that these principles are situated within a context of increasing ML equity and do not occur in a vacuum (see Figure 1.3). We will dive into each of these topics in much more depth in Chapter 3 through Chapter 7.

Figure 1.3   Principles of ML Equity

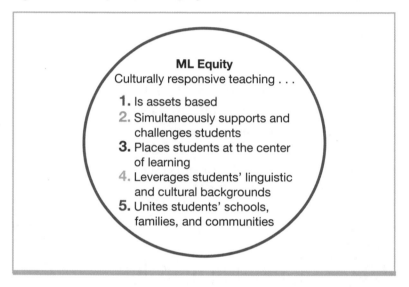

ML Equity
Culturally responsive teaching . . .

1. Is assets based
2. Simultaneously supports and challenges students
3. Places students at the center of learning
4. Leverages students' linguistic and cultural backgrounds
5. Unites students' schools, families, and communities

Guiding Principle 1: *Culturally responsive teaching is assets-based.*

There are multiple media outlets that espouse ways in which some believe multilingual learners are draining resources from our schools and economy. While it may sometimes pain us to hear such language about MLs, we feel it's important to be aware of how students may be perceived by others. In addition, in our professional development and technical assistance work with educators we sometimes hear comments unknowingly framed in deficit views about MLs. While we believe most educators don't intentionally think of MLs in terms of their deficits, deficit-based language sometimes subconsciously may surface. When we consider the obstacles that MLs must surmount in order to learn academic content in a context that may not be culturally relevant, it can be easy to default to a deficit-based approach. **A deficit perspective is**

one in which we focus on students' challenges and frame our interactions with them in terms of these challenges. Using a deficit lens, educators tend to view MLs' home language(s) and culture(s) as hindrances to overcome or, even worse, broken components that need to be fixed instead of shifting the school culture in a more systematic way (Hammond, 2015; National Education Association [NEA], 2015). Educators may attribute what they consider poor performance to MLs' linguistic abilities in English, low motivation, lack of parental or guardian involvement, or similar factors that place blame on students and/or their families (González, 2005; Valencia, 1997; Valenzuela, 1999).

In contrast, an assets-based perspective values students' home languages and cultures and sees them as a springboard for future learning (González, 2005; Valencia, 1997; Valenzuela, 1999; Zacarian & Staehr Fenner, 2020). To that end, an assets-based perspective recognizes that parents of MLs are involved in their children's education and support their children in ways that might not be so obvious to many educators who do not have knowledge of individual ML family routines and beliefs (Staehr Fenner, 2014). An additional benefit of educators adopting an assets-based perspective is that it provides multiple entry points and opportunities to honor students' cultural and linguistic backgrounds and build teaching upon what students already know (Hammond, 2015).

Guiding Principle 2: *Culturally responsive teaching simultaneously supports and challenges students.*

Our second principle is based on the importance of having high expectations for the MLs in your classes while at the same time giving them the support that they need to achieve. MLs should have access to the same grade-level content and texts as their non-ML peers, but they should feel safe and also be given sufficient instructional support for this work as needed. Hammond (2015) refers to this combination of creating a safe space for students while setting high expectations for them

and holding them accountable to meet those expectations as taking a "warm demander" stance. When teachers operate from a warm demander framework, students are less likely to become dependent on others for their learning. Hammond notes, "Your role as an ally in the learning partnership calls for you to know when to offer emotional comfort and care and when to not allow the student to slip into learned helplessness" (p. 97).

This second principle is also framed around the idea that within our society certain groups are bestowed privileges that are not granted to individuals outside these groups. As part of our second principle, culturally responsive teachers collaboratively develop lessons that include the history and experiences of diverse groups and explicit instruction about structures that reinforce power, privilege, and discriminatory practices in society. In addition, culturally responsive teachers provide opportunities for students, families, and educators to think critically about institutionalized inequity, how inequity and injustice impact their lives, and steps they can take to address inequity (National Center for Culturally Responsive Educational Systems, 2008).

Guiding Principle 3: *Culturally responsive teaching places students at the center of learning.*

Student-centered learning is not a new concept in the field of education, and there are a variety of approaches that fit under

the umbrella of student-centered learning, such as collaborative learning, inquiry-based learning, and project-based learning. **Student-centered learning can be defined as an instructional approach in which the students in the classroom shape the content, instructional activities, materials, assessment, and/or pace of the learning.**
Student-centered learning also focuses on the idea that students are provided with opportunities to learn from one another rather than solely from the teacher. There has been little research on how to reframe collaborative learning and groupwork for language learners (WIDA, 2014). One

step toward student-centered learning for MLs in particular is making sure that learning goals and objectives—including language objectives for ELs as appropriate—are explained in student-friendly language so that students of all levels of English proficiency can participate in setting goals for their learning and assessing their learning (Gottlieb, 2016; Stiggins et al., 2004).

Guiding Principle 4:
Culturally responsive teaching leverages students' linguistic and cultural backgrounds.

The fourth principle focuses on ways that teaching and learning can give value to students' home language(s), cultures, and experiences. A common misconception in teaching MLs is that they should be discouraged from speaking their home language with their families and peers and that home language use should not be incorporated into instruction. However, research indicates that families should speak their home language with their children, as  providing them exposure to the rich, complex language in which they are the most proficient has a positive impact on MLs' development of their home language and also English. This concept may seem counterintuitive to families, who may have been told by esteemed members of their communities, such as teachers, administrators, and even pediatricians, that they need to speak only English at home. Further, instruction that incorporates and builds on MLs' home language(s) will support them in developing literacy in English (August et al., 2009; Carlo et al., 2004; Liang et al., 2005; Restrepo et al., 2010). As educators of MLs, we also need to consider the benefits of a powerful tool for learning that is receiving more attention in today's classroom—translanguaging, or using languages together to maximize communicative potential (García, 2009a).

Hand in hand with building upon students' home languages is learning about and leveraging students' cultures in instruction (Staehr Fenner & Snyder, 2017). To respect and value students' home cultures, educators should recognize the funds of knowledge, or the linguistic, cognitive, and sociocultural resources MLs bring to the classroom, and build on these resources during their teaching (August & Shanahan, 2006; Moll et al., 1992; Riches & Genesee, 2006). By providing MLs multiple opportunities to draw from and use their home language(s) and cultures, teachers validate students' cultural and linguistic backgrounds and elevate the benefits of being multilingual and multicultural.

Guiding Principle 5: *Culturally responsive teaching unites students' schools, families, and communities.*

Undergirding all four of these principles is our fifth principle—that CRT can serve as a uniting force to bring together students, schools, families, and communities. We first note that we use the term "family" instead of "parent" to recognize the concept of the entire family (e.g., siblings, cousins, aunts, uncles, grandparents, and other caregivers or guardians) having an impact on an ML's education, not only parents. When examining the relationship between schools and families, we know that when MLs feel welcomed in their classrooms and schools, this positive sentiment can extend to their families, helping cement their trust. We also need to consider the shift from the term "family involvement," or families being physically present in the school building, to "family engagement," or considering multiple ways in which families may contribute to their children's education (Baker et al., 2016). It is also well documented that family engagement is a predictor of students' academic achievement (Arias, 2015; Breiseth et al., 2011; Hattie, 2009, 2012). In addition, communities play a vital role in supporting CRT. Community-based organizations and partnerships also play a vital role in rounding out and supporting the relationship between schools and families, enabling them to feel they truly belong in both contexts (Arias, 2015). Not only do MLs benefit from culturally responsive instruction, but their non-ML peers, teachers, families, and communities do as well.

Application Activity 1b. Rank the Guiding Principles

Directions: Rank the five guiding principles in order of importance to you. (*Note*: You will be asked to rank them again in the final chapter of this book.)

_____ Culturally responsive teaching is assets-based.

_____ Culturally responsive teaching simultaneously supports and challenges students.

_____ Culturally responsive teaching places students at the center of learning.

_____ Culturally responsive teaching leverages students' linguistic and cultural backgrounds.

_____ CRT unites students' schools, families, and communities.

Reflection Question

Why did you rank them in the order that you did?

THE ML CULTURALLY RESPONSIVE TEACHING CYCLE

While culturally responsive teaching may not yet be on everyone's radar, all educators need to see themselves as culturally responsive. Previously, we have stressed that all teachers need to share the responsibility for teaching MLs, and all teachers should teach academic language and culture simultaneously (Staehr Fenner, 2014; Staehr Fenner & Snyder, 2017). Similarly, all teachers need to teach in their area of expertise in a way that is culturally responsive for all learners. To do so, we recommend educators address our five cyclical CRT cycle components, as detailed in Figure 1.4.

Figure 1.4   CRT Cycle Components

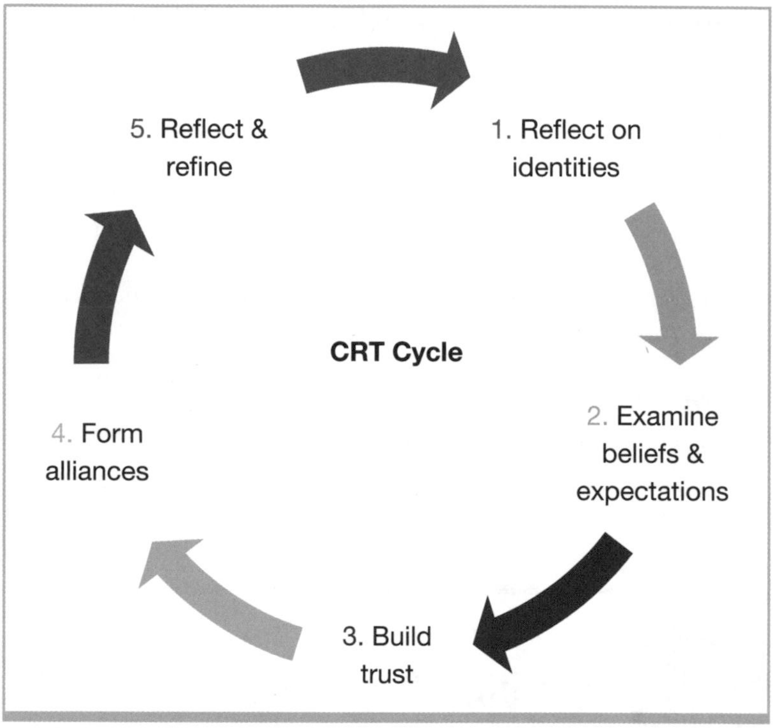

1. **Reflect on implicit personal identities, including biases.** Hammond (2015) notes that "culture is like the air we breathe, permeating all we do. And the hardest culture to examine is often our own because it shapes our actions in ways that seem invisible and normal" (p. 55). Similarly, Staehr Fenner (2014) urges educators of MLs to reflect on their own culture and the impact it may unwittingly have on the way in which educators engage with students. As educators, we will not make progress until we move out of our comfort zones and confront anything standing in the way of us growing as CRT educators, recognizing that discomfort means we are making progress.

2. **Examine beliefs and expectations about MLs and their families.** After reflecting on their own cultures and implicit biases, we recommend educators expand their sphere

to look more deeply at their beliefs and expectations when it comes to MLs and their families. We encourage educators to determine what they already know and believe, think about where there are misunderstandings, and learn where to find more information to have a more complete picture of their students and families.

3. **Build trust with MLs and their families.** The next step in becoming a more culturally responsive educator is to increase trust among MLs as well as their families. Trust is crucial in creating a safe classroom space in which MLs feel free to take risks with language and content (Staehr Fenner, 2014; Staehr Fenner & Snyder, 2017). In addition, an established sense of student–teacher trust enables students' brains to focus on activities that include creativity, learning, and higher-order thinking (Hammond, 2015).

4. **Form alliances with educators and students to do the hard work of CRT.** At this point, educators are ready to collaborate to leverage each other's expertise to make progress in furthering their journey as CRT educators. To do so, it is important for educators to determine who their allies might be, joining forces with fellow educators who also seem open to the idea of growing as CRT educators (NEA, 2015). Critical to the work is also forming alliances with ML students, who often get left out of the equation. Alliances with students offer the opportunity for teachers to practice validation, or acknowledging the inequities inside and outside the school walls that impact MLs and validating their ways of speaking and being that may have been labeled "wrong" in the mainstream school culture (Hammond, 2015).

5. **Reflect, refine, and begin the process again.** In our work as educators, we should never be satisfied with the status quo. Therefore, this process is cyclical; we need to constantly reflect on our progress, refine our approaches, and keep going. We recommend taking notes in this book as well as keeping a reflection journal that allows you to hit the pause button and be honest about the areas that are going well and about places you

Something I learned about myself that might impact my teaching is...

may need to refine your approach. Then, you can discuss the impact of your work with your allies (including ML students and families) to also determine areas that can be improved to carry over into your work in Step 1.

Reflection Journal

Something I learned about myself that might impact my teaching is . . .

Summary of Key Ideas

- This book is an important addition to the field because we need to examine and repair systemic inequities in ML education.

- Multilingual learners are students whose parent or guardian reports speaking one or more languages other than English at home. They may or may not qualify for ESOL, depending on their level of English proficiency.

- There are multiple definitions of culture and CRT. No matter the definition, we must ensure that CRT is used as a means to ameliorate inequity for MLs.

- CRT is critical for MLs because of mismatches between MLs, teachers, and families; the bullying of MLs; and the focus on CRT in the TESOL standards, among many other reasons.

- Five guiding principles of CRT frame our work, all situated within a context of increasing MLs' equity:

  1. Culturally responsive teaching is assets-based.

  2. Culturally responsive teaching simultaneously supports and challenges students.

  3. Culturally responsive teaching places students at the center of learning.

  4. Culturally responsive teaching leverages students' linguistic and cultural backgrounds.

  5. CRT unites students' schools, families, and communities.

- The culturally responsive teaching cycle allows educators to enter into and constantly refine their work as CRT educators.

Chapter 1 Reflection Questions

1. How would you define your own sense of urgency in ensuring CRT for multilingual learners?

2. Reflect on the five guiding principles for CRT. Which is an area of strength for you? Which principle might you wish to work on?

3. What are you wondering about as you move on to Chapter 2?

References

Anne Arundel County Public Schools. (n.d.). *Global community citizenship (GCC) course.* https://www.aacps.org/globalcitizenship

Arias, B. (2015). Parent and community involvement in bilingual and multilingual education. In W. E. Wright, S. Boun, & O. García (Eds.), *The handbook of bilingual and multilingual education* (pp. 282–298). Wiley-Blackwell.

August, D., Branum-Martin, L., Cardenas-Hagan, E., & Francis, D. J. (2009). The impact of an instructional intervention on the science and language learning of middle grade English language learners. *Journal of Research on Educational Effectiveness, 2*(4), 345–376.

August, D. E., & Shanahan, T. E. (2006). *Developing literacy in second-language learners: Report of the national literacy panel on language-minority children and youth.* Lawrence Erlbaum Associates.

Baker, T. L., Wise, J., Kelley, G., & Skiba, R. J. (2016). Identifying barriers: Creating solutions to improve family engagement. *School Community Journal, 26*(2), 161–184.

Barnshaw, J. (2008). Race. In R. T. Schaefer (Ed.), *Encyclopedia of race, ethnicity, and society* (Vol. 1, pp. 1091–1093). SAGE.

Breiseth, L., Robertson, K., & LaFond, S. (2011). *A guide for engaging ELL families: Twenty strategies for school leaders.* Colorín Colorado.

Calderón, M., Slavin, R., & Sánchez, M. (2011). Effective instruction for English learners. *The Future of Children, (21)*1, 103–127.

Carlo, M. S., August, D., McLaughlin, B., Snow, C. E., Dressler, C., Lippman, D. N., Lively, T. J., & White, C. E. (2004). Closing the gap: Addressing the vocabulary needs of English-language learners in bilingual and mainstream classrooms. *Reading Research Quarterly, 39*(2), 188–215.

Cooper, R. S., Kaufman, J. S., & Ward, R. (2003). Race and genomics. *New England Journal of Medicine, 348*(12), 1166–1170.

Cummins, J. (1986). Empowering minority students: A framework for intervention. *Harvard Educational Review, 56*(1), 18–37.

Delpit, L. (1995). *Other people's children: Cultural conflict in the classroom.* The New Press.

Delpit, L. (2006). Lessons from teachers. *Journal of Teacher Education, 57*(3), 220–231. https://doi.org/10.1177/0022487105285966

DiAngelo, R. (2018). *White fragility: Why it's so hard for white people to talk about racism.* Beacon Press.

Erickson, F. (2007). Culture in society and educational practices. In J. Banks & C. A. Banks (Eds.), *Multicultural education: Issues and perspectives* (6th ed.; pp. 31–61). John Wiley & Sons.

Ethnic. (n.d.). *In Merriam-Webster.com.* https://www.merriam-webster.com/dictionary/ethnic

Ethnicity. (n.d.). In *Merriam-Webster.com.* https://www.merriam-webster.com/dictionary/ethnicity

García, O. (2009a). Education, multilingualism and translanguaging in the 21st century. In A. Mohanty, M. Panda, R. Phillipson, & T. Skutnabb-Kangas (Eds.), *Multilingual education for social justice: Globalising the local* (pp. 128–145). Orient Blackswan.

García, O. (2009b). Emergent bilinguals and TESOL: What's in a name? *TESOL Quarterly*, *43*(2), 322–326.

Gay, G. (2002). Preparing for culturally responsive teaching. *Journal of Teacher Education*, *53*(2), 106–116.

Gay, G. (2010). *Culturally responsive reaching: Theory, research, and practice* (2nd ed.). Teachers College Press.

Gay, G. (2013). Teaching to and through cultural diversity. *Curriculum Inquiry*, *43*(1), 48–70.

González, N. (2005). Beyond culture: The hybridity of funds of knowledge. In. N. Gonzalez, L. C. Moll, & C. Amanti (Eds.), *Funds of knowledge: Theorizing practices in households, communities and classrooms* (pp. 29–46). Erlbaum.

Gorski, P. (2016). Rethinking the role of "culture" in educational equity: From cultural competence to equity literacy. *Multicultural Perspectives*, *18*(4), 221–226.

Gorski, P. C., & Swalwell, K. (2015). Equity literacy for all. *Educational Leadership*, *72*(6), 34–40.

Gottlieb, M. (2016). *Assessing English language learners: Bridges to educational equity*. Corwin.

Hall, E. T. (1976). *Beyond culture*. Doubleday.

Hammond, Z. (2015). *Culturally responsive teaching and the brain*. Corwin.

Hattie, J. (2009). *Visible learning: A synthesis of over 800 meta-analyses relating to achievement*. Routledge.

Hattie, J. (2012). *Visible learning for teachers: Maximizing impact on learning*. Routledge.

Heath, S. (1983). *Ways with words: Language, life and work in communities and classrooms*. Cambridge University Press. https://doi.org/10.1017/CBO9780511841057

Ingersoll, R. M., Merrill, E., Stuckey, D., & Collins, G. (2018). *Seven trends: The transformation of the teaching force*. CPRE Research Reports.

Kieffer, M. J., & Thompson, K. D. (2018). Hidden progress of multilingual students on NAEP. *Educational Researcher*, *47*(6), 391–398.

Ladson-Billings, G. (1992). Reading between the lines and beyond the pages: A culturally relevant approach to literacy teaching. *Theory Into Practice*, *31*(4), 312–320.

Ladson-Billings, G. (1994). *The dreamkeepers: Successful teachers of African American children*. Jossey-Bass.

Ladson-Billings, G. (1995). Toward a theory of culturally relevant pedagogy. *American Research Journal*, *32*(3), 465–491.

Ladson-Billings, G. (2006). It's not the culture of poverty, it's the poverty of culture: The problem with teacher education. *Anthropology & Education Quarterly*, *37*(2), 104–109.

Liang, L. A., Peterson, C. A., & Graves, M. F. (2005). Investigating two approaches to fostering children's comprehension of literature. *Reading Psychology*, *26*(4–5), 387–400.

Los Angeles Unified School District. (2018). *Master plan for English learners and standard English learners*. https://achieve.lausd.net/cms/lib/CA01000043/Centricity/domain/22/el%20sel%20master%20plan/2018%20Master%20Plan%20for%20EL%20and%20SEL.pdf

Moll, L. C., Amanti, C., Neff, D., & Gonzalez, N. (1992). Funds of knowledge for teaching: Using a qualitative approach to connect homes and classrooms. *Theory Into Practice*, *31*(2), 132–141.

Nagel, J. (1994). Constructing ethnicity: Creating and recreating ethnic identity and culture, *Social Problems*, *41*(1), 152–176. https://doi.org/10.2307/3096847

Natanson, H., Woodrow Cox, J. & Stein, P. (2020, February 13). Trump's words, bullied kids, scarred schools. *The Washington Post*. https://www.washingtonpost.com/graphics/2020/local/school-bullying-trump-words/

National Center for Culturally Responsive Educational Systems (NCCREST). (2008). *Module 6: Culturally responsive response to intervention*. Mary Lou Fulton College of Education. http://www.niusileadscape.org/docs/pl/culturally_responsive_response_to_intervention/activity1/RTI%20Academy%201%20FacMan%20ver%201.1%20FINAL%20kak.pdf

National Education Association. (2015). All In! How educators can advocate for English language learners. Washington, DC: National Education Association. https://www.nea.org/resource-library/english-language-learners

NCES. (2017). Digest of education statistics. *U.S. Department of Education*. https://nces.ed.gov/programs/digest/d18/tables/dt18_204.20.asp?current=yes

Ogbu, J. U. (2003). *Sociocultural, political, and historical studies in education. Black American students in an affluent suburb: A study of academic disengagement*. Lawrence Erlbaum Associates.

Park, Y. (2005). Culture as deficit: A critical discourse analysis of the concept of culture in contemporary social work discourse. *Journal of Sociology and Social Welfare, 32*(3), 11–33.

Restrepo, M. A., Castilla, A. P., Schwanenflugel, P. J., Neuharth-Pritchett, S., Hamilton, C. E., & Arboleda, A. (2010). Effects of a supplemental Spanish oral language program on sentence length, complexity, and grammaticality in Spanish-speaking children attending English-only preschools. *Language, Speech, and Hearing Services in Schools, 41*(1), 3–13.

Riches, C., & Genesee, F. (2006). Crosslinguistic and cross-modal issues. In F. Genesee, K. J. Lindholm-Leary, W. M. Saunders, & D. Christian (Eds.), *Educating English language learners: A synthesis of research evidence* (pp. 64–108). Cambridge University Press.

Rivera, D. (2011, January 23). Bullying & microaggressions. *Psychology Today*. https://www.psychologytoday.com/us/blog/microaggressions-in-everyday-life/201101/bullying-microaggressions

Saifer, S., Edwards, K., Ellis, D., Ko, L., & Stuczynski, A. (2011). *Culturally responsive standards-based teaching: Classroom to community and back*. Corwin. http://dx.doi.org/10.4135/9781452219639

Southern Poverty Law Center. (2016). *After election day: The Trump effect*. https://www.tolerance.org/sites/default/files/2017-06/After%20the%20Election%20Trump%20Effect%20Report.pdf

Staehr Fenner, D. (2014). *Advocating for English learners: A guide for educators*. Corwin.

Staehr Fenner, D., & Kuhlman, N. (2012). *Preparing effective teachers of English language learners: Practical applications for the TESOL P–12 professional teaching standards*. TESOL International Association.

Staehr Fenner, D., & Snyder, S. (2017). *Unlocking English learners' potential: Strategies for making content accessible*. Corwin.

Stiggins, R. J., Arter, J. A., Chappuis, J., & Chappuis, S. (2004). *Classroom assessment for student learning: Doing it right, using it well*. Assessment Training Institute.

Sue, D. W. (2010). *Microaggressions in everyday life: Race, gender, and sexual orientation*. John Wiley & Sons.

Sue, D. W., Capodilupo, C. M., Torino, G. C., Bucceri, J. M., Holder, A., Nadal, K. L., & Esquilin, M. (2007). Racial microaggressions in everyday life: Implications for clinical practice. *American Psychologist, 62*(4), 271.

Sugarman, J. 2020. *Which English learners count when? Understanding state EL subgroup definitions in ESSA reporting.* Migration Policy Institute.

TESOL International Association. (2019). *Standards for initial TESOL Pre-K–12 teacher preparation programs.* https://www.tesol.org/docs/default-source/books/2018-tesol-teacher-prep-standards-final.pdf?sfvrsn=23f3ffdc_6

U.S. Census. (2017). https://factfinder.census.gov/faces/tableservices/jsf/pages/productview.xhtml?pid=ACS_15_5YR_S1603&prodType=table

U.S. Department of Education, National Center for Education Statistics, Common Core of Data (CCD). (2018). *Local education agency universe survey, 2000–01 through 2016–17.* https://nces.ed.gov/programs/digest/d18/tables/dt18_204.20.asp?current=yes

Valencia, R. R. (1997). Conceptualizing the notion of deficit thinking. In R. R. Valencia (Ed.), *The evolution of deficit thinking: Educational thought and practice* (pp. 1–12). Palmer Press.

Valenzuela, A. (1999). *Subtractive schooling: Issues of caring in education of US–Mexican youth.* State University of New York Press.

WIDA. (2014). *Collaborative learning for English language learners.* https://wida.wisc.edu/sites/default/files/resource/Brief-CollaborativeLearningforELLs.pdf

WIDA. (2019). *WIDA guiding principles of language development.* https://wida.wisc.edu/sites/default/files/Website/Misc%20Pages/2020StandardsVision/2020-vision-guiding-principles-flyer.pdf?fbclid=IwAR2Wg9ChBLGhN52ccACox6s7uSaGC7YQ-xfpMCmdBPiyj4Oo6CHU6cI2U8I

Zacarian, D., & Staehr Fenner, D. (2020). From deficit-based to assets-based. In M. E. Calderón, D. Staehr Fenner, A. Honigsteld, S. Slakk, D. Zacariam, M. G., Dove, M. Gottlieb, T. Ward Singer, & I. Soto (Eds.), *Breaking down the wall: Essential shifts for English learners' success.* Corwin.

Building Cultural Competency

Scenario: Lian, Lestari, and Ms. Morgan

Ninth-grader Lian is a multilingual learner (ML) from China who immigrated to the United States three years ago with her mom and younger brother. Although quiet in class, she has developed close friendships with other MLs as well as with a couple of girls on the junior varsity volleyball team that she plays on. One of her closest friends is Lestari, an Indonesian student who entered the school last year.

Early in the school year, Lian's biology teacher, Ms. Morgan, asks her to stay after class one day. Ms. Morgan explains that, despite the fact that Lian did an excellent job on a model of a cell, she has to give Lian a zero because Lestari (who is a student in another section of the class) submitted the same work. Ms. Morgan assumed that—because Lian is getting an *A* in the course, speaks English more fluently, and consistently submits high-quality work—she allowed Lestari to copy from her. Lian explained to Ms. Morgan that they worked on the assignment together, and they didn't know that each submitting the same work wasn't allowed. Ms. Morgan is sympathetic but still feels that Lian and Lestari cheated and should be graded accordingly.

Scenario Reflection Questions

After reading the scenario, consider the following questions:

1. What cultural beliefs or expectations might Ms. Morgan have that led her to respond how she did?

2. What cultural beliefs or expectations might Lian have brought to this situation?

3. How could Ms. Morgan and/or Lian resolve this situation?

CHAPTER OVERVIEW

In this chapter, we'll discuss what it means to build cultural competency and provide five elements of cultural competency, ranging from understanding your own culture to looking at the role of culture at an institutional level. You will have an opportunity to reflect on your own cultural beliefs and expectations and also explore personal bias that you might bring to your interactions with students. We'll conclude the chapter with three steps that you can take next to continue your exploration of this topic at an individual and school level.

WHAT IT MEANS TO BUILD CULTURAL COMPETENCY

In order to engage in the work of culturally responsive instruction, it is essential to build your cultural competency. **Cultural competency is the ability to successfully and effectively interact with individuals from cultures other than your own in cross-cultural situations.** The term "cultural competency" was coined by Cross and colleagues (1989) to analyze interactions and relationships in the health care field. When thinking about cultural competency in the field of education, the term highlights the knowledge, skills, and attitudes needed to effectively teach students from other cultures and engage with families from cultures other than your own.

Reflection Questions

What do you think are the two most critical areas of knowledge, skills, or attitudes that are needed to effectively interact and build relationships with ML students and families? Why did you choose these?

Knowledge, Skill, or Attitude Needed	Why You Think It's Important
I.	
2.	

While there are various descriptions of the characteristics included in cultural competency, we would like to focus on five key elements (adapted from Diller & Moule, 2005; Lindsey et al., 2019; National Education Association, n.d.; Quezada et al., 2015). We will introduce these five elements here and then explore them more deeply in the remainder of this chapter.

1. **Be culturally self-aware.** Self-awareness is the first step in building cultural competence. As anthropologist Edward T. Hall (1959) explains, "Culture hides much more than it reveals, and strangely enough what it hides, it hides most effectively from its own participants. Years of study have convinced me that the real job is not to understand foreign culture but to understand our own" (p. 30). In order to begin the work of building cultural competence, it is essential that you understand the various beliefs and experiences that shape your cultural identity and recognize the impact your identity has on how you teach and interact with others. Self-awareness requires you to acknowledge personal bias and take opportunities to reflect on this bias and the implications that it has on your interactions with others.

2. **Assess cultural knowledge and seek knowledge about other cultures**. This skill means that as an educator you evaluate your understanding of your students' cultures and endeavor to learn more in those areas where you may have gaps. One concern when discussing cultures is the potential to group students into a single category or make assumptions about that student based on what you believe to be true about his or her culture (e.g., He is Asian American, so he must be good at math; she is from the Caribbean, so she probably has a relaxed attitude about punctuality). Learning about the history and background of students' home cultures is just one piece in understanding your students.

3. **Value diversity.** Valuing diversity and understanding the strength that diverse perspectives can offer is essential to culturally responsive teaching (CRT). A commitment to CRT requires the fundamental understanding that everyone benefits from the sharing of varied viewpoints and experiences. If you value diversity, you look for opportunities to engage in new cultural experiences and provide opportunities for your students to share their unique perspectives with you and with one another.

4. **Appreciate the dynamics of difference.** Appreciating the dynamics of difference requires an understanding that cultural differences can, and often do, lead to misunderstandings, miscommunication, and resistance. We have noticed in our own experience as teachers that these misunderstandings can increase when students are developing proficiency in English and are still learning nuances of the language. To be culturally competent in this area requires learning to problem solve and being open to conflict. It necessitates speaking honestly about cultural differences, power differences, and inequity. It requires acknowledging privilege that you have that others may not have. It also requires risk-taking.

5. **Institutionalize cultural knowledge**. The skill of institutionalizing cultural knowledge extends the work of being culturally competent beyond the boundaries of our classroom. It speaks to the way we as educators must look to embed our understandings and our practices of CRT into the larger context. For example, rather than focusing only on making use of more culturally responsive materials in our classroom, we seek to examine the school curricula as a whole and the presence of culturally inclusive materials throughout the school. The institutionalizing of cultural knowledge builds on the work of element number four in which we take steps to address inequities and push back against discourse and actions that narrow the opportunities and understandings of certain groups of students, particularly marginalized students.

Let's now take a deeper dive into each of these five areas. You'll have an opportunity to engage in reflection activities and explore tools for strengthening cultural competency in each area.

KEY ELEMENT 1: *BE CULTURALLY SELF-AWARE.*

In order to support you in building your cultural self-awareness, we are going to ask you to take part in a series of reflection activities. You can complete these activities individually or, whenever possible, complete and then discuss them with colleagues. Some of these activities can also be adapted for use in the classroom to help students explore their own cultural identities.

Application Activity 2a. My Multifaceted Identity[1]

In the profile that follows, write five aspects of yourself that shape who you are. These aspects might be related to nationality, racial or gender identity, religion, role, hobby, and so forth. Try to consider those aspects of yourself that most profoundly influence how you see and respond to events and people around you. For each aspect of your identity, write how it shapes how you see the world. We have shared a partially completed example with you.

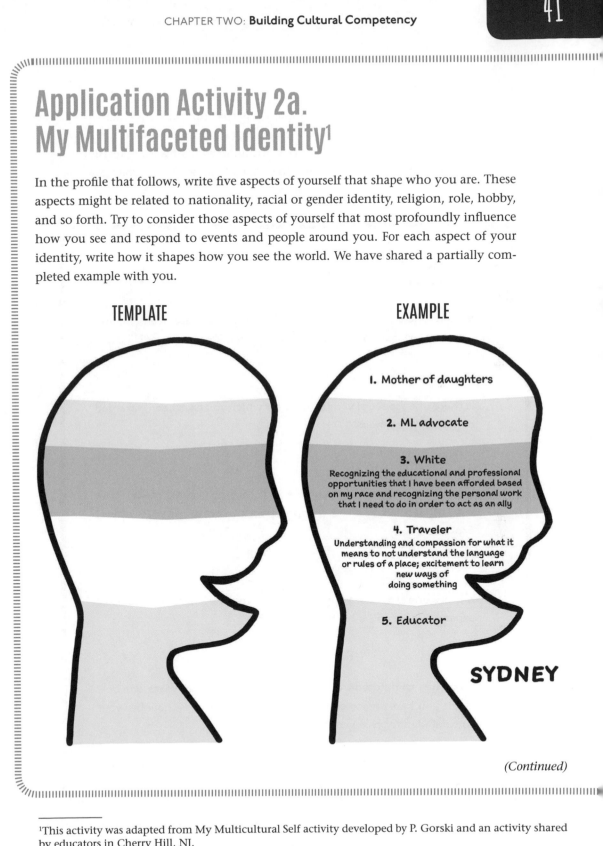

TEMPLATE

EXAMPLE

1. Mother of daughters

2. ML advocate

3. White
Recognizing the educational and professional opportunities that I have been afforded based on my race and recognizing the personal work that I need to do in order to act as an ally

4. Traveler
Understanding and compassion for what it means to not understand the language or rules of a place; excitement to learn new ways of doing something

5. Educator

SYDNEY

(Continued)

---

[1]This activity was adapted from My Multicultural Self activity developed by P. Gorski and an activity shared by educators in Cherry Hill, NJ.

(Continued)

Based on your profile, consider the reflection questions that follow. As you answer the questions, take notice of your feelings. Consider how honest you are able to be in your responses. Some of the questions might challenge you, and you might want to revisit them at a later time. Also consider if you would be able to be equally honest about your responses if sharing them with others.

Reflection Questions

1. Is there one aspect of your identity for which you have been discriminated against, teased, or misunderstood? If so, what happened?

2. Is there one aspect of your identity for which you have been rewarded or valued? If so, how?

3. Is there one aspect of your identity that you don't easily share with others, but you feel it impacts your interactions with others? Explain.

4. Is there one aspect of your identity that you work hard to develop or expand or that you want to be known for?

5. If you had completed this same activity five, 10, or 20 years ago, how might you have answered differently? In other words, how has your cultural identity changed throughout your life?

Application Activity 2b. My Teachers

Next, we would like to turn the discussion to the impact that culture can have on teaching and learning. In the following section, think back on your educational experiences. Consider the questions in the My Teachers activity and complete the table.

- Think of one teacher in your life that you had a positive relationship with. What drew you together? In what ways might your cultures have been similar? What did you appreciate about that teacher?

- Next, think of a teacher that you did not have a positive relationship with. What prevented you from having a positive relationship? How were you different? What might have the teacher done differently to improve your relationship?

A Teacher You Connected With	A Teacher You Did Not Connect With

(Continued)

(Continued)

Reflection Questions

1. How might you apply your experiences with these two teachers to your role as an educator and your work with MLs?

2. Have you ever had a teacher who had a cultural background that was different than your own? Why is this question significant?

Hand in hand with understanding your own culture and school culture is recognizing personal bias and how it might impact your interactions with students of other races, cultures, or socioeconomic groups. *Teaching Tolerance* (n.d.) has a Common Beliefs Survey that asks educators to rate themselves in response to the following statement: *I don't think of my students in terms of their race or ethnicity. I am color-blind when it comes to my teaching.*

Strongly Agree		*Neither Agree nor Disagree*		*Strongly Disagree*
1	*2*	*3*	*4*	*5*

How accurate is that statement for you? Why did you select the number that you chose?

While being color-blind in relation to your teaching may seem like an effective way to treat all students fairly and equally, ignoring cultural, racial, and linguistic differences actually undermines the potential of being able to connect with each student based on her or his unique background. Being color-blind inherently denies students an opportunity to share facets of their identity. When individuals profess to be color-blind, they may also overlook the role that implicit bias can play in their interactions with students and families who come from cultures other than their own. Implicit bias is a result of our brain's work of categorizing and stereotyping as a way to process large amounts of information (Hammond, 2015; Kirwan Institute for the Study of Race and Ethnicity, 2013). Bias can lead you to make assumptions about others and ignore the inherent inequities that exist in education, such as inequitable access to college preparation and honors courses, greater numbers of disciplinary referrals, lower scores on state achievement tests, and lower graduation rates, among many others.

To further explore your own cultural identity, consider the following recommendations adapted from Nieto's *On Becoming Sociocultural Mediators* (2017):

- **Keep a journal.** You can use a journal to reflect on what you learn about yourself through your interactions with others, about privileges that you have that others may not have, or about steps that you are taking toward CRT or building a culturally responsive school climate.

- **Start a reading or inquiry group** framed around CRT or equity. You can determine the topic that you would like to focus on in this group. For example, you might choose to read books that provide historical insight on the home countries of your students. You might choose to explore books that offer multifaceted perspectives on a unit of study and discuss how you could incorporate those ideas into your teaching. In Appendix F, we have provided a list of books and resources that you might consider for an inquiry group. Instead of engaging in a book study, you might, instead, focus on an advocacy issue that you feel needs to be addressed in your context and explore steps that you can take as a team to address those problems. For some tools and strategies for engaging in advocacy work, please refer to Chapter 8.

- **Conduct a critical family history.** "Critical family history" is a term coined by Christine Sleeter (2008) to describe a process in which individuals use a critical lens to analyze the experiences of their ancestors in an effort to understand the power relationships among different groups at that time, the position of their ancestors within those power dynamics, ways those relationships were maintained or changed over time, and seek to understand if and how these dynamics have a lasting impact today.

- **Explore your privilege.** Seek out resources that offer tools to help you unpack privilege that you may have based on your race, ethnicity, socioeconomic status, and citizenship, as well as other aspects of your identity that may grant you access to freedoms, opportunities, and resources that others do not have.

Talking about privilege—and especially white privilege—can be incredibly uncomfortable. It is not easy to acknowledge unearned advantages that we have. Collins (2018), in his article on white privilege explains, "White privilege is both unconsciously enjoyed and consciously perpetuated. It is both on the surface and deeply embedded into American life" (para. 18). Figure 2.1, Examples of White Privilege in Schools, provides some illustrations that Greenberg (2017) shares of what privilege may look like for you or your children if you are white.

Figure 2.1   Examples of White Privilege in Schools

- I have the privilege of learning about my race in school.

- I have the privilege of finding children's books that overwhelmingly represent my race.

- I have the privilege of being favored by school authorities and leaders.

- I have the privilege of attending affluent or well-funded schools.

- I have the privilege of being insulated from the daily toll of racism.

Source: Greenberg, J. (2017). *Ten examples that prove white privilege exists in every aspect imaginable.* Yes! https://www.yesmagazine.org/social-justice/2017/07/24/10-examples-that-prove-white-privilege-exists-in-every-aspect-imaginable/

For white educators, Robin DiAngelo's *White Fragility* (2018) and Peggy McIntosh's *White Privilege: Unpacking the Invisible Knapsack* (1988) can be solid starting points for thinking about how you may benefit from white privilege in different aspects of your life. Other books to help educators explore the ways that systemic racism impacts education include books by Monique Morris—*Pushout: The Criminalization of Black Girls in Schools* (2018) and *Sing a Rhythm, Dance a Blues: Education for the Liberation of Black and Brown* Girls (2019)—and Lisa Delpit's *Other People's Children: Cultural Conflict in the Classroom* (2006). For more anti-racism and anti-bias resources, please take a look at Appendix F.

Reflection Question

What is an example of privilege in your own life?

As you think about the role that your culture plays in teaching and learning, it is also important to consider the school culture. Let's return to the Lian, Lestari, and Ms. Morgan scenario at the beginning of the chapter. A student may come from a culture where there are strong expectations around working collaboratively and supporting members of their community. This may be different from the teacher's culture or the school culture in the United States, in which the importance of demonstrating independence is highly valued. Cultural differences such as this example can lead to miscommunication and misunderstandings about expectations, which will in turn impact student learning. Our colleague Dr. Ayanna Cooper developed the following model to help us think about the convergence of these three cultures (i.e., student, teacher, and school) and the impact that they have on teaching and learning. Consider the model, and then complete Application Activity 2c. My School Culture.

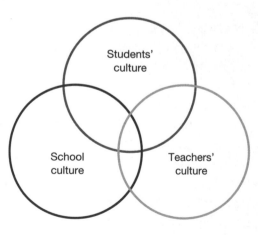

Source: Ayanna Cooper, 2019 (personal communication).

Application Activity 2c.
My School Culture

Reflect on either your current school culture or the culture of a school that you attended in the past. Consider the three levels of culture (i.e., surface, shallow, and deep) that we discussed in Chapter 1.

Reflection Questions

1. What are the elements of the school culture that are visible?

2. What are the beliefs and values of the school culture that may not be easily observable?

3. How are the beliefs and values that are embedded in school culture manifested in expectations for students and teachers?

4. To what extent does your personal culture align with the school culture?

Next, let's turn our focus to a second element of cultural competency, assessing cultural knowledge.

KEY ELEMENT 2: *ASSESS CULTURAL KNOWLEDGE.*

Sonia Nieto (2017), in her paper titled *On Becoming Sociocultural Mediators*, emphasizes the importance of educators taking steps to learn about their students and their communities in respectful ways that build trust and relationships. She explains that sociocultural mediators "not only introduce students to other perspectives and experiences, but also that they encourage students to carry who they are along with them" (p. 10). Hammond (2015) urges educators to expose themselves to cultural experiences similar to those of their students in order to "experience alternative ways of doing and being" (p. 62). Consider the following steps that you might take (adapted from Nieto, 2017, and Hammond, 2015):

- Explore the history of students' home countries and cultures.

- Visit students' families in their homes or communities.

- Conduct family interviews.

- Develop family and community surveys.

- Write letters to students sharing about yourself and ask students to write you back. The questions in 2d might be a good starting place for the type of information you could share with students.

- Watch movies or television series that can help you step into another culture and that portray that culture in a positive and accurate light. Reflect on patterns of both verbal and nonverbal communication.

For this next activity, identify one ML that you would like to learn more about. If you aren't currently in the classroom, try this activity with a student at your school or a neighbor or colleague. You don't need to answer all the questions. See what you might be able to learn from an informal conversation. It's important to share about yourself in the process, to be respectful of the student's comfort level, and refrain from questions that might raise fear or be a trigger for the student.

Application Activity 2d. Learning About My Student

Select one ML student that you teach or work with. Perhaps choose a student that you would like to improve your relationship with. How many of the following questions can you answer about that student? What steps could you take to learn the information that you don't know in a respectful way so as to build a positive relationship with that student? When asking questions of your student, be mindful of how your questions might be perceived and consider whether you would feel comfortable being asked these types of questions:

1. Where was the student born?

2. Where were the student's parents born?

3. What do you know about the history of your student's or her or his parents' home country?

4. What languages does the student speak? With whom does he or she speak these languages?

5. Whom does the student live with?

6. What responsibilities does the student have outside of school?

7. What is something that the student is interested in or passionate about?

8. What goals does the student have for the future? These could be educational goals, career goals, or personal goals.

(Continued)

(Continued)

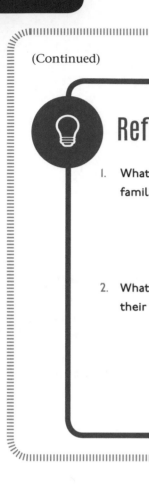

Reflection Questions

1. What is one step that you will take to learn more about the families of the students that you work with?

2. What is one step that you will take to help your students and their families learn more about you?

After reflecting on your cultural identity and your knowledge of the cultures of your students, it is important to consider the extent to which you value the benefit of diversity and the impact cultural differences can have in your school and classroom.

KEY ELEMENT 3: *VALUE DIVERSITY.*

According to Amy Stuart Wells, Lauren Fox, and Diana Cordova-Cobo (2016), scholars at Teachers College, Columbia University, "Diversity makes us smarter." A critical step in building cultural competency is appreciating the benefit and importance of diversity. Diversity in the workplace is understood to increase creativity and drive innovation. The same is true in schools. Stuart Wells and her colleagues (2016) write, "researchers have documented that students' exposure to other students who are different from themselves and the novel ideas and challenges that such exposure brings leads to improved cognitive skills, including critical thinking and problem solving" (p. 2).

Seymour Dual Language Academy in New York State's Syracuse City School District (SCSD) presents a strong model for what it means to honor and value diversity. Respect for diversity can be seen through SCSD's dual language program model, the attitudes of their staff, and the vast multilingual resources throughout the school. To learn a little more about the work that is being done at Seymour and to hear Seymour social worker Pedro Abreu talk about strategies for building relationships with families who come from cultures that are different than ours, watch the video *What It Means to Value Diversity*.

Video 2.1

What It Means to Value Diversity

resources.corwin.com/CulturallyResponsiveTeaching

Cummins (2000) states that through personal interactions between educators and students an interpersonal space is created in which identities are negotiated. These negotiated identifies are critical to student success.

> When students' identities are affirmed and extended through their interactions with teachers, they are more likely to apply themselves academically and participate actively in instruction. . . . By contrast, when students' languages, cultures, and experiences are ignored or excluded in classroom interactions, these students are at a disadvantage. Everything they have previously learned about life and the world is dismissed as irrelevant to school learning. There are few points of connection between their life experiences and curriculum materials or instruction; students are expected to learn in an experiential vacuum. (p. 166)

Thus, how we speak about and respond to the diversity in our classroom is critical to ML student achievement.

For educators who are positioned within the dominant culture, it can be uncomfortable to recognize, embrace, and discuss the power dynamics associated with difference. We can be afraid to make mistakes, be fearful that we will say something that might offend those who are different from us, or find discomfort in talking about privileges that we are born with based on our ethnicity, race, gender, and/or socioeconomic status. Robin DiAngelo in *White Fragility* (2018) writes,

> The key to moving forward is what we do with our discomfort. We can use it as a door out—blame the messenger and disregard the message. Or we can use it as a door in by asking, Why does this unsettle me? What would it mean for me if this were true? (p. 14)

At this time, take a moment to reflect on your own beliefs about diversity in your school and classroom by answering the questions in Activity 2e, Beliefs About Diversity in My Context. Then, take the next step to share your reflection with a colleague, classmate, or coworker. Begin the important conversation of talking about diversity in your context.

Application Activity 2e. Beliefs About Diversity in My Context

1. In your context, do you believe that cultural and linguistic differences are seen as sources of strength or sources of conflict? Explain.

2. To what extent are discussions of difference embraced or avoided? Explain.

3. How do you feel about taking part in discussions about diversity related to socioeconomic status, ethnicity, culture, race, or other areas of difference with colleagues and in your classroom?

4. How do you feel about facilitating discussions about diversity related to socioeconomic status, ethnicity, culture, race, or other areas of difference with colleagues and in your classroom?

5. What resources or training would you like to have in order to feel more comfortable and confident having these conversations?

School Activity Idea

At a school in Cherry Hill Public Schools, New Jersey, students and teachers filled in aspects of their identities on the profile of a person's head (just as you did in Application Activity 2a). The teachers completed the activity first, and these were hung in the school hallways. Initially, all names were covered. Next, students completed their heads. Again, names were covered. Then all at once, all names were revealed. Students and teachers had an opportunity to look for others that shared aspects of their identity. This was a powerful activity in that it helped build appreciation for difference as well as make connections in the community that might not otherwise have existed. For example, one teacher described building a relationship with a student in a different class that shared her love and appreciation for a certain type of East Indian dance.

KEY ELEMENT 4: *APPRECIATE THE DYNAMICS OF DIFFERENCE.*

In addition to valuing diversity, it is important to appreciate that differences do exist. Lindsey et al. (2019) describe the need to "reframe the differences so that diversity is not perceived as a problem to be solved" and to take steps to "teach and learn about differences and how to respond to them effectively" (p. 9).

One area of difference that can have a significant impact in the classroom is related to cultural values around the role of the group and the role of the individual. Take a minute to respond to the following reflection questions.

Reflection Questions

1. Do you prefer to celebrate group successes or individual successes? Give an example.

2. Do you prefer to work on projects individually or with a team? Give an example.

Cultural psychologist Geert Hofstede developed a cultural index that evaluates cultures based on six dimensions. One dimension is the level of individualism versus collectivism within a culture. **In individualist cultures, there is a greater focus on independence and individual achievement.** Self-reliance is emphasized and learning is completed through individual study. In addition, individual contributions and status are important. Individualist cultures tend to be competitive, technical, and analytical. **In collectivist cultures, there is a strong focus on interdependence and group success.** There is an emphasis on collective wisdom and shared resources. Learning occurs through group interactions, and group dynamics and harmony are very important (Hofstede et al., 2010, as cited in Hammond, 2015, p. 27.).

Hammond (2015, p. 25) explains that our brains are, in fact, generally structured with a preference toward a communal understanding of the world, with 80 percent of the world following a collectivist mindset and 20 percent following an individualistic view of the world (Hofstede et al., 2010). While collectivist and individualist cultures fall on a continuum and these traits will be expressed differently among different cultures, understanding some of the key differences between individualist and collectivist cultures and the impact that these differences can have in the context of education can be helpful on your path toward becoming a culturally responsive educator. Figure 2.2 highlights some of the differences between collectivist and individualist cultures and provides some recommendations for supporting students from collectivist cultures in your classroom.

To hear more about possible differences between individual and collectivist cultures, watch Sangita Chadha's interview about her role as a nationality worker in the Syracuse City School District. Nationality workers are school employees that come from the home cultures of the district's English learner (EL) and immigrant families. They provide instructional support in classrooms and also act as liaisons to assist school personnel to communicate effectively with families.

Figure 2.2   Differences Between Individualist and Collectivist Cultures

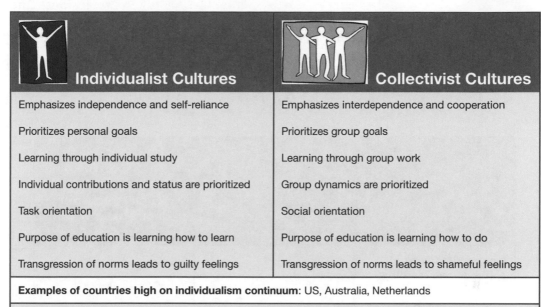

Individualist Cultures	Collectivist Cultures
Emphasizes independence and self-reliance	Emphasizes interdependence and cooperation
Prioritizes personal goals	Prioritizes group goals
Learning through individual study	Learning through group work
Individual contributions and status are prioritized	Group dynamics are prioritized
Task orientation	Social orientation
Purpose of education is learning how to learn	Purpose of education is learning how to do
Transgression of norms leads to guilty feelings	Transgression of norms leads to shameful feelings

Examples of countries high on individualism continuum: US, Australia, Netherlands

Examples of countries with low individualism continuum: Indonesia, Pakistan, Guatemala

Recommendations:

- Build both individual and group accountability into group projects.
- Give students the choice to work independently or in pairs or groups.
- Seek to establish relationships with students by sharing about yourself and learning about them.
- Foster a supportive classroom community where students feel a sense of belonging.
- Celebrate group successes (e.g., class party for everyone's hard work on a project).

Resources: Hofstede, 2003, 2011; Hammond, 2015.

Video 2.2

Understanding and Appreciating Cultural Differences

resources.corwin.com/CulturallyResponsiveTeaching

Once you have watched Sangita's video, complete Application Activity 2f, Reflecting on Your Cultural Beliefs and Expectations to think more critically about how differences between individual and collectivist cultures may be impacting your teaching or your interactions with students.

Application Activity 2f. Reflecting on Your Cultural Beliefs and Expectations, Part 1

Topic and Reflection Questions	Your Beliefs or Expectations	How Your Beliefs and Expectations Are Represented in Your Instruction or Interactions With Students
Independent versus collaborative learning • What are your expectations for when students should work independently? • What are your expectations for when and how they should work collaboratively?		
Role of teacher in class • What do you think is the teacher's role in terms of managing a class, interacting with students, and supporting student learning?		
Student interactions with teacher • What are your expectations in terms of how [or if] a student should address a teacher, ask questions, or disagree with a teacher?		

Source: Adapted from Staehr Fenner and Snyder, 2017, p. 35.

Application Activity 2f. Reflecting on Your Cultural Beliefs and Expectations, Part 2

Read the following cultural considerations and reflect on how your beliefs and expectations may be different from those of your students.

Topic	Cultural Consideration
Independent versus collaborative learning	Students from collectivist cultures (e.g., Japan, Brazil, India) may value working together interdependently rather than working alone independently. Contributing to a group's well-being is valued more than one's individual achievement (Rothstein-Fisch & Trumbull, 2008). In contrast, students from individualist cultures (e.g., Greece, New Zealand, US) may see greater value in working independently toward individual goals and achievement.
Role of teacher in class	The role of the teacher may vary between collectivist and individualist cultures. Collectivist cultures are those in which group goals and needs are generally placed above individual needs. In contrast, individualist cultures tend to value individual goals, individual rights, and independence. Students from collectivist cultures (e.g., Mexico, Korea, Somalia) may have been taught that they should show respect for teachers at all times by carefully listening to their teacher and not asking questions or disagreeing (Rothstein-Fisch & Trumbull, 2008). Group harmony is considered most important. In contrast, students from individualist cultures (e.g., Australia, Germany, US) recognize that they will be valued for speaking out for their unique ideas and opinions. They also tend to expect a more student-centered approach to teaching and learning.
Student interactions with teacher	In some cultures, there is greater "power distance" between leaders and followers than in other cultures. Power distance refers to how people from a specific culture view power relationships. For example, in high power distance cultures (e.g., Guatemala, Malaysia, Saudi Arabia) the relationship between a teacher and a student would be very formal and respectful. In these cultures, there tends to be more focus on titles, formality, and authority. Students from these cultures may not feel comfortable talking to teachers, and parents may take the teacher's word without question (Hofstede, 2003). In contrast, in cultures where there is less power distance (e.g., Netherlands, Norway, US) relationships are usually more informal. Parents or guardians may work together with teachers for the student's best interest, and the teacher may provide a more student-centered classroom, giving choice and autonomy to students.

Source: Adapted from Staehr Fenner and Snyder, 2017, pp. 36–37.

(Continued)

(Continued)

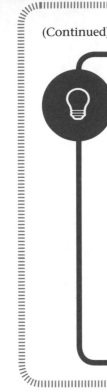

Reflection Questions

1. What do you notice about how your cultural beliefs and expectations may differ from those of your MLs?

2. How might you address these differences in your classroom or school?

KEY ELEMENT 5: *INSTITUTIONALIZE CULTURAL KNOWLEDGE.*

The reflective work and practice that we have described up to this point in the chapter have been primarily focused on having a better understanding of yourself and recognizing the culture that you carry with you (knowingly or unknowingly). However, the critical work of CRT must extend beyond ourselves and our classrooms. The fifth element of cultural competence is focused on the integration of CRT into the heart of a school and/or district. While much has been written about processes for institutional change, our focus here is to provide some general considerations if you have an opportunity to use a team-based approach to this work. In Figure 2.3., Steps Toward Institutionalizing Cultural Knowledge, we have provided four goals that could be a good starting point for your school-based CRT work, as well as some action steps to consider.

Figure 2.3 Steps Toward Institutionalizing Cultural Knowledge

Goal	Action Steps
1. Set CRT priorities.	• Form a team of interested stakeholders who will meet regularly (if possible, include content teachers, ESOL teachers, administrators, staff, parent liaisons, family members, and community members). • Assess strengths and needs of the school through surveys, interviews, and CRT checklist (Appendix B). • Develop a CRT vision for the school and share this vision with all stakeholders. • Determine CRT priorities and corresponding action steps that are both feasible and measurable; assign responsibilities to align with action steps.
2. Engage staff in CRT work.	• Demonstrate the value of CRT to all school stakeholders by sharing research, success stories, and need. • Create shared definitions of key terminology for CRT work. • Provide professional development to educators focused on bias, equity, and CRT strategies. • Provide training to staff on strategies for having cross-cultural, anti-racism conversations and open conversations about difference. • Examine school policies, procedures, and structures for potential bias or inequity (e.g., hiring practices).
3. Evaluate educational outcomes.	• Establish educator teams to assess and address issues related to achievement and access disparities, cultural responsiveness, and academic rigor. • Familiarize the inquiry teams (or designate one person to be the expert) with all of the assessments (e.g., federal, state, local, formative) that students take, the implications of those assessments for students, how the results can serve teachers, and what options students have if they don't do as expected. • Develop a common rubric to evaluate how CRT techniques or interventions have improved educational outcomes for MLs.
4. Incorporate multiple voices, angles, viewpoints, and stories in classroom materials and school culture.	• Shadow an ML throughout the day to experience the school and curriculum from her or his perspective. • Use the Determining ML Family Engagement Scale (found in Chapter 7) to assess the extent to which your school welcomes MLs and their families. • Set goals to strengthen family and community engagement in the school. • Evaluate the school curriculum to look for resources, activities, and perspectives that could offer richer insight into the experiences of your students and other cultures.

Source: Synthesized from The Aspen Education & Society Program and the Council of Chief State School Officers, 2017; Byrd, 2016; Gonzalez, 2016; NYSED, 2019; NYC DOE, 2020.

Reflection Questions

As you read Figure 2.3, what stood out for you as a need in your school or district? What might be a good first step toward institutionalizing cultural knowledge?

DISTRICT PROFILE

Cherry Hill Public Schools in New Jersey have a long-standing commitment to diversity and, more recently, cultural proficiency. They have created a district committee that focuses exclusively on issues of cultural proficiency, equity, and character education. The district committee includes representatives from schools, parent groups, and community organizations. It also includes high school students who are advocates. The committee meets monthly, and their work is grounded in a district five-year plan that includes seven key goals and corresponding action steps. Some examples of their goals include the following:

- Recruiting, hiring, and retaining staff of color
- Increasing the cultural proficiency of all teachers, administrators, and staff through the adoption and implementation of a framework for culturally responsive teaching and learning
- Increasing outreach for the purpose of improved student achievement through community engagement with parents and community members of diverse backgrounds (Cherry Hill Public Schools, 2017)

To support their work in increasing the cultural proficiency of teachers, administrators, and staff, select district personnel receive professional development related to such topics as courageous conversations on race (Singleton, 2014), cultural competency, bias, and microaggressions. These educators then facilitate a professional development session to all staff at their individual schools as a way of building a shared understanding of and a collaborative effort toward meeting district goals.

When Cherry Hill principal and committee cochair George Guy was asked about the cultural proficiency work occurring in Cherry Hill, he also described an initiative to support greater access to higher-level math classes to historically underserved students (i.e., African American, Latino, students receiving free and reduced lunch). He emphasized the need for districts to look at their data and see who is making progress and who is not. He explained,

> The time to have this conversation is when there is not something that the board, or the state, or the community is calling the school or school district out on. This is really, in my mind, work that needs to be done with boards and school districts in the summer when they are . . . looking at their data, and they are saying who's making accomplishments in our system and who is not. That's the time to start having conversations about equity, culturally responsive systems, culturally responsive pedagogy, microaggressions, implicit bias, cultural proficiency, race, and courageous conversations about race. . . . But I also encourage people that once they are doing that in the summer, they have to begin to look at their capacity. What is the one thing when you see that inequity about who is making strides in your system and who isn't, what is that one thing from a capacity standpoint that you can begin to ask questions about and effect change with so that by the end of that school year, you've been able to ask those questions and answer those questions using the resources . . . that you have available to you. (G. Guy, personal communication, January 22, 2020)

As you think about the work that is being done in Cherry Hill Public Schools, consider the steps you can take to continue toward cultural proficiency.

THREE STEPS THAT YOU CAN TAKE

Now that we have explored the five elements of cultural competency, we'd like to offer you three steps that you can take to continue on the path toward strengthening it in yourself and your community. When discussing cultural competency, it is important to remember that we are all at various points along the continuum, and there is always more to learn. What is important is how you approach the journey and how open you are to the challenge.

Step 1: *Explore your bias.*

In speaking about the bias work that educators are doing in the Cherry Hill Public Schools, George Guy explains,

> Our own personal values and beliefs will always have a bias. Our job is to detect that bias and see how it is being played out in procedures within our classrooms, procedures within our schools, procedures within our school district that inadvertently disenfranchise underserved demographics. (G. Guy, personal communication, January 22, 2020)

For Step 1, select one of the following tools for analyzing your bias. Then, discuss what you learned with a friend or colleague or write a journal reflection on what you learned.

1. Take an Implicit Association Test (IAT; 1998). Project Implicit is a nonprofit organization that collects data through online bias testing with the goal of educating the public about hidden biases. Some of the possible tests are related to bias in race, skin tone, Arab Muslims, and Asian Americans, among others. However, keep in mind that there is some controversy about the validity of IATs to measure biases rather than familiarity with certain groups (Ottaway et al., 2001).

2. Watch Jose Antonio Vargas's documentary *White People* and reflect on what you learned. If possible, watch with a colleague and discuss your takeaways from the film. (www .defineamerican.com/white-people)

3. Complete the Cultural Awareness Knowledge and Skills Assessment. This tool—seen in Application Activity 2g—was adapted from the Central Vancouver Island Multicultural Society's cultural competence self-assessment checklist. Please refer to this chapter's references to access the link for the complete tool.

Application Activity 2g. Cultural Awareness, Knowledge, and Skills Self-Assessment

Read the list of characteristics in each of three categories (awareness, knowledge, and skills). For each category, identify one area of strength and one area where you think you can improve. Then, answer the reflection questions.

Awareness	
Share my culture.	*I am aware that in order to learn more about others, I need to understand and be prepared to share my own culture.*
Be aware of areas of discomfort.	*I am aware of my discomfort when I encounter differences in race, color, religion, sexual orientation, language, and ethnicity.*
Reflect on how my culture informs my judgment.	*I am aware of how my cultural perspective influences my judgement about what are "appropriate," "normal," or "superior" behaviors, values, and communication styles.*
Be curious.	*I take any opportunity to put myself in places where I can learn about difference and create relationships.*
Be aware of my privilege if I am white.	*If I am a white person working with a Native American or person of color, I understand that I will likely be perceived as a person with power and racial privilege and that I may not be seen as "unbiased" or as an ally.*
An area of strength for me:	
An area where I can improve:	

(Continued)

(Continued)

Knowledge	
Gain from my mistakes.	*I will make mistakes and will learn from them.*
Assess the limits of my knowledge.	*I will recognize that my knowledge of certain cultural groups is limited and commit to creating opportunities to learn more.*
Acknowledge the importance of difference.	*I know that differences in color, culture, ethnicity, and so on are important parts of an individual's identity, which they value and so do I. I will not hide behind the claim of "color-blindness."*
Know the historical experiences of non-European Americans.	*I am knowledgeable about historical incidents in my country's past that demonstrate racism and exclusion toward individuals of non-European heritage.*
Commit to lifelong learning.	*I recognize that achieving cultural competence involves a commitment to learning over a lifetime.*
An area of strength for me:	
An area where I can improve:	

Skills	
Challenge discriminatory and/ or racist behavior.	*I can effectively intervene when I observe others behaving in a racist and/or discriminatory manner.*
Communicate across cultures.	*I am able to adapt my communication style to effectively communicate with people who communicate in ways that are different from my own.*
Seek out situations to expand my skills.	*I seek out people who challenge me to maintain and increase the cross-cultural skills I have.*
Become engaged.	*I am actively involved in initiatives, small or big, that promote understanding among members of diverse groups.*

Skills	
Act as an ally.	*My colleagues who are Native American, immigrants, and/or people of color consider me an ally and know that I will support them in culturally appropriate ways.*

An area of strength for me:

An area where I can improve:

Source: Adapted from the Central Vancouver Island Multicultural Society's cultural competence self-assessment checklist (n.d.).

Reflection Questions

1. What do you notice about your cultural competence strengths? How do you think you developed these areas of strengths?

2. What steps could you take in those areas you would like to improve?

Step 2: *Learn more about the history and language of another culture.*

Learning about other cultures is a lifelong journey. For this step, choose a culture that you do not know much about, with the understanding that specific cultures are not monolithic. Take steps to learn as much as you can about that culture through individual research. Consider how what you have learned will impact your teaching and interactions with ML students and families who share that home culture. As a reminder, it is important to avoid making assumptions about ML students and families based on what you learn; instead, use your new knowledge to generate appropriate questions you might ask a student. Consider using Figure 2.4, Learning About Another Culture, to guide your work.

Figure 2.4   Learning About Another Culture

Items to research about another country's culture:

- Language (how is it similar to or different from English)
- Historical events that shaped the country
- Cultural group and factors that may have impacted immigration to the US
- Religious beliefs or foundations
- Beliefs about family and kinship
- Sports or hobbies enjoyed in the culture
- An interesting fact

Step 3: *Identify patterns of inequity that may exist and begin a conversation about this in your school.*

Lindsey et al. (2019) describe that culturally proficient change initiatives can raise awareness about practices and policy changes that need to be made in schools or school districts. The following topics are some possible areas of inequity that may exist for ML students and their families. Look at the list in Figure 2.5, Exploring Inequity in My Context, and identify one area that you feel you would like to explore. You could choose one area from the list or another possible source of inequity based on your own experience. Determine the data that you will need to have an informed understanding of the issue. Then, determine what steps you will take to collect the data that you need. Consider who may be an ally who would support you in your work. Once you have collected your data, reflect on what you learned, who you would like to share the information with, and what steps you will take next.

Figure 2.5   Exploring Inequity in My Context

Exploring Inequity in My Context
Possible areas of inequity
• ML students are educated by teachers who do not have training in educating culturally and linguistically diverse students.
• ML students are disproportionately identified as needing special education services.
• ML students are underrepresented in gifted and talented programs. Possible areas of inequity might include identification based primarily on language-based assessment, scores on student achievement tests, and teacher recommendation.
• ML students are underrepresented in honors, advanced placement (AP), and college preparation courses.
• ML students are overrepresented in disciplinary referrals, suspensions, and/or bullying referrals.
• ML students have lower graduation rates and higher dropout rates.
• ML students perform below school averages on school-based and state assessments.
• School assignments or family communications require technology that ML families may not have access to.
• Meetings and school activities are scheduled at times that make it challenging for ML families to participate.
• ML students are disproportionately represented in extracurricular activities.
• Other: _____
Area of focus:
Data needed:
Steps to take: 1. 2. 3.
Potential allies:

(Continued)

Figure 2.5   **(Continued)**

Reflection questions

1. What did you learn?

2. What surprised you?

3. Who would you like to share your information with?

4. What steps will you take next to follow up on what you learned?

Source: Adapted from Lindsey et al., 2019, pp. 61 and 63.

Summary of Key Ideas

- Building cultural competency is a lifelong process.

- We all have bias. It is how we identify and respond to our biases that is important.

- Cultural competency includes the following:

  o Being culturally self-aware

  o Assessing your cultural knowledge and seeking knowledge about other cultures

  o Valuing diversity

  o Appreciating the dynamics of difference

  o Institutionalizing cultural knowledge

Chapter 2 Reflection Questions

1. What have you learned about yourself through the activities in this chapter? What surprised you?

2. What steps would you like to take to build your cultural competence?

References

The Aspen Education & Society Program and the Council of Chief State School Officers. (2017). *Leading for equity: Opportunities for state education chiefs*. The Aspen Education & Society Program.

Byrd, C. M. (2016). *Does culturally relevant teaching work? An examination from student perspectives. SAGE Open, 6*(3), 1–10. https://doi.org/10.1177%2F2158244016660744

Central Vancouver Island Multicultural Society's Cultural competence self-assessment checklist. (n.d.). http://www.coloradoedinitiative.org/wp-content/uploads/2015/10/cultural-competence-self-assessment-checklist.pdf

Cherry Hill Public Schools. (2017). *Cherry Hill Public Schools cultural proficiency/equity/character education five-year working document*. https://www.chclc.org/cms/lib/NJ50000493/Centricity/Domain/941/Five_Year_Working_Document.pdf

Collins, C. (2018, Fall). What is white privilege, really? *Teaching Tolerance, 60*. https://www.tolerance.org/magazine/fall-2018/what-is-white-privilege-really

Cross, T., Bazron, B., Dennis, K., & Isaacs, M., (1989). *Towards a culturally competent system of care, Volume I*. Georgetown University Child Development Center, CASSP Technical Assistance Center.

Cummins, J. (2000). *Language, power and pedagogy: Bilingual children in the crossfire*. Multilingual Matters.

DiAngelo, R. (2018). *White fragility: Why it's so hard for white people to talk about racism*. Beacon Press.

Diller, J., & Moule, J. (2005). *Cultural competence: A primer for educators*. Wadsworth.

Gonzalez, J. (2016, July 10). *A 4-part system for getting to know your students*. https://www.cultofpedagogy.com

Greenberg, J. (2017). Ten examples that prove white privilege exists in every aspect imaginable. Yes! https://www.yesmagazine.org/social-justice/2017/07/24/10-examples-that-prove-white-privilege-exists-in-every-aspect-imaginable/

Greenwald, A., McGhee, D., & Schwartz, J. (1998). Measuring individual differences in implicit cognition: The Implicit Association Test. *Journal of Personality and Social Psychology, 74*(6), 1464–1480.

Hall, E. T. (1959). *The silent language*. Doubleday.

Hammond, Z. (2015). *Culturally responsive teaching and the brain*. Corwin.

Hofstede, G. (2003). *Culture's consequences: Comparing values, behaviors, institutions and organizations across nations* (2nd ed.). SAGE.

Hofstede, G. (2011). Dimensionalizing cultures: The Hofstede model in context. *Online Readings in Psychology and Culture, 2*(1). https://doi.org/10.9707/2307-0919.1014

Hofstede, G., Hofstede, G. J., & Minkov, M. (2010). *Cultures and organizations: Software of the mind*. McGraw-Hill.

Kirwan Institute for the Study of Race and Ethnicity. (2013). *Understanding implicit bias: The state of science*. Author.

Lindsey, R. B., Nuri-Robins, K., Terrell, R. D., & Lindsey, D. (Eds). (2019). *Cultural proficiency: A manual for school leaders*. Corwin.

McIntosh, P. (1988). *White privilege and male privilege: A personal account of coming to see correspondences through work in women's studies* (Working Paper No. 189). Wellesley College Center for Research on Women.

Morris, M. (2018). *Pushout: The criminalization of Black girls in schools*. The New Press.

Morris, M. (2019). *Sing a rhythm, dance a blues: Education for the liberation of Black and Brown girls*. The New Press.

National Education Association Diversity Toolkit. (n.d.). *Cultural competence for educators*. http://www.nea.org/tools/30402.htm

Nieto, S. (2017). *On becoming sociocultural mediators*. TeachingWorks University of Michigan Working Papers. http://www.teachingworks.org/

NYC DOE. (2020). *Culturally responsive-sustaining education*. NYC Department of Education. https://www.schools.nyc.gov/about-us/vision-and-mission/culturally-responsive-sustaining-education

NYSED. (2019). *Culturally responsive-sustaining education framework*. New York State Education Department.

Ottaway, S. A., Hayden, D. C., & Oakes, M. A. (2001). Implicit attitudes and racism: Effects of word familiarity and frequency on the implicit association test. *Social Cognition, 19*(2), 97–144.

Quezada, R., Lindsey, D., & Lindsey, R. (2015). 5 elements of cultural proficiency. *Communicator, 38*(12).

Rothstein-Fisch, C., & Trumbull, E. (2008). *Managing diverse classrooms: How to build on students' cultural strengths*. Association for Supervision & Curriculum Development.

Singleton, G. (2014). *Courageous conversations about race: A field guide for achieving equity in schools* (2nd ed.). Corwin.

Sleeter, C. E. (2008). Critical family history, identity, and historical memory. *Educational Studies, 43*, 114–124.

Stuart Wells, A., Fox, L., & Cordova-Cobo, D. (2016, February 9). *How racially diverse schools and classrooms can benefit all students*. https://tcf.org/content/report/how-racially-diverse-schools-and-classrooms-can-benefit-all-students/

Teaching Tolerance. (n.d.). *Common beliefs*. http://www.tolerance.org/sites/default/files/general/common_beliefs_descriptions.pdf

Operating From an Assets-Based Approach

Scenario: Manny—My Name, My Identity

It's the beginning of the school year, and you're the third-grade classroom teacher of a boisterous group of 25 students who represent seven different home languages. Eleven of your students are at varying levels of English language proficiency (ELP) and qualify for ESOL services, while five of your students exited from ESOL services in the first or second grade. The remainder of your students are a diverse group of native English speakers. Three of your students receive special education services.

You finally get your class list and see that one of your students, Manuel, exited ESOL services in the second grade. You notice his reading score was the lowest of all four domains (reading, writing, speaking, and listening) assessed on his annual ELP assessment.

On the first day of school, you review the class roster with your students, read each name out loud, and ask the students to introduce themselves to the class. When it's Manuel's turn, he quickly corrects you and says that his name is Mike, not Manuel. After school, you ask him why he's called Mike, and he responds that his kindergarten teacher gave him that name *"and it's kind of stuck with me."* He notes, shyly, that his family calls him Manny for short and asks if you can call him that name this year.

Application Activity 3a. Consider Student Identity

Consider students you have previously taught or are currently teaching. Reflect on the following:

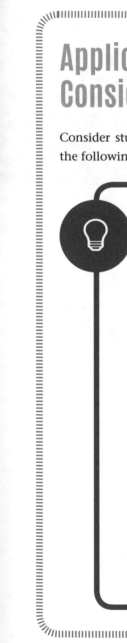

Reflection Questions

1. What is your immediate reaction when you read Manny's statement?

2. Why do you think Manny's kindergarten teacher gave him a nickname?

3. How much do you know about your students' names?

4. What would you do in this situation? Why?

CHAPTER OVERVIEW

This chapter is framed around the first guiding principle for the culturally responsive teaching of multilingual learners (MLs): **Culturally responsive teaching is assets-based**. The chapter will provide an opportunity for educators to get to the heart of what it means to operate from an assets-based approach with multilingual students and their families so that all educators can feel ownership for multilingual learners' success within and beyond classroom walls. Through case studies and reflection exercises, you will apply tools to respond to and mitigate deficit-thinking related to multilingual students to embody an assets-based perspective at the school and district level as well as at the classroom level during instruction.

WHY AN ASSETS-BASED PERSPECTIVE IS CRUCIAL

As educators of MLs, we hear deficit-based statements more often than we might like to admit. We sometimes encounter bias against MLs and their families when we work with teachers and administrators. This bias can occur to varying levels, even with ESOL or bilingual teachers, who we typically expect to serve as unwavering stewards for MLs' assets. Bias can range anywhere from subtle and subconscious to loud and bold.

When thinking about shifting to an assets-based perspective of MLs, it may seem daunting. However, we encourage you to reflect on Desmond Tutu's quote: "There is only one way to eat an elephant: a bite at a time." While it may prove ineffective to confront every aspect of a system that disadvantages MLs at one time, we suggest being intentional about where you can begin to make an impact. We suggest reflecting on which areas you may be able to change as opposed to what you think you may not be able to change (Gorski, as cited in Staehr Fenner, 2014) and begin with an area in which you have some agency. We firmly believe that all educators—no matter what their title or how many years of experience they have—are positioned to serve as agents of change to promote and champion MLs' assets. We would also like to note that we use the term "assets" in the plural to stress that MLs and their families bring multiple strengths with them; it's our job to uncover these strengths and incorporate them into MLs' education.

Finally, as we begin this chapter we would like you to keep in mind that helping others shift from a deficit- to an assets-based perspective of MLs involves both changing individuals' hearts and minds as well as chipping away at policies that maintain discrimination of MLs on a more systematic level. While we can eat that elephant a bite at a time with individuals, we also need to simultaneously confront the larger, policy-related pieces of the elephant that hold MLs back from realizing their full potential. **Where individual hearts and minds intersect with sound policy that positions MLs for success is where the true change will happen.**

DEFINING AN ASSETS-BASED APPROACH TO MLs

To ensure we're on the same page when it comes to what an assets-based approach is for MLs, we will first define it. **An assets-based perspective values students' home languages and cultures and sees these gifts as foundations for future learning rather than as obstacles or even hindrances to overcome.** An assets-based perspective also recognizes that parents/guardians and families of MLs are engaged in their children's education and support their children in varied and perhaps unrecognized ways rather than blaming them for their children's perceived lack of academic skills (Staehr Fenner, 2014). For example, while parents of MLs may not attend in-school events on the same scale as non-ML parents without unique supports being put in place, parents of MLs may be ensuring that homework is completed and speaking with students about trying hard in school on a regular basis. In addition, an assets-based perspective provides multiple opportunities to honor ML students' rich cultural and linguistic backgrounds and incorporate what students already know (which is a lot!) into their learning.

An assets-based perspective stands in direct contrast to a deficit perspective, in which the focus is on MLs' challenges and actually results in educators as well as policymakers blaming students or their families for their perceived lack of academic success. **A deficit perspective is one in which we focus on MLs' challenges and frame our interactions with them solely in terms of these challenges.** When operating from a deficit perspective, educators tend to view MLs' home language(s) and culture(s) as hindrances to overcome instead of as gifts to be treasured. Figure 3.1 outlines three aspects of an assets-based approach versus a deficit-based approach with MLs. We leave space for you to contribute your own insights in the final row.

Figure 3.1   Assets-Based Approach Versus Deficit-Based Approach

Factor/Aspect	Assets-Based Approach	Deficit-Based Approach
Home language and culture	• Gifts to be recognized • Foundations for future learning	Hindrances to overcome
Families of MLs	• Engaged in children's education • Interact with children in their rich home language • Share their home cultural practices	• Blamed for students' perceived lack of academic skills • Do not learn English quickly enough • Not engaged in their child's learning
Connection with student learning	Direct correlation between building instruction around students' life experience and positive impact on learning	Disconnect between students' lives and learning
Other		

In order to see how Syracuse City School District (SCSD) educator Angela Matarazzo describes steps that she takes to build on students' assets, watch the video clip *Building on Students' Assets*.

Video 3.1

Building on Students' Assets

resources.corwin.com/CulturallyResponsiveTeaching

RESEARCH ON ML ASSETS

Now that we have defined an assets-based perspective and compared it with a deficit approach, let's take a deeper look at the interplay between students' home languages, cultures, and their learning. Students' home languages and culture play a key role in their academic and social-emotional development (Staehr Fenner, 2014; Staehr Fenner & Snyder, 2017; Zacarian, 2012; Zacarian, 2013).

As educators, it is essential to learn as much as we can about our MLs' backgrounds. What a student already knows and is familiar with can affect his or her understanding and interpretation of new content and new texts (Hammond, 2015; Shanahan, 2013). Because MLs bring such varied backgrounds and experiences, it is essential that educators reflect on students' prior knowledge and experiences in order to make connections to new concepts as well as look for background information that students might need to make connections to new content (Fisher et al., 2012). Learning more about individual students also allows for teams of educators to collaborate in order to advocate for MLs both inside and outside the classroom and to develop an instructional plan that addresses their strengths and meets the unique needs of each student.

Some tools that will provide educators with this type of student information include student and family surveys, home visits, formative and summative assessment data, student work samples, and home language formative assessments. Educators can collaborate with a team to gather and share individual student information and its relevance to instruction (Fairbairn & Jones-Vo, 2016; Staehr Fenner, 2014). Saifer and colleagues (2011) recommend a variety of activities for getting to know students better, such as student surveys, poetic introductions in which students write a poem about themselves, and cultural boxes in which students fill a box with objects that are meaningful to them and then share with the class. In addition to in-class activities, educators can learn more about their students through informal conversations and attending school and community events that students are involved in (Staehr Fenner, 2014).

In order to support the effective instruction and assessment of MLs, educators must also have knowledge of individual student characteristics on an academic level, including their educational history, language skills in English, literacy skills in the home language, academic strengths and challenges, and learning preferences (Fairbairn & Jones-Vo, 2016; Saifer et al., 2011; Staehr Fenner, 2014). Fairbairn & Jones-Vo (2016) emphasize the importance of learning about individual students' family backgrounds, cultural backgrounds, living situation, home language literacy skills, English skills, and a variety of other factors that may impact student performance.

Once we know more information about our students' personal histories as well as academic backgrounds, MLs' home language use and literacy practices should be used as rich resources in designing effective instruction. Educators can incorporate instructional practices into their lessons that provide students the opportunity to build on their knowledge and skills in their home language or languages (August et al., 2009). Some strategies that support the practice of building on home language include instruction on using cognates, providing supporting content materials in home languages, using bilingual glossaries or dictionaries when students are literate in the home language, intentionally grouping students that share a common home language, and assigning bilingual homework tasks (August et al., 2014; Staehr Fenner & Snyder, 2017).

Within the larger group of MLs, educators should be aware of the smaller group of students with limited or interrupted formal education (SLIFE) as well as other students who may have limited literacy in both their home language and English. Some strategies to support this smaller group of MLs include ongoing use of pair or small-group work, beginning lessons with conversational interactions, and emphasizing the connection between the new learning and students' lives (DeCapua, 2020; Robertson & Lafond, 2008; Salva, 2017, WIDA, 2015).

To get a sense of how this guideline of assets-based perspectives can be operationalized in the classroom, read the look-fors in Figure 3.2. Please note that these look-fors are not an exhaustive list.

Figure 3.2   Look-Fors for Guiding Principle I: *Culturally responsive teaching is assets-based.*

✓   Administrators, teachers, and staff pronounce students' names correctly.

✓   Administrators, teachers, and staff show interest in MLs' home languages by learning at least a few words or phrases.

✓   Students' cultural, historic, and linguistic backgrounds are incorporated into instruction.

✓   Teacher uses home language cognates to reinforce vocabulary comprehension.

✓   Administrators, teachers, and staff are aware of each student's interests and challenges outside of the classroom.

✓   School puts supports in place to help students overcome obstacles that may get in the way of their learning (e.g., snacks for students who may not have had breakfast, system for catching up on missed work, and written agenda for MLs to follow).

Source: Adapted from Staehr Fenner and Snyder, 2017.

Reflection Question

What additional look-fors would you recommend to ensure an assets-based perspective of your MLs?

CASE STUDIES

Let's take a deeper look at how MLs' backgrounds can affect their instructional outcomes. Please read the two case study scenarios and reflect on your answers to the guiding questions. You can choose one or both of the case studies to focus on.

Manny: Third Grade

Ms. Ruiz, Manny's third-grade teacher, has noticed that Manny is especially quick at math and seems to be getting bored during instruction. Manny finishes all his tasks quickly and immediately asks for something else to do. It's October, and parents and guardians have just been invited to attend a special presentation about the gifted and talented (GT) program. Ms. Ruiz would like to nominate Manny for consideration in the district's GT program. She initially sent an email about the meeting to Manny's parents, but she did not hear back from them. After not receiving a response to her email, she spoke with Manny's parents about it with the support of an interpreter. If Manny qualifies for the program, he would need to attend a separate GT center outside his community school, but Manny's parents seem reluctant to do that. She also told them that in order for Manny to be considered, they need to sign a permission letter, write an essay about why they believe their son qualifies for GT, and complete a three-page parent inventory in English.

After receiving the GT paperwork (all in English), Manny's parents decide they do not wish to proceed with the GT nomination after all. Ms. Ruiz is frustrated with Manny's parents because she thinks Manny is missing out on a special opportunity that could change the trajectory of his education.

Application Activity 3b.
Put Yourself in Their Shoes

Think of how Manny's parents might complete the Sample Parent or Guardian Inventory Questions (see Figure 3.3) as one facet of the GT recommendation process. Keep in mind why this abridged version of the form might be daunting and/or confusing for ML families.

(Continued)

(Continued)

Figure 3.3   Sample Parent or Guardian Inventory Questions

Directions: Please check the box that describes how often you observe the following behaviors in your child.

Behavior or Characteristic	Seldom or Never (1)	Sometimes (2)	Regularly (3)	Almost Always (4)
1. **Artistic**: creates art and/or music that is advanced for his or her age				
2. **Extracurricular talents**: excels at activities beyond schoolwork (e.g., clubs, volunteering)				
3. **Independence**: prioritizes on own ideas over contributing to a group				
4. **Athletic**: is noticed for athletic skills (e.g., tennis, crew, lacrosse)				
5. **Verbal**: learns to speak and read considerably earlier than peers; uses extensive abstract vocabulary and sentence structure; gifted at public speaking				
6. **Achievement**: unwavering drive to be noticed as "the best," be recognized as expert				
7. **Dominant**: in groups, establishes him- or herself as the group leader				
8. **Positive**: unwaveringly confident about his or her own academic and extracurricular abilities				
9. **Risk-taker**: easily assumes academic risks (e.g., raising hand to orally answer difficult questions)				
10. **Admired**: classmates want to be with him or her and emulate his or her behavior				

Reflection Questions

1. What is problematic about this form when used by ML parents or guardians as part of the GT nomination?

2. What impact does your understanding of collectivist versus individualist culture have on parental nomination for this school's GT program?

3. What other effects of implicit cultural bias in the GT identification process do you note?

Lian: Ninth Grade

Ms. Pepper, Lian's English language arts teacher, has noticed that Lian often brings a book to lunch and reads while the other students talk and laugh with each other. Some of Lian's other content teachers have noted that Lian does not contribute to whole-group class discussions and only speaks when spoken to when working in small groups, not making eye contact with her peers or teacher. Lian seems to be slipping through the cracks socially and not engaging with the content in her high school classes since she is quiet. Because of her reticence to communicate orally, some of her content teachers worry that she is not learning as much content as she should be. However, she has made some friends with a couple of other girls in her ESOL class and is an active participant in that class, offering her opinions and engaging in dialogue. Ms. Pepper has recently begun an international club at Lian's high school and thinks Lian might benefit from the club, where she could possibly make some new friends. However, Lian has not been able to attend after-school meetings since she takes care of her younger brother in the afternoons while her mother works. Ms. Pepper is not certain about what she can do to make sure Lian feels included in her new high school and more fully engages with the content of instruction.

Reflection Questions

1. What do you think is happening in this situation?

2. What impact does school or district policy have on this situation?

3. What is the impact of your identity, role, cultural understandings, personal biases, and/or knowledge of US culture on your interpretation of this situation?

4. If you were the student's teacher, how would you learn about your student's assets (e.g., interests, motivations, strengths, and his or her family)?

5. How would you use the information you learn about the student's assets to address the situation?

6. What would you do in this situation?

STRATEGIES FOR PROMOTING MLs' ASSETS

Engaging in an assets-based approach with MLs requires a shift in our thinking from what we believe is lacking in our students to the many strengths and assets that they and their families already possess. To do this, we must take time to learn about our MLs' and their families' invaluable personal, cultural, social, and world experiences and draw from these strengths-based understandings to create instructional opportunities that are meaningful, purposeful, and appealing to our students. Not only will our MLs benefit, but native English-speaking students will learn from their ML peers and see them in a new light. We share several replicable ways with you to promote MLs' assets.

SCSD kindergarten teacher Gloria Kimmich uses a variety of collaborative games and activities to build community in her classroom and teach students the benefits of working together and being persistent. To see one of the activities she uses, watch *Building a Collaborative Community in the Classroom.*

Video 3.2

Building a Collaborative Community in the Classroom

resources.corwin.com/CulturallyResponsiveTeaching

Encourage Storytelling

We all love to hear a good story, and MLs sharing their own stories is one way we can build bridges and help foster connections with ML students. Teachers of younger MLs can first model the task of students drawing a personal narrative storyboard or series of images, then have students write a response to the sentence prompt of their choice, such as "What's your least favorite part of school? Why?" or "Share a favorite memory you have with a family member." Teachers can ask older newcomer students to write a personal narrative and then share it with colleagues and school administrators. To begin this project, teachers can interview students using guiding questions. Students at lower levels of proficiency who are literate in their home languages can write about themselves in their home languages. Each of these activities supports the process of learning more about students' lives and experiences so that we, as educators, develop a better understanding of the linguistic and cultural assets that our students bring to our classrooms.

We do offer one piece of advice: Be sure to give MLs the choice to tell as much of their stories as they feel comfortable with or to have the option to not share them at all, as students may have experienced traumatic events that they wish not to divulge. Students and their families who are open to the idea could also publish their stories in school newspapers to reach a wider audience. Artwork can provide an alternative way for students to contribute their stories.

Use Mentor Texts as Way for MLs to Share Stories

Mentor texts are works of literature that teachers and students can return to and reread for a multitude of different purposes. They are texts that teachers and students can study as well as imitate, helping students take risks in their writing (Schulten, 2019). Teachers Brittanie Peterson and Shawna Whitford in Montgomery County Public Schools, Maryland, used the mentor text "The Best Part of Me" by Wendy Ewald (2002) to inspire and provide a model for their students' writing. In using this mentor text, the students imitated the techniques used in the book by choosing one feature that was the best part of them. Their teachers took a picture of their feature to illustrate their writing.

Play a Game

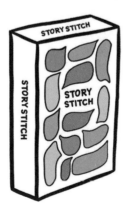

Green Card Voices' "Story Stitch" game, introduced in 2019 (www.greencardvoices.com/programs/storystitch), was created as a way to support exchanging stories and mutual understanding between immigrants, refugees, and US-born neighbors. Through Story Stitch, players use a deck of cards with story questions and connecting cards to connect with each other and discover shared feelings and experiences. Some sample questions include positives such as "Describe your favorite smell and what it reminds you of" and "Tell a story of a time when someone was kind to you." Some questions are also of a thought-provoking nature, such as "Tell a story about a time you felt mistreated by other people" and "Tell about a time you felt marginalized." Using these stories, MLs and their families can build relationships with native English speakers in and beyond the classroom. We recommend using an interpreter and/or written translated versions of the questions as appropriate. Please see Chapter 5 for more information on Green Card Voices.

Have Students Tell Stories Through Artwork

Artwork can provide an alternative way for students to share their stories. Through the "Finding Home" art outreach project with the Toronto District School Board and the Aga Khan Museum, newcomer English learners (ELs) worked with artists to share their experiences of home through multidimensional artwork of structures based on what the concept of home meant to them. (See photographs from the Aga Khan exhibits on www.tdsb.on.ca.)

Create ML Student Info Cards

You can assist all students, not only MLs, in creating info cards that highlight students' learning style, strengths, and/or interests. You can scaffold this for students at different levels of proficiency by modeling a finished product and also providing sentence stems or frames. On one side of the card, students can include a "selfie," or an image of themselves. On the other side, they might describe themselves in writing as a learner and include some of their outside interests. Students can also create infographics or images to highlight aspects of themselves.

Take Student Storytelling to a Deeper Level

Winnie Yeung, an English language arts teacher in Edmonton, Alberta (Canada), wrote the award-winning book *Homes: A Refugee Story* (2018). This book came to be through a Syrian newcomer student named Abu Bakr al Rabeeah telling his refugee story to his teacher. The story began with his teacher asking him what his secret wish was. Although he said it was to play soccer, Ms. Yeung suspected there was more depth to his wishes. Abu expressed a desire to share his story, and the stories turned into more formal interviews with Abu and his family. Together, they went on to write a self-published book, and then publisher Freehand Books fine-tuned it into its current form as a creative work of nonfiction.

Share Qualitative Stories About MLs' Success

In addition to students sharing their own stories, we also encourage you to share news of MLs' successes—both great and small—with your school, district, and/or community. Stories need to come from both MLs and their families as well as from educators in order to foster more connection and recognition of MLs' assets. There are lots of examples— if we are more aware of where to find them—of ways to demonstrate MLs' growth academically or on a personal, social-emotional level.

Highlight MLs Who Excel or Are Valedictorians

We are so proud when we learn each spring about MLs who have become high school valedictorians, even if we don't personally know the MLs. These success stories highlight the metalinguistic superpowers students develop (not to mention hard work and persistence) as they learn content in a new language.

Invite ML Visitors

You can also invite successful MLs who have graduated— including those in college, receiving technical training, or in careers—back to your school in person or by video. These visits can highlight their recollections of what helped them be successful in school and beyond.

Disseminate the Positive Stories of MLs

We suggest that you investigate multiple ways to share your message of ML success, such as in assemblies, local newspapers, and/or on your school or district's social media channels (with students' and families' permission).

One new, innovative program took place in Jefferson County Public Schools, Kentucky, in the summer of 2019. The district offered an interpreter training course to train bilingual high school students to serve as community interpreters. As the district experienced a high level of growth of its EL students, it chose to leverage the students' unique strengths to serve an urgent need in the community. The district also chose to publicize this opportunity on the local TV station and through the local newspaper, highlighting one tangible way for ML students to contribute to the community.

Spend Time in ML Communities

Oftentimes, we have found that people who lack an understanding of MLs and have a deficit perspective of them have not spent any amount of time in their communities. We have noticed through our own experience that a significant increase in the number of ML families present in a community may provoke feelings of panic and resentment from some community members. Some community members—especially those who have not spent time in a culture other than their own—may fear that ML families will take away resources and jobs from the community, will decrease home values, and will lessen their school's academics. Along those lines, educators may not feel prepared to teach MLs, especially those who qualify for EL services and are at lower English proficiency levels. However, there are ways to challenge these issues at the community level.

The following example (Samuels, 2017) speaks volumes about how contact with ML families can actually change someone's heart and mind. John Dutcher, a 61-year-old house cleaner from Omaha, Nebraska, described himself as a person who hated Muslims, his hatred stemming from the September 11 attacks. He recounts that he would "sneer at" women wearing hijabs—even though he had never actually met a Muslim person before. His previous US-born neighbors had issues with substance abuse, which irritated him. Then, six families of Muslim refugees, including families from Syria and

Afghanistan, moved into his apartment building. He describes his reaction: "The Muslims here were all about family and they just loved everyone." He continues: "I remember the people who lived here before; they took for granted everything this country gave them. These people (the refugees), they really changed my heart." He shared how he learned of the families' stories of fleeing war with the help of interpreters. His new neighbors brought him plates of food, and he got to know their children. He shared that, after a very short time being in Omaha, the families settled in to the community, securing jobs, cars, and sending their children to school. He sums up his feelings of the new community members: "They took the hatred out of me."

Community Walks

One way to explore MLs' assets is through community walks. These experiences, which take place on foot, provide participants (e.g., educators, community members) the opportunity to glimpse neighborhoods in which ML families live. Community walks could include visits to houses of worship, community centers, a student's home, and/or a meal at a local restaurant (Edutopia, 2017). Please see Chapter 7 for more in-depth information on community walks.

Be a Warm *and Informed* Demander

In Spanish, "pobrecito" means poor little one. The term "pobrecito syndrome" is attributed to Pedro Noguera, who uses it to describe well-meaning educators who have subconsciously set low expectations for students from lower socioeconomic status and whose parents or guardians are not native English speakers (Cepeda, 2013). While these educators who operate from a "pobrecito" mindset may think they have good intentions or sympathy for MLs, Noguera emphasizes that MLs need empathy instead of pity and need to be challenged academically. This idea leads to the notion of being a warm *and informed* demander. We agree that educators need to be warm demanders (see Hammond, 2015, referenced in Chapter 1), but in order to do so, they need to also be informed about their multifaceted MLs' lives. We have to be aware of our students' past histories and present context in order to help shape their futures.

Consider Systematic Factors in MLs' Education

When MLs struggle, as warm and informed demanders we should first reflect on extrinsic factors and systematic inequities that might be impacting student learning instead of beginning with a deficit view of the student as being "at fault." It's crucial to ensure that when we are thinking about interventions and support for MLs, we are getting the whole picture of that student. Hamayan et al. (2013) outline seven integral factors that enable educators to collect more nuanced data that represents the whole student, not merely one-dimensional academic performance data.

Their seven factors include the following:

1. Learning environment factors

2. Academic achievement and instruction factors

3. Oral language and literacy factors

4. Personal and family factors

5. Physical and psychological factors

6. Previous schooling factors

7. Cross-cultural factors

The seven factors include the student's personal and family history as well as the areas of instruction and academic achievement. Colleagues are encouraged to collaborate on a case-by-case basis for MLs who are struggling and to do some detective work and learn the potential causes of academic issues those MLs may be exhibiting. They will need to have dialogues with the students' caregivers and previous teachers to find out the missing information that makes up the complete picture of the student. Then, they can continue this collaboration and sharing of expertise to determine a path forward for struggling MLs.

Share Quantitative Data About MLs' Achievement

In addition to collaborating when MLs are not performing as expected and sharing qualitative success stories of individual students, we also highly encourage you to share quantitative data about MLs' academic achievement. While we find that stories are effective in helping some stakeholders recognize MLs' assets, for others it takes quantitative data to help shift people's mindsets to recognizing MLs' numerous assets. When we work with school districts and state departments of education, one of our first questions is how well former ELs (sometimes called "ever Els," depending on the district) do on content area assessments. We believe that all educators should welcome current ELs, former ELs, and MLs into their classrooms and schools. We applaud those educators that welcome these students naturally, but other colleagues may need more convincing. Two examples of how data can do the talking about the benefits of multilingualism are the New York City Department of Education and the Arkansas Department of Education.

- **New York City**. It was recently determined that when former ELs, or MLs who were once considered ELs and eligible for ESOL services, were included in content assessment data, these former ELs in New York City Schools outscored native English speakers on the state English language arts (ELA) assessments (Jorgensen, 2019).

- **Arkansas**. When we were planning on presenting at the ARKTESOL annual conference, we asked for data on EL performance so we could situate our work and gain a deeper understanding of the local context. We were initially given data that showed former ELs outscored current ELs on state content assessments in English language arts and mathematics. While knowing this data in and of itself was meaningful, we followed Rosling's (2018) suggestion to always have a counterpoint for the data so that it is more contextual.

So we dug a little deeper and asked for non-ELs' performance on those same assessments. We were provided Figures 3.4 and 3.5.

As you analyze these two figures, think about the following: (1) What does this data say to you? (2) What impact does this data have on your understanding of MLs' assets?

(3) Why do you think MLs scored this way? You will respond to these reflection questions after you analyze the figures.

Figure 3.4   Percentage of Students Scoring *Ready* and/or *Exceeding* on ACT Aspire, ELA

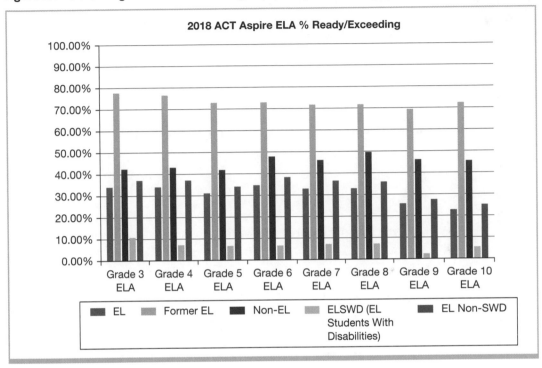

Source: Arkansas Department of Education.

Figure 3.5   Percentage of Students Scoring *Ready* and/or *Exceeding* on ACT Aspire, Mathematics

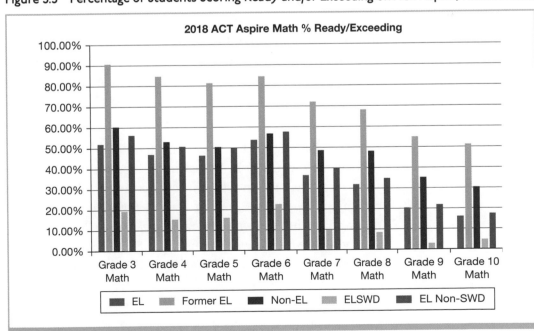

Source: Arkansas Department of Education.

Reflection Questions

1. What does this data say to you?

2. What impact does this data have on your understanding of MLs' assets?

3. Why do you think MLs scored this way?

In the case of the Arkansas state-level data, when former ELs' assessment results were analyzed, it was clear to see that they outperformed native English speakers at every grade level in both English language arts and mathematics. In the course of our review of the Arkansas data, we learned about this note-worthy achievement only when we asked to see the data displayed in this way.

It can be challenging to think long term when it comes to ELs' language acquisition. By nature of taking content assessments in a language in which they are not yet fluent, these assessments in English are not a valid measure of what ELs know and can do; they are a de facto measure of language proficiency. While they are still considered ELs, it is very unlikely that they will score on par with native English speakers or former ELs. It's much more common for educators to think of ELs as deficient in English and always scoring low on content assessments given in English. But when we look long term, we see that some former ELs outscore their native English-speaking peers.

- **Seek out the data**: We wonder if teachers, administrators, parents/guardians, and students are privy to these types of data in their schools, districts, and states. We strongly encourage you to seek out the data about how former ELs fare in your schools and districts after they exit from ESOL services and/or are no longer considered ELs.

- **Share achievement data**: If you find that former ELs outscore native English speakers, we encourage you to collaborate with colleagues to share this information widely. It's our imperative to spread the word that our efforts with MLs will eventually come to fruition; we should always think about and promote the long-term benefits of multilingualism. Showing them data you have gathered and displayed in easy-to-comprehend tables on how the benefits of multilingualism play out positively in their schools, districts, and/or states might help turn the tides.

The Every Student Succeeds Act of 2015 requires states to include data on "the number and percentage of English learners meeting challenging state standards for each of the four years after such children are no longer receiving services under this part" [ESEA, Title III, Section 3121, (a)(5)]. In other words, state education agencies must now provide data on how former ELs (for four years) perform on state content assessments.

Now that we have explored some strategies for fostering an assets-based perspective of MLs, we'd like you to think about the implications of deficit perspectives and how you might respond if you hear a deficit perspective being used by a colleague in Application Activity 3c.

Application Activity 3c. Moving From a Deficit Perspective to an Assets-Based Perspective

PART 1

1. Complete the table. In the first column is a statement that you might hear an educator saying about a multilingual student and his or her family. In the second column, dig a little deeper and write what you think the educators may actually mean by the statement. In the third column, write what the educator may accomplish by making that statement. We've modeled the first row for you.

2. Select one of the statements and decide what you might say as a response to move from a deficit perspective to an assets-based perspective of MLs.

What Educators Say About a Student	What They May Mean	What They May Accomplish by Saying This
1. *To an ESOL teacher*: "Your student isn't doing very well in my class."	That student is the ESOL teacher's responsibility only.	The educator may remove responsibility from her- or himself for meeting the needs of the student.
2. "His name was too difficult to pronounce, so I gave him an American nickname."		
3. "Her parents don't seem to care how well she does in school."		
4. "The assignment that I gave to the class is just too hard for him."		
5. "She doesn't want to fit in with the American students."		

What Educators Say About a Student	What They May Mean	What They May Accomplish by Saying This
6. "He only has friends who speak Spanish and always chooses to work with them."		

Source: Adapted from the National Education Association, 2016, The Hidden Power of Words activity in *Issues of Equity and Culture for English Language Learners.*

PART 2

Choose one scenario. Write your possible response to the educator. What might you say to help change the perspective? Include the following:

- Empathy for the teacher's position or situation

- The underlying concern being raised by the teacher (e.g., student's academic performance)

- A recommendation to address the situation

Scenario:

My response:

PART 3

Consider your own teaching context. Is there a need for an assets-based perspective related to multilingual students and their families?

- What is the issue?

- What assets are the students and their families bringing?

- What steps might you take to shift the way the issue is being discussed and responded to?

THREE STEPS YOU CAN TAKE

Now that you have looked at the definition of an assets-based perspective, examined some of the relevant research that supports an assets-based perspective, and reflected on some case studies, let's become familiar with some tools and strategies to support MLs' assets in their educational settings. We will share one tool you can use to support each step.

Step 1: *Learn about your MLs' assets.*

One of the first steps in operating from an assets-based perspective is learning about your individual students and their families. The "What I Know About My ML" tool (see Figure 3.6) provides a space for you and your colleagues to collect information on individual students. It is framed around discovering more about students' strengths in an effort to make more connections between students' languages, cultures, interests, and their impact on their education.

Figure 3.6 What I Know About My ML

Name:	Country of birth or family's country of birth:
Home language(s): _____ Comments related to strengths in home language (e.g., oracy and literacy in home language, identity as a speaker of home language):	If applicable English proficiency level: _____ English language proficiency scores from _____ (date) Composite (the combined score): _____ Speaking: _____ Reading: _____ Listening: _____ Writing: _____
Relevant educational experiences (e.g., amount of time in US schools, educational experience in home country, areas of strength in current school):	

Cultural connections with schooling (e.g., individualist vs. collectivist, nonverbal communication preference, interactions with teacher):
Family background (e.g., who student lives with, what family likes to do together, family interests):
Student interests (e.g., sports, animals, video games, musical artists):
Student plans and/or goals (e.g., high school graduation, career and technical education courses, college):
Inequities student may face (e.g., microaggressions, bullying, access to technology, child care duties):

Source: Adapted from Staehr Fenner and Snyder, 2017.

Step 2: *Eliminate deficit-based ML policies.*

In addition to your entry point of focusing on individual ML strengths, we also need to approach the eradication of deficit thinking from a policy standpoint. Instead of focusing on a perceived personal deficit of the ML or family (e.g., they don't care about their child's education), we encourage you to devote resources to examining what current policies and practices in your school or district may be preventing MLs' assets to shine. When you're prioritizing which policies you may wish to focus on, remember to act on policies you have the ability to change instead of expending energy and resources on those aspects you are not likely to change (Staehr Fenner, 2014). Then, brainstorm actionable solutions that you can put in place with colleagues to support your MLs and promote their assets. Figure 3.7 provides a space to reflect on deficit-based policies in place in your context—a chance to determine what about this policy makes it deficit-based—and offers a place to brainstorm potential solutions. We share an example to get you started in this reflective process.

Figure 3.7   Deficit-Based ML Policies and Solutions

ML Deficit-Based Policy Example	Why It Operates From a Deficit	Potential Solution
Ninth-grade ESOL is not a credit-bearing course that counts toward high school graduation. It is considered an elective.	This policy penalizes students who are receiving ESOL services and might prevent them from accruing enough credits to graduate from high school.	Research other school districts that offer ESOL or ELD for credit at the high school level. Share recommendations with district policymakers.

Step 3: *Thoughtfully confront individuals' ML deficit mindset.*

On your journey of helping your colleagues shift from a deficit- to an assets-based mindset about MLs, you will undoubtedly encounter deficit-based statements from your colleagues and community. This occurrence gives you the opportunity to support a colleague's shift from a deficit- to an assets-based disposition. We need to be thoughtful about challenging others' thinking in order to do so without disrupting our crucial relationships with our colleagues. But how can we best challenge others' deficit thinking when we find ourselves in the uncomfortable space in which we hear someone apply a deficit perspective in describing an ML or an ML's family? When you encounter such a situation, we suggest following the steps found in Figure 3.8 (adapted from Zacarian & Staehr Fenner, 2020; originally adapted from Staehr Fenner, 2017).

Figure 3.8   Protocol to Counter ML Deficits and Promote an Assets-Based Approach

Step for Moving From ML Deficits to Assets	Guidance
1. Approach a deficit-focused situation thoughtfully.	Take a minute to think about the situation, who the players are, and the possible ramifications of your actions on MLs and their families. Many teachers and administrators haven't received coursework or training on educating MLs. Keep in mind that their deficit perspective may come from a lack of confidence or strategies in working with MLs.
2. Recognize and acknowledge other colleagues' expertise aloud.	When you point out something positive a colleague is doing (e.g., their expertise in their content area), you'll start to build their trust or continue to build the trust you've already established.
3. Model unwavering empathy for MLs.	Demonstrate your character and leadership by remaining an empathetic ally for MLs and their families. In this way, others will look to you as an expert on ML assets and education.
4. Try to first listen and understand others' perspectives, even if you may not agree with them on their approach.	Try to put yourself in someone else's shoes to understand where they may be coming from in focusing on MLs' deficits. This openness to understanding others' frustrations will provide you a greater depth of understanding of their perspective. Your listening to them will also help strengthen their trust in you.
5. Consider what might be happening on a systematic level to promote deficit thinking around this issue.	Reflect on what is happening to cause your colleague to focus on MLs' deficits. Think of some potential ways to address systematic inequalities that promote ML deficit thinking (e.g., programming, scheduling, training for all teachers of MLs).

(Continued)

Figure 3.8   (Continued)

Step for Moving From ML Deficits to Assets	Guidance
6. Suggest some potential solutions and/or strategies to them.	After you've listened to their frustration, recognize when to gently shift the narrative to what you can do to support MLs and/or their families in this situation. By offering concrete support (e.g., modeling a culturally responsive instructional strategy or reviewing materials to suggest some culturally responsive texts), you can help them see the potential for a focus on ML assets instead of deficits. You can also lighten their load, which may make them feel less apprehensive.
7. Follow up on your support and solutions for MLs.	To demonstrate your commitment to MLs and their families' assets, regularly check in with a colleague who you've already helped to see how your suggestions are working. Revisit your plan regularly and revise your approach as needed, based on the outcome of your collaboration.

Source: Adapted from Zacarian and Staehr Fenner, 2020, *Breaking Down the Wall*. (Originally Staehr Fenner, 2017)

Summary of Key Ideas

- We all have the ability to spread a culture of ML assets in our sphere of influence.

- If you approach your work with MLs with their assets in mind, you and your colleagues will be better positioned to create a more welcoming environment for our MLs who have so much to contribute and offer.

Chapter 3 Reflection Questions

1. What is one strategy for building an assets-based perspective of MLs that you would like to implement in your context?

2. What will your first step be? Describe.

3. What is your timeline for this first step?

4. What will your second step be? Describe.

5. What is the timeline for this second step?

6. Who might you collaborate with on your work?

7. What possible pushback do you anticipate?

8. How will you respond to that pushback?

References

al Rabeeah, A., & Yeung, W. (2018). *Homes: A refugee story*. Freehand Books.

August, A., Branum-Martin, L., Cardenas-Hagan, E., & Francis, D. J. (2009). The impact of an instructional intervention on the science and language learning of middle grade English language learners. *Journal of Research on Educational Effectiveness*, *2*(4), 345–376.

August, D., Staehr Fenner, D., & Snyder, S. (2014). *Scaffolding instruction for English language learners: A resource guide for English language arts*. American Institutes for Research. https://www.engageny.org/resource/scaffolding-instruction-english-language-learners-resource-guides-english-language-arts-and

Cepeda, E. J. (2013). Cepeda: In education, a "pobrecito" syndrome. *The Washington Post*. https://archive.sltrib.com/article.php?id=56717963&itype=CMSID

DeCapua, A., Marshall, H., & Tang, F. (2020). *Meeting the needs of SLIFE: A guide for educators* (2nd ed.). University of Michigan Press.

Edutopia. 2017. *Community walks*. www.edutopia.org/blog/community-walks-create-bonds-understanding-shane-safir

Every Student Succeeds Act of 2015, Pub. L. No. 114-95 § 114 Stat. 1177 (2015-2016).

Ewald, W. (2002). *The best part of me*. Little, Brown Books for Young Readers.

Fairbairn, S., & Jones-Vo, S. (2016). *Engaging English learners through access to standards: A team-based approach to schoolwide student achievement*. Corwin.

Fisher, D., Frey, N., & Lapp, D. (2012, January). Building and activating students' background knowledge: It's what they already know that counts. *Middle School Journal*, *43*(3), 22–31.

Hamayan, E., Marler, B., Sanchez-Lopez, C., & Damico, J. S. (2013). *Special education considerations for English language learners: Delivering a continuum of services*. Caslon.

Hammond, Z. (2015). *Culturally responsive teaching and the brain: Promoting authentic engagement and rigor among culturally and linguistically diverse students*. Corwin.

Jorgensen, J. (2019). *Statewide English test finds ELLs performed better than native English speakers*. www.ny1.com/nyc/all-boroughs/news/2019/10/19/statewide-english-test-finds-ells-performed-better-than-native-english-speakers?cid=share_twitter

Robertson, K., & Lafond, S. (2008). *How to support ELL students with interrupted formal education (SIFEs)*. https://www.colorincolorado.org/article/how-support-ell-students-interrupted-formal-education-sifes

Rosling, H. (2018). *Factfulness*. Flatiron Books.

Saifer, S., Edwards, K., Ellis, D., & Stuczynski, A. (2011). *Culturally responsive standards-based teaching: Classroom to community and back*. Corwin.

Salva, C. (2017). *Boosting achievement: Reaching students with interrupted or minimal education*. Seidlitz Education.

Samuels, R. (2017). How to be an American: Syrian refugees find a home in Trump country. *The Washington Post*. https://www.washingtonpost.com/politics/in-nebraska-syrian-refugees-find-a-warm-and-welcoming-community/2017/02/05/5615c82a-eb9b-11e6-9973-c5efb7ccfb0d_story.html

Schulten, K. (2019). Introducing a new feature: Mentor texts. *The New York Times*. https://www.nytimes.com/2019/09/04/learning/introducing-nyt-mentor-texts.html

Shanahan, T. (2013). Letting the text take center stage: How the Common Core State Standards will transform English language arts instruction. *American Educator*, *37*(3), 4–11.

Staehr Fenner, D. (2014). *Advocating for English learners: A guide for educators*. Corwin.

Staehr Fenner, D. (2017). *SupportEd's top 10 ways to support English learners in 2017*. https://getsupported.net/supporteds-top-10-ways-support-english-learners-2017/

Staehr Fenner, D., & Snyder, S. (2017). *Unlocking English learners' potential: Strategies for making content accessible*. Corwin.

WIDA. (2015). *Students with limited or interrupted formal education*. https://wida.wisc.edu/resources/students-limited-or-interrupted-formal-education-slife

Zacarian, D. (2012). *Transforming schools for English learners: A comprehensive guide for school leaders*. Corwin.

Zacarian, D. (2013). *Mastering academic language: A framework for supporting student achievement*. Corwin.

Zacarian, D., & Staehr Fenner, D. (2020). From deficit-based to assets-based. In M. E. Calderón, M. G. Dove, D. Staehr Fenner, M. Gottlieb, A. Honigsfeld, S. Singer, I. Soto, & D. Zacarian (Eds.), *Breaking down the wall: Essential shifts for English learners' success* (pp. 1–20). Corwin.

Simultaneously Supporting and Challenging Students

Scenario: Manny's Math Class

Math is one of Manny's favorite subjects, and his teacher, Ms. Ruiz, uses a variety of strategies to support students in learning both math skills and the language of math. For example, she teaches students which mathematical terms are multiple-meaning words and asks students to compare the everyday and mathematic meanings of such words as "table," "product," and "expression." She also develops math problems that are rel-

evant to students' lives. She provides sentence stems to help students describe their mathematical thinking orally and in writing as well as steps that they take to solve math problems. She also pairs them up to work with manipulatives as they solve problems. Manny is a strong math student, and Ms. Ruiz often pairs him with another Spanish-speaking student so that they can discuss

(Continued)

(Continued)

the problem in Spanish and then write the steps to solve the problem and the solution in English. At the end of a lesson, Ms. Ruiz frequently asks students to complete math journals in which they can write about what they have learned in the language of their choosing and ask any questions that they have.

Scenario Reflection Questions

1. What steps is Ms. Ruiz taking to build students' identities as strong math students?

2. What other types of support might a student who is not a confident math student need to successfully learn both math skills and the language of math?

CHAPTER OVERVIEW

Our second guiding principle is **"Culturally responsive teaching simultaneously challenges and supports students."** This principle emphasizes the need for students to have access to standards-based, grade-level material while at the same time recognizing that some multilingual learners (MLs) will need very specific kinds of support in order to be able to access this material and content. principle #2 also includes the important idea that all students should have opportunities to think critically about issues of social justice and equity in order to push them to understand and identify injustice in their own communities and to inspire them to work for change.

In this chapter, we are going to ask you to take a closer look at equitable education opportunities for MLs in your schools and districts and also reflect on how you can support all learners on their academic journeys. We are going to focus on three key areas:

1. MLs' **access** to content and programs
2. Ways to **support** MLs as they acquire language and content
3. How to **challenge** MLs to think critically and build cross-curricular connections

In this chapter, we will begin by looking at what it means to simultaneously support and challenge students as well as give you an opportunity to reflect on where your students may need additional support and also where students may need to be pushed to expand their learning. Next, we'll discuss what it means to provide equitable access to MLs and how to foster an academic mindset for all students, including building MLs' academic language. Following the discussion of access, we will talk about strategies for supporting MLs through scaffolded instruction. Then, we will explore strategies for challenging MLs through using interdisciplinary, project-based learning and social justice units. We will end the chapter by providing three steps that you can take in your context to simultaneously support and challenge MLs.

WHAT IT MEANS TO SIMULTANEOUSLY SUPPORT AND CHALLENGE MLs

At the heart of culturally responsive teaching (CRT) is instruction that supports students in becoming critical, self-directed learners who can bring all of themselves to the learning. In other words, students' academic identities should be developed and nurtured while being inclusive of students' home cultures and backgrounds. As briefly mentioned in Chapter 1, Hammond (2015) describes the need for educators to be *warm demanders*. This term was originally coined by educator Judith Kleinfeld (1975) to describe the type of relationships needed when teaching Inuit or Yupik children in urban schools in Alaska. Warm demanders are educators who have high expectations of all students in order to push them to become more independent learners but at the same time provide the support that students need in order to take the steps toward greater autonomy. Hammond writes, "The ultimate goal as a warm demander is to help students take over the reins of their learning" (2015, p. 100). In order to strengthen the role that MLs have in their learning, educators must provide the tools and resources so that "students cultivate positive self-efficacy beliefs and a positive academic mindset" (Hammond, 2015, pp. 88–89).

Just as we want educators to view MLs from an assets-based perspective in which they see and value what each student brings to their learning, we also want MLs to see in themselves someone who can be a successful learner. Farrington (2013) describes four characteristics of an academic mindset:

1. I belong here.
2. I can succeed at this.
3. My ability and competence grow with my effort.
4. This work has value for me.

The third characteristic in the list, often referred to as a growth mindset, is defined by Snipes and Loan (2017) as students' "beliefs about the malleability of ability and the payoff for student effort." Carol Dweck (2015), who coined the term "growth mindset," makes the distinction between a growth mindset (the belief that intelligence can be developed) and fixed mindset (the belief that intelligence is static). Students with a growth mindset understand and believe that their effort will positively impact their learning and growth.

In addition to fostering an academic and growth mindset, educational institutions need to examine policies and procedures that may result in inequitable opportunities for particular groups of students. James Banks (2007), an influential leader in the area of multicultural education, specifies the need for schools to examine their school cultures and the impact that those school cultures have on disproportionality in achievement, enrollment in gifted and talented programs, and identification for special education services, as well as the interactions of staff and students across ethnic and racial groups.

In considering the achievement of MLs, it is important to examine the extent to which effective instructional practices that support ML learning and growth are being used and the types of professional development that educators are receiving related to MLs. While there has been research on subgroups within the ML category (e.g., Latino students, English learners), there is much less research related to effective instructional practices for MLs as a whole. However, we do know that instructional recommendations for ELs often include practices that can benefit other learners. In a synthesis of effectives strategies for supporting ELs, Baker and colleagues (2014) highlight the importance of integrating oral and written English language practice into content instruction and providing regular structured opportunities for developing written language skills. Similarly, August (2018), in her synthesis of research for supporting ELs, recommends developing ELs' academic language. She also specifies the importance of providing scaffolded support to help ELs master core content and skill. In this chapter, we will offer some key strategies for MLs related to this research.

In terms of challenging MLs, interdisciplinary and project-based units are two areas to consider. Interdisciplinary or thematic units of study can support MLs by making individual subject areas more coherent and interconnected (Aslan, 2016). Collaborative project-based learning units can foster student agency when students receive sufficient support and guidance (Lenz & Larmer, 2020). We must also challenge students by engaging in social justice and anti-racist work. Ibram X. Kendi, in his book *How to Be an Antiracist* (2019), writes, "The opposite of racist isn't 'not racist.' It is 'anti-racist.'. . . One either allows racial inequities to persevere, as a racist, or confronts racial inequities, as an anti-racist. There is no in-between safe space of 'not racist'" (p. 9). Accordingly, we must create a space in our classrooms in which there is a place for discussions of race and racism and students can critically examine the ways in which particular narratives and resources do or do not share the perspectives, experiences, and voices of people of color (Simmons, 2019).

As in Chapter 3, we have provided a list of look-fors that you would see if this principle is being successfully implemented in the classroom. We have compiled the complete list of look-fors in the Culturally Responsive Teaching Checklist that is provided in Appendix B.

Figure 4.1   Look-Fors for Guiding Principle 2: *Culturally responsive teaching simultaneously supports and challenges students.*

✓   MLs are taught grade-level content and texts. Instructional texts include a balance of grade-level texts and texts at students' reading and language levels.

✓   MLs are provided clear visual and oral instructions for activities. All new activities are modeled.

✓   Instruction and materials are appropriately scaffolded so MLs are able to access and engage with grade-level content and texts.

✓   The classroom contains visual supports for MLs (e.g., word wall with visual and/or home language translation).

✓   Instruction includes regular, structured small-group and pair work.

✓   Instruction includes activities that foster critical thinking and reflection (e.g., open-ended discussion prompts and student monitoring of their learning).

✓   Instruction includes interdisciplinary and project-based learning.

✓   Instruction includes activities that require students to make connections with their prior learning.

✓   Instruction includes activities that require students to consider alternative ways of understanding information and push students to challenge the status quo (e.g., analyzing the change that some states have made from celebrating Columbus Day to celebrating Indigenous People's Day).

✓   MLs have access to and the support needed to be successful in gifted, honors, and/or college preparatory classes.

Source: Adapted from Staehr Fenner and Snyder, 2017.

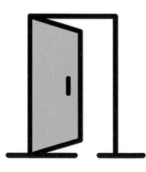

PROVIDE ACCESS TO MLs

Critical to the equitable education of MLs is their access to standards-based, grade-level content and course materials (August, 2018). In order to set the stage for student engagement with rigorous content, ML educators must work to foster an academic mindset in all students.

Building an Academic Mindset

During a recent classroom visit, we observed an eighth-grade English learner in his science class. The student was still

Reflection Questions

What does it look like to have an academic mindset? What student behaviors might you expect to see? What is an educator's role in helping all students build an academic mindset?

developing his language abilities, but he clearly already had an academic mindset. The student sat in front of the teacher, listened attentively to what the teacher said, raised his hand to answer questions, and stayed on task throughout the lesson despite the challenging language demands of the content. We all know students like the one we are describing. The question, though, is what steps we can take to build this academic mindset in students who may not yet see themselves as learners. The following three strategies can be a starting point in helping to build this academic mindset:

1. **Provide models of academic mindsets.**

As teachers, we can model what it means to have an academic mindset by describing our own challenges and how we work to overcome them. We can acknowledge that challenge and failure are both a normal and temporary part of the learning process. It is critical for us as educators to express our vulnerabilities so that students know it's OK to feel the same way. We can also set up procedures where students can model their problem-solving strategies and academic mindsets for other students. It is important to consider how you can provide an opportunity for students to model their own academic mindset throughout the year.

Another strategy is to explicitly identify and describe the academic mindsets that we are working on to help students cultivate and explain why they are important. We can provide models of academic mindsets through the

> I can try
> **different strategies**
> to find the solution
> to the problem.

books and stories that we share. For example, in the book *The Most Magnificent Thing* (2014) by Ashley Spires, the main character perseveres through multiple failed attempts to build a device that she has imagined. In Appendix F: Supporting Resources, we have included booklists that provide models of perseverance and growth mindsets that might be beneficial for students.

2. **Ask students to reflect on their academic mindset.**

Academic mindset exit tickets, goal-based journaling, and success folders are three ways to help students to think about their learning and to see themselves as learners. For example, as part of an exit ticket or as a journal prompt you might ask students to reflect on something that was challenging about the day's lesson and one strategy that they used to meet that challenge. Other items you might include on an exit ticket or as a journal prompt are asking students to explain a way in which they thought like a learner, to explain a new academic term they learned, to write the steps they took to make today successful, or to describe something they were most proud of related to their learning.

Success folders are compilations of student work. Each week or every two weeks, you can return student work and ask your students to select a piece of work that they are most proud of or that they worked hard to complete. When you are setting up this procedure, be sure to model the process for students and talk about what work they might want to include as an example. You can have students write a short explanation of why they included a particular piece of work on an index card that you attach to the piece of work. These success folders can

be a great resource for parent or guardian conferences and student goal-setting meetings.
You can also have students decorate their folders with inspirational quotes or images that
represent success for them.

3. **Foster students' academic language
   use.**

In order for students to see themselves as
academics, we need to support all students
in using academic language and recognizing
the different registers that we use to communicate for different purposes. Academic language is the specialized, often
decontextualized language that is needed to engage with the
school curriculum and academic learning tasks (Bailey, 2007).
Academic language is distinct from the everyday social language that students use on the playground and during lunch
in terms of the complexity of the grammatical structures and
vocabulary used (WIDA Consortium, 2012). We also like to
stress that *all* students benefit from a focus on academic language instruction, not only English learners or MLs. Many
native English speakers do not have access to academic
language outside the school walls and need to be well-versed
in academic language to be successful in school, college,
and/or career.

One way that we can support students in using academic
language is by explicitly teaching language functions for different academic tasks that students are expected to engage
in, such as agreeing and disagreeing, asking for clarification,
providing evidence, adding on, and so forth. When we ask
students to expand on their ideas or provide evidence to support their thinking, we are helping to develop their academic
language as well as academic mindset. For more ideas about
supporting MLs' engagement in academic conversations,
see Chapter 5. For two activities that you could try with
your students, see Application Activity 4a and Application
Activity 4b.

Application Activity 4a. Exploring Language Registers

You are in the park with one of the four people below. For each person, imagine what he or she might say to you.

Your best friend	Your new neighbor
A park employee	A botanist giving a tour on native plants

Reflection Questions

1. What do you notice about the language that is used by each (e.g., verb choice, level of formality)?

2. How would your response vary for each of these people?

Application Activity 4a can support students in recognizing how language changes across settings and with different people. You could even expand the discussion of registers to explore how students might communicate differently based on cultural expectations. For example, how might a student communicate differently with her grandmother than with a classmate when talking about the same topic? By being explicit about language use, we can help students recognize different parts of their identities and foster the skills needed to transition smoothly among cultures.

Zwiers and Soto (2016) developed an activity that they call Fortify a Conversation, which we highlight in Application Activity 4b. For this activity, students write down an informal conversation on a topic that is being studied. In a second column, students are then asked to "fortify" the conversation by developing more academic statements and responses. Such changes might include increasing the academic language that is used; increasing the length of the statements and responses; using expressions such as *in order to, however,* or *in addition;* using words such as *some, could,* and *might* to soften the message; and using evidence to support thinking. Then, students are asked to practice the revised conversation with their partner and reflect on their language use. In order to scaffold this activity, you can provide the starting conversation and then work with small groups of students to have them fortify the conversation using word banks and/or sentence stems.

Let's give this activity a try. In Application Activity 4b, Fortifying Conversations, rewrite the dialogue to increase the use of academic language, soften the language if needed, and increase the use of evidence to support the ideas in the conversation.

Application Activity 4b.
Fortify a Conversation

Basic	Fortified
Person A: We have to recycle if we want to save the planet.	In my opinion, an important step in protecting the environment is recycling.

(Continued)

(Continued)

Basic		Fortified
Person B:	I don't think we should be forced to recycle. It's not fair.	
Person A:	But not enough of us are doing it on our own.	
Person B:	Aren't there other ways to get people to do it without making it law?	
Person A:	What about giving people rewards for recycling?	
Person B:	Like what?	

Source: Adapted from Zwiers and Soto, 2016.

To see strategies that Syracuse City School District (SCSD) educators use to help students build their academic mindset, take a look at the *Building Students' Academic Identities Through Academic Language Use* video. Once you have watched the video, consider the video reflection questions.

 Video 4.1

Building Students' Academic Identities Through Academic Language Use

resources.corwin.com/CulturallyResponsiveTeaching

Reflection Questions

1. What did you notice about the different ways that the three educators in the video helped build students' academic language?

2. Why do you think using academic language is important to building students' academic identity?

3. What is a strategy that you use or have seen modeled to support students' academic language use?

SUPPORT MLs

Going hand in hand with building students' academic identity is providing sufficient support so that students, regardless of language proficiency level, can engage with grade-level texts and academic content. The inclusion of scaffolded instruction is a critical instructional tool needed to support MLs' learning.

Scaffolded Instruction to Support ML Learning

Reflection Questions

1. How do you define scaffolded instruction?

2. How can scaffolded instruction support MLs in engaging with standards-based, grade-level content?

3. Why do you think scaffolded instruction is a component of culturally responsive teaching?

Scaffolded instruction is defined as the temporary supports that an instructor or more capable peer provides another student that allow a student to perform a task he or she could not do without help (Gibbons, 2015; National Governors Association for Best Practices, Council of Chief State School Officers, 2010; Staehr Fenner & Snyder, 2017). A scaffold is not meant to be a permanent support. Rather, the ultimate goal of scaffolded instruction is to facilitate a student in completing the same type of task independently in the future once they have acquired the necessary language and/or skill. As our colleague Tonya Ward Singer instructs, you need to both "use *and lose*" scaffolds (2018).

Because of the support that they provide, scaffolds can help make rigorous grade-level curriculum accessible to all students by providing what Krashen (1977) refers to as comprehensible input. Academic texts and concepts can be broken down into meaningful pieces and be presented with key instructional supports in order to strengthen MLs' understanding of and engagement with this content. For example, if MLs are engaging with a chunk of grade-level text, they may benefit from such scaffolds as the use of graphic organizers, bilingual or English glossaries of key vocabulary, scaffolded text-dependent questions to help them get at the key ideas of the text, pair or small-group work, and supporting material in their home language (if they are literate in it). Scaffolds can also provide opportunities to model academic language and academic ways of thinking, such as when students work in pairs or small groups with non-MLs or through using sentence stems and frames. When using scaffolds, it's important to recognize that they aren't a one-size-fits-all. They should be provided to MLs based on each student's strengths and needs (Staehr Fenner & Snyder, 2017).

Based on the work of the WIDA Consortium (2012), scaffolds can be grouped into three categories: materials and resources, instruction or instructional practices, and student grouping. At this time, we would like you to complete a self-assessment related to your use of different types of scaffolds with MLs. Please complete Application Activity 4c, Scaffolding for MLs Self-Assessment, and answer the reflection questions. For each scaffold decide the following:

1) If you are not familiar with the scaffold

2) If you are familiar with it, but don't regularly use it with MLs

3) If you regularly use it with MLs

If you are not currently in the classroom, consider the extent to which you see each scaffold being used with MLs in your school or district.

Application Activity 4c. Scaffolding for MLs Self-Assessment

Scaffold	I am not familiar with this scaffold.	I am familiar with this scaffold, but don't regularly use it with MLs.	I regularly use this scaffold with MLs.
Materials and Resources			
Graphic organizers	☐	☐	☐
Visuals	☐	☐	☐
Manipulatives	☐	☐	☐
Word banks or word walls	☐	☐	☐
Sentence stems, frames, paragraph frames	☐	☐	☐
Adapted texts and/or audio texts	☐	☐	☐
English and/or bilingual glossaries	☐	☐	☐
Supporting materials in home language	☐	☐	☐
Instruction or Instructional Practices			
Repeat and paraphrase language	☐	☐	☐
Provide interactive modeling	☐	☐	☐
Preteach vocabulary and academic language structures	☐	☐	☐
Provide concise instruction of background knowledge	☐	☐	☐
Practice academic skills and language with a nonacademic topic	☐	☐	☐
Reinforce concepts and skills using multiple modalities	☐	☐	☐
Implement routines to support reading and writing	☐	☐	☐
Student Grouping			
Structured pair work	☐	☐	☐
Structured small-group work (may be teacher-led)	☐	☐	☐

Source: Adapted from Staehr Fenner and Snyder, 2017.

Reflection Questions

1. What are one or two scaffolding strategies that you feel you are using consistently in your work with MLs?

2. How do you feel these strategies benefit MLs?

3. What is one strategy that you would like to learn more about or try out in your classroom?

Many of the scaffolds in the self-assessment checklist, such as graphic organizers and visuals, are probably very familiar to you. We explore other scaffolds, such as home language materials and providing concise instruction of background knowledge, in upcoming chapters of this book. In the remaining section of this chapter, we would like to highlight four scaffolding strategies that you may be less familiar with and provide a tool for thinking about how and when to use scaffolds for MLs. Just as with academic language, *all* students may benefit from using scaffolds, not only students who live in a home in which they speak or are exposed to a language other than English. Particularly in distance-learning[1] environments, students are often asked to complete tasks independently—without the benefit of having a teacher in the same room to provide support. Scaffolds may especially be beneficial for all students in these distance learning environments where help is not immediately available by raising a hand.

---

[1]Distance learning may also be referred to as remote or online learning.

Scaffolding Strategy 1: Modeling and Think-Alouds

Modeling, an essential scaffold for MLs, involves the teacher or another student demonstrating a new concept or approach to learning, and the students learn by observing. Teachers can model behaviors, language, thinking, and/or steps to an activity. A strategy for engaging students during the modeling process is to ask students what they notice during the modeling. Modeling through a think-aloud can also provide an opportunity to bring the learning process out in the open. Ness (2018) suggests the following steps in planning for a think-aloud related to text analysis:

1. **Identify juicy stopping points:** To prepare for a think-aloud, Ness suggests using sticky notes to identify places in a text where you could make inferences, synthesize information, ask a question, or consider the author's purpose. She also suggests identifying areas that might cause confusion to students.

2. **Determine where and when to think aloud:** Next, Ness suggests narrowing down your think-alouds to five to seven stops per text. In identifying where to stop, consider your objectives for the lesson, what strategies you have or haven't covered with students, and why the text was selected.

3. **Write scripts on sticky notes:** Finally, Ness suggests writing your script on sticky notes using the first person—for example, "I am a little confused about what is happening at this point. I think perhaps the author is using a flashback to provide background information to the reader. I am going to keep reading to see if my prediction is correct."

As you prepare for your think-aloud, also consider how you will assess student understanding. For example, could you have students respond to a question in pairs on a whiteboard? Might you ask students to give a quick thumbs-up or thumbs-down response to a question? Look for ways that all students can demonstrate their engagement.

Scaffolding Strategy 2: Practicing Academic Skills and Language With Familiar Content

Practicing academic skills and language with familiar content can be an excellent strategy to introduce students to new academic skills and the language needed for those academic skills. For example, if you are going to have students compare and contrast the viewpoints of two characters from a text you are reading, you might have them first compare and contrast their opinions on a familiar topic (e.g., the best summer activity) with the opinions of a peer. Ward Singer (2018) recommends that teachers begin with the language the students use during this initial discussion to create response frames (sentence stems or frames). Then, teachers can teach new sentences structures that students can try out. For example, in working on comparisons, you might introduce and have students practice using words or phrases such as *whereas, on the one hand,* and *on the other hand.* Figures 4.2 and 4.3 provide a model of a graphic organizer and sentence frames that you might use to introduce and practice language of comparison.

Figure 4.2 Graphic Organizer for Making Comparisons About a Familiar Topic

Student's Name	Favorite Summer Activity	Reason

Figure 4.3 Practice Language for Comparing and Contrasting

Language for Comparing

Both _____ and _____ like _____ because
_____.

_____ and _____ are similar because they _____.

Language for Contrasting

Whereas _____ likes _____, _____
likes _____.

On the one hand, _____ likes _____ because _____.

On the other hand, _____ likes _____ because _____.

Scaffolding Strategy 3: Reinforcing Concepts and Skills Using Multiple Modalities

Using multiple modalities to reinforce concepts and skills provides MLs an opportunity to practice concepts or skills in a variety of ways. The use of multimodal learning opportunities can foster student engagement and appeal to learners' varied learning preferences. The Barometer and Argument Balance Scale are two examples of multimodal activities.

Barometer: Taking a Stand (Post-It Note Barometer). For this activity, place signs labeled *Strongly Agree* and *Strongly Disagree* at opposite ends of the room or put two contrasting statements at either end. Then, ask a compelling question that can be answered with a yes or no response. For example, a compelling question could be, "Should schools have dress codes?" Give students time to consider the question and develop their opinion. Next, ask students to position themselves in the room based on their response.

This activity could be used to introduce a topic, serve as a formative assessment, or be used at the end of a unit. You could also assign students roles and have them respond to the question with their new role. For example, if studying the American Revolution, you might assign students to be either a Patriot or a Loyalist. To incorporate additional modalities as well as provide additional scaffolding, you can ask students to jot down a reason for their opinion on a sticky note before they move. For MLs needing additional support, you could provide sentence stems or frames to support their writing. Once students have positioned themselves in the room, you can ask students to share their response with a classmate and also ask a couple of students in each category to share their thinking with the whole group.

Argument Balance Scale (Zwiers & Soto, 2016). For this activity (see Figure 4.4), students create either a two-dimensional or three-dimensional scale that they use to evaluate an argument. The issue is placed in the center of the scale. For example, if students are debating the benefits and risk of space exploration, the phrase "space exploration" would go into the center. Students work in pairs to list supporting evidence for both sides of the argument. Students are asked to consider the strength of each argument that they provide. For example, the pair might decide that one piece of evidence is weaker than another. They could use a smaller-sized card for that argument or tear off the corner of the card to indicate weaker evidence. To learn more about this activity or to see a video of it in action, take a look at the Zwiers's Argument Balance Scale in Appendix F.

Figure 4.4   Argument Balance Scale Visual Organizer

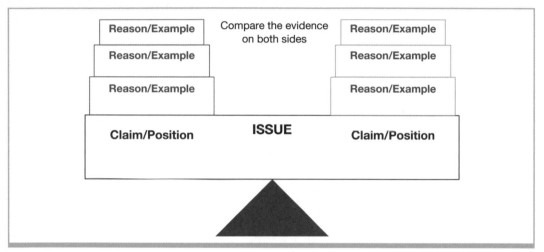

Source: Zwiers, J., and Hamerla, S. (2017). *The K–3 guide to academic conversations: Practices, scaffolds, and activities.* Thousand Oaks, CA: Corwin.

Take a minute to reflect on a concept or skill that students in your content area or teaching context often struggle to understand. Complete Application Activity 4d. Planning for Multimodal Practice to think about how you might incorporate multimodal practice with the skill or big idea. An example has been provided for you first as a model.

Application Activity 4d. Planning for Multimodal Practice (Example)

Skill or Big Idea: Estimating and language for making estimates	
Reading	**Speaking and Listening**
In this carousel activity, students will move around the room reading estimation word problems written	Students will work in pairs to complete a gap activity in which they estimate how long it will take for someone

on poster paper. Pairs will write their estimates on index cards that they tape face down on the poster paper. Once each pair has made an estimate, the cards can be turned over.	to complete a series of tasks. For example, Student A will have some of the activities, and Student B will have the others. They will need to share their information and then decide on an estimate together. Students should sit back to back or across the table from one another to complete this task.
Writing Students will write estimation problems for their peers using a word bank of terms related to estimating (e.g., *approximately, about, more than, less than, rounding, nearest*).	**Other (e.g., seeing, touching, moving)** Students will use their estimating skills to match jars of objectives with index cards with estimates on them.

Application Activity 4d.
Planning for Multimodal Practice

Skill or Big Idea:	
Reading	**Speaking and Listening**
Writing	**Other (e.g., seeing, touching, moving)**

Scaffolding Strategy 4: Implement Routines to Support Reading and Writing

In order to foster equitable education opportunities for MLs, it is essential that they have access to grade-level texts and opportunities to develop standards-aligned reading and writing skills across content areas. The inclusion of routines around reading and writing practices can be an excellent way to scaffold learning for MLs and support the use and development of the critical academic language that we described earlier in this chapter.

Close Reading Routines

Close reading is a concept based on the idea that by engaging in a process of reading, interpreting, and evaluating a complex text, readers can gain access to the meaning that resides within texts (Shanahan, 2013). When engaging in close reading, Fisher and Frey (2015a, 2015b) recommend several instructional components to effectively support all students in the process. They explain that students should engage in multiple reads of short, complex passages that warrant a close read. Students should read the message multiple times and annotate the text as they read. Fisher and Frey (2015b) also recommend the incorporation of collaborative conversations about the text and the use of text-dependent questions.

In her book *EL Excellence Every Day* (2018), Tonya Ward Singer provides a four-step process that can be used to engage students in collaborative conversations during the close reading process. For each step, Ward Singer provides some guiding questions that students can discuss. As with all routines, it is essential to model each step in the process. See Figure 4.5, Collaborative Conversations for Close Reading, for an example. However, once students become familiar with the routines and language needed, they could collaboratively work through the close reading process with greater autonomy. In addition to modeling of routines, some MLs may also benefit from other scaffolds

Figure 4.5   Collaborative Conversations for Close Reading

Steps	Questions for Discussion
1. Anticipate	• Based on the title, what do we predict the text will be about? • After looking at the headings and the images, what do we predict the text will be about? • What questions do we think the text might answer?
2. Read to understand	• What is the gist (the main point) of what we read? • What don't we understand? • How do our predictions about the text compare to what we read?
3. Reread to analyze and infer	• What inferences can we make about what we read? • What conclusions can we make about what we read? • What connections can we make between this text and what we have read about or discussed in the past?
4. Collaborate to write with text evidence	• What is our claim? • What evidence from the text best supports our claim? • How can we explain the connection between our evidence and the claim?

Source: Adapted from Ward Singer, 2018, p. 175.

such as building background knowledge, using sentence stems and frames, and using graphic organizers for organizing ideas.

Building Writing Routines With Mentor Sentences

A strategy for supporting MLs' writing and language development is the implementation of routines focused on mentor sentences. This strategy is designed to teach writing conventions and patterns (Anderson & La Rocca, 2017). In Figure 4.6, The Mentor Sentence Routine, we have added possible considerations for MLs to the mentor sentence routine that Anderson and La Rocca (2017) propose.

Figure 4.6   The Mentor Sentence Routine

Steps	Example	Considerations for MLs
1. **Select a mentor sentence:** To begin the routine, you should select a mentor sentence that demonstrates an area of focus that you want to work on and is aligned to the standards. For example, you might focus on capitalizing proper nouns, pronoun use, or including text quotation in a text. Anderson and La Roca recommend selecting a piece of writing that "demonstrates the convention's power and purpose" (p. 23).	Example mentor sentence: "Everyone was running—men, children, women carrying babies." —Linda Sue Park, *A Long Walk to Water* (regular and irregular plurals, use of dash)	In selecting sentences, you'll want to be sure to preteach or explain any vocabulary needed for the sentence or select sentences that are comprehensible to all students.
2. **Develop a focus phrase:** Based on your area of focus, you develop a focus phrase to guide students. This should be written in student-friendly language and clearly define the learning goal.	I use plural nouns to show more than one person, place, or thing.	Depending on the needs of your MLs, you may need to provide additional opportunities for students to practice the skill. For example, with irregular nouns, you might consider providing a resource that they could use for their work or assigning some small-group work to facilitate extra practice with the skill.
3. **Invite students to notice:** Explain to students that rather than looking at a sentence that needs to be fixed, you'll be focusing on great sentences. Read the sentence aloud two times. Ask students what they notice about the mentor sentence.	• The -*y* changed to -*ies* in "babies." • Men and women don't have an -*s* at the end. • There is a dash before more details are added.	As with all routines, students will need modeling and practice with the process the first couple of times. It is also important to give students wait time. It can be beneficial to have students talk in pairs in order to provide more think time and opportunities for language practice.
4. **Invite students to compare and contrast:** Develop an imitation sentence and ask students to compare the original sentence with an imitation sentence that you have created. This imitation sentence should closely mirror the mentor sentence but also provide an opportunity to demonstrate how the pattern can be applied to other situations and content.	Everyone was swimming—ducks, fish, and ponies carrying children.	Consider modeling this process through a think-aloud. Provide sentence stems and modeling of language used to compare and contrast (e.g., In the first sentence, I see _____, but in the second I don't).

Steps	Example	Considerations for MLs
5. **Give students an opportunity to imitate:** Next, it is the students' turn to create an imitation sentence. This can be done as an interactive or whole-group writing activity, pair writing, and/ or independent writing. You might have students first develop an imitation sentence in pairs, and then have them create an imitation sentence independently.	Everyone was flying—fairies, witches, and dragons carrying children.	Be intentional about your pairings in order to provide scaffolded support. For example, you might pair students who share the same home language groups so they can discuss their sentence in their home language. Consider additional scaffolds that students might need to complete this next step, depending on the convention that you're working on (e.g., a list of adjectives, list of irregular plural nouns).
6. **Share and celebrate**: Anderson and La Rocca specify that during the sharing it is important to celebrate the students' work. We want students to associate positive feelings with their writing. This is a time for students to listen to each other's ideas and also to notice how writing conventions connect across topics.	• Students share sentences with class. • Set up mentor sentence walls with a focus phrase along the top. • Make mentor sentence books. • Share mentor sentences with students in lower grades.	Give an opportunity for students to practice reading their sentences aloud in pairs or to you before they share with the whole class. Consider developing a student-friendly checklist that students can use when writing their sentence (e.g., I capitalized the first letter of the sentence).
7. **Invitation to edit:** Anderson and La Roca specify that having students edit their own writing is the main skill that it is important for students to master. The invitation to edit can be used to help them hone their "editing eyes" (p. 39). You can ask students what they learned from the mentor sentence. Then, show students the mentor sentence again, followed by two to three other sentences that include errors in the focus area.	Everyone was running—cats, mouses, and dogs carrying childs.	Some MLs could benefit from additional supports with this process. For example, students could work in pairs and be provided a resource such as a list of irregular plural nouns. Also, when introducing this activity, it would be good to practice the language that students can use to describe and explain errors.

Source: Adapted from Anderson and La Rocca, 2017.

Reflection Questions

1. What routines do you use in your classroom to support students in developing their literacy skills, fostering academic language use, and/or engaging with grade-level content?

2. If you are not currently in the classroom, what routines do you see being used in your context or what routines have you learned about to support students in developing their literacy skills, fostering academic language use, and/or engaging with grade-level content?

Matching appropriate scaffolds to the needs of a particular ML is a bit like a puzzle for the teacher to solve. In some instances, a scaffold such as a graphic organizer (see Figure 4.7) will benefit a significant number of students when working on an academic task. However, there will be other times when we don't know exactly which particular scaffold or combination of scaffolds is going to effectively provide the support an ML needs to be successful with a given academic task.

At this time, we would like you to put on your detective hat and think about a particular student that struggles in your class or in your school. If you aren't currently in the classroom, think about a former classmate of yours who may have struggled academically. Consider what supports you have tried with that student and what supports from the scaffolding checklist that you haven't tried but you think might be beneficial to the student. Also, consider what steps you need to take to teach the student to use the scaffold. For example, a word wall is an ineffective instructional support if it isn't used by students who might benefit from it. Similarly, pair work isn't a scaffold if one student in the pair does all the work. Finally, assess how effective the scaffold was in supporting the student in accomplishing the learning task. What formative assessment tools will you use to measure student success (e.g., rubric, checklist) and to identify areas where the student may need more support?

Figure 4.7   Selecting and Implementing Scaffolds

Student name:

Academic task:	Possible challenges student may have with task:

Scaffolds to address those challenges:

Scaffolds that have been successfully used with student in past:	New scaffolds to try (or formerly used scaffolds) to present in new ways:

Steps for effectively implementing the scaffold:

What could go wrong in implementing the scaffold?	What steps can you take to increase the effectiveness of the scaffold?

Assessing scaffold:

How effective were the scaffolds in supporting the student in accomplishing the learning task?	What would you change for next time?

To strengthen the use of scaffolds, we can also involve students in reflecting on the types of supports that they need to complete tasks and decisions about when to remove scaffolding. In the section on fostering an academic identity at the beginning of the chapter, we discussed using exit tickets to encourage students to think about academic challenges and how they were met during learning tasks, as well as student reflection on their completed work. Both of these tools can also be useful to engage students in the metacognitive task of thinking about their use of scaffolds.

CHALLENGE MLs

Before we begin the section on challenge, we would like you to take a minute to reflect on your own experiences as a learner.

Directions: Recall a time that you were challenged. It might be something that challenged you in a formal educational setting or something that pushed you to new learning in a nonacademic setting. What happened? What was difficult? What did you learn? What supported you with your learning? What impact did the learning or experience have on you? Jot your answers down in this box.

There is a wide variety of ways to challenge MLs. In this chapter, we would like to take a look at curricular units and coursework that push students to make connections across disciplines, to think critically and problem solve, and to challenge inequitable monolingual and monocultural policies and practices. Kinloch (2017) describes the need for CRT to provide a space for students to critique institutional barriers that stand in the way of their academic success by having educators position "multiculturalism, multilingualism, and racial, cultural, and social justice at the center of teaching and learning" (p. 39). We recognize that this aspect of CRT could be a book in itself. However, in the remainder of the chapter, we'll highlight some areas for consideration when challenging ML students, and we will also provide additional resources for you to explore.

Interdisciplinary and Project-Based Learning Units

Implementing interdisciplinary and project-based learning units into the curriculum is one way of challenging students to think critically about content as it relates to different disciplines and to engage in collaborative problem-solving as a tool for learning. Let's take a look at a definition of each.

- **Interdisciplinary study** is "a curriculum approach that consciously applies methodology and language from more than one discipline to examine a central theme, topic, issue, problem, or work" (Jacobs, 1989).

- **Project-based learning (PBL)** is "a teaching method in which students gain knowledge and skills by working for an extended period of time to investigate and respond to an authentic, engaging, and complex question, problem, or challenge" (Wolpert-Gawron, 2018).

Figure 4.8, Comparing Interdisciplinary and PBL Units, provides a synthesis of some key differences and similarities between the two.

Figure 4.8   Comparing Interdisciplinary and PBL Units

Interdisciplinary Unit	PBL Unit	Both
• Is framed around a central theme or topic and two to five essential questions • Explores topic through the lens of more than one discipline (often includes teacher collaboration across disciplines) • Can be independent or group-oriented • Unit example: Art and Literature During U.S. Civil Rights Movement (combines disciplines of art, literature, and history)	• Is framed around a complex question, problem, or challenge • Often includes an authentic or real-life scenario • Is group-oriented • May or may not be multidisciplinary • Unit example: In the Quadrats Biodiversity Unit, students conduct a quadrat survey to measure the health of a local ecosystem such as a park near their school (pblworks. org, n.d.).	• Include an end product • Offer opportunities for language development and use of language in four modalities • Offer opportunity for social justice and anti-racism lens • Should include scaffolded support for MLs

Interdisciplinary and project-based learning units can support MLs in accessing challenging content and also foster the sharing of diverse perspectives. These units can be cross-curricular, meaning they address a topic from more than one content area, and multimodal in that they integrate practicing the four skills (reading, writing, speaking, and listening) into the lessons. These types of units also benefit MLs because they do these things:

- Offer opportunities for oral language practice through collaborative work

- Offer authentic learning experiences framed around a common theme

- Provide opportunities to practice language in context across content areas

- Support the development of higher-order thinking skills

- Provide an opportunity for educators to collaborate in support of MLs' language development and content learning (McAdoo, 2014; Wolpert-Gawron, 2018)

Before we explore strategies for developing interdisciplinary or PBL units to use with MLs, consider the following reflection questions.

Reflection Questions

1. How might you equitably assess MLs at different levels of language proficiency on an interdisciplinary or PBL project?

2. How can you ensure that MLs at varying proficiency levels are engaged in the work?

3. How might you build a classroom culture where all students can give and receive constructive feedback?

Both types of units begin with the development of a guiding question or questions that are framed around the benchmarks or standards. Generally, interdisciplinary units are guided by two to five themes or essential questions. For PBL, the questions are often linked to a real-world problem that connects to students' experiences or communities (Farber, 2017). Projects that result in real-world outcomes can be especially powerful for students (Lenz & Larmer, 2020).

For both types of units, you'll need to select the end project or product. Consider how you might give students some choice in determining the final project. As you develop your unit, you'll also want to give careful consideration to the timeline you'll follow, how you scaffold the project for students of varying language proficiency or skill levels, and how you'll build in opportunity for assessment and reflection. To help you plan a unit and think through considerations for MLs, we have created Figure 4.9, Differentiating for MLs in Planning Interdisciplinary and Project-Based Learning Tool, and Figure 4.13, Interdisciplinary, Project-Based Learning, or Social Justice Themed Unit Planning (p. 145). In addition, we have included some supporting resources in Appendix F at the end of the book.

One PBL example is a project completed by students of Shelburne Community School in Shelburne, Vermont. The

Figure 4.9   Differentiating for MLs in Planning Interdisciplinary and Project-Based Learning Tool

1. How will you provide students voice and choice in the unit (e.g., topic, grouping, final project)?

2. How will you strategically group students in order to incorporate peer scaffolding (e.g., home language, language proficiency level consideration, skill level considerations, personality)?

3. How will you build in both individual and group accountability?

4. How will you develop a timeline that allows for the chunking of larger tasks, regular checkpoints, opportunity for revision, and continuous progress toward the end goal?

5. How can you incorporate learning centers and focused minilessons as a tool to scaffold instruction for those students that need extra support in a particular area?

6. What supporting resources will you provide (e.g., home language resources, resources at different Lexile levels)?

7. What instructional scaffolds will you provide (e.g., sentence stems, bilingual glossary, paragraph frame, model)?

8. What formative and summative assessment tools will you use? How might you differentiate these tools if needed?

9. What steps will you take to include students in goal setting, reflection, and self-assessment?

10. How will you celebrate student successes throughout the unit and at the end of the unit?

Source: Adapted from Miller, 2012; Boss and Larmer, 2018.

students collected data related to carbon emissions that came from idling cars in front of their school. The project was framed around an authentic problem related to measuring the quality of the air students breathed (Farber, 2016). If you would like to explore additional examples of different types of project-based learning units, please refer to the additional resources In Appendix F at the end of the book. When developing interdisciplinary and PLU units, consider how you can embed a social justice and/or anti-racism lens to your unit.

The Role of Social Justice and Anti-Racism Education

Reflection Questions

What do you think it means to teach for social justice and anti-racism? What is an activity, a lesson, or a unit that you teach or have seen taught or have read about that supports social justice or anti-racism pedagogy?

In a school culture that simultaneously challenges and supports all students, students should also be engaged in activities that support them in becoming socially and politically aware. For example, students might explore a unit that looks at an environmental issue or take part in a community-based volunteering effort. Students should also be pushed to think critically about dominant cultural narratives and the role that student voices can have in shifting the narrative. To do so, you must challenge white students from the dominant culture to critically look at their privilege and question the way in which narratives are told. At the same time, students of color and students from other historically oppressed communities (e.g., immigrant students, LGBTQ students) must also be given a safe space to explore their cultural practices and challenge dominant ways of knowing and understanding information.

Paris and Alim (2017) describe the importance of culturally responsive teaching, taking into account the fact that culture "both remains rooted *and* continues to shift in the ways that culture always has" (p. 9). By embracing this essential idea, we can provide a space for students to honor the cultural practices that are deeply embedded in their communities as well as celebrate the ways in which these practices may also be changing.

To hear how Syracuse City School District educator Angela Matarrazo engages students in social justice education, watch the video clip titled *Building on Students' Backgrounds in Support of Social Justice Education.*

Video 4.2

Building on Students' Backgrounds in Support of Social Justice Education

resources.corwin.com/CulturallyResponsiveTeaching

Figure 4.10, a Linguistic Autobiographies Unit, is an example of a project-based unit focused on language and culture. This unit is included in the California Department of Education's English Language Arts/English Language Development Framework (2015). In this unit, students reflect on their own language use and how it varies across different contexts, such as at home with family, with friends, at school, and when interacting with strangers. They also watch the documentary *Precious Knowledge*, which gives an account of the fight over a Mexican American Studies program in Arizona public schools. The film includes the stories of several students enrolled in the Mexican American Studies program at Tucson High School, with interviews with teachers, parents/guardians, school officials, and the lawmakers who wish to outlaw the classes.

Figure 4.10   Linguistic Autobiographies Unit

Unit: Linguistic Autobiographies, Ninth Grade

Unit Summary: "Students spend much of their class time engaging in collaborative conversations about challenging topics, including their reactions to negative comments in the media about their primary languages, "nonstandard" varieties of English (e.g., African American English), accents (e.g., Southern), or slang. Through these conversations, students learn to value linguistic diversity—their own and others—and develop assertive and diplomatic ways of responding to pejorative comments regarding their primary languages or dialects. For various projects, students work in collaborative groups to generate interview questions, peer-edit drafts, and produce media. This collaborative academic learning environment strengthens the bonds between students but also supports them to engage in the types of tasks that will be expected of them in college, community, and careers" (California Department of Education, 2015).

Unit Tasks:

- View and discuss documentary films and other multimedia resources related to language and culture and creative uses of language and dialects (e.g., *Precious Knowledge;* TED Talk "Reggie Watts: Beats That Defy Boxes").

- Read and discuss short essays and memoir excerpts by bilingual authors to explore the writers' experiences and provide models for the students' writing.

- Analyze and discuss poetry and contemporary music to explore how artists' language choice represent their values and identity (e.g., the poem "In Lak'ech: You Are My Other Me" by Luis Valdez).

- Reflect on and discuss students' own multilingual or multidialectal experiences and how others have responded to their use of different languages or dialects.

- Conduct oral interviews and write about their families and communities' language use.

- Develop a variety of writing around the topic of language and culture. Writing tasks might include personal narratives, poems, blog posts, informative reports, and argumentative essays.

- Research, produce, and present original multimedia pieces related to language and culture. These presentations might include visual presentations or short documentary films.

Source: Adapted from California Department of Education, 2015.

In the following bullets and in Appendix F: Supporting Resources, we have provided a description of other social justice and anti-racism themed units and resources that can support your social justice and anti-racism work.

- Teaching Tolerance is an organization focused on helping teachers and schools educate students to be active participants in a diverse democracy. They provide a variety of free resources to educators, including lesson plans, student texts and tasks, and recommendations for specific teaching strategies. Their materials focus on social justice and anti-bias education.

  o Teaching Tolerance offers a series of 12 lessons called *Using Photographs to Teach Social Justice.* These lessons are designed for students in Grades 6–12 and cover three themes: (1) understanding people's perspectives, (2) exposing injustice, and (3) confronting injustice. As an example, in one lesson on gender stereotyping, students compare two different images of a female construction worker. For each image, they consider whether the woman in the photo is actually a construction worker, what features of the individual are emphasized, and other questions related to the details of each picture (Teaching Tolerance, n.d.).

○ Teaching Tolerance has also put together a series of articles, professional development resources, and classroom resources related to racism and police violence. These resources are excellent resources to further your own learning and support discussions with your students (Teaching Tolerance, 2020).

- Facing History and Ourselves has developed a unit called *The Power to Change the World: A Teaching Unit on Student Activism in History and Today* (https://www.facinghistory.org/educator-resources/current-events/youth-taking-charge-placing-student-activism-historical-context). In this unit, students begin by analyzing the student activism of Marjory Stoneman Douglas High School students against gun violence. This unit asks students to explore the role that teenagers can have in activist movements.

- The Global Oneness Project (www.globalonenessproject.org) offers a series of lesson plans that include films and articles on various topics related to issues such as migration, water scarcity, food insecurity, climate change, poverty, and endangered cultures.

- Radical Math (www.radicalmath.org) is a website and group of educators who teach math from a social justice perspective with the goal of improving math and science literacy and fostering economic access for individuals from low socioeconomic status households and people of color.

- UNICEF Canada (www.unicef.ca/en/elementary-resources) offers a series of lesson plans and resources for elementary school teachers on such topics as global citizenship.

Ethnic Studies

Ethnic studies are interdisciplinary courses framed around the study of race and ethnicity from the perspective of under-represented racial groups. Examples of ethnic studies might include Middle Eastern Studies, Native American Literature, and Puerto Rican and Latino or African American history. Research shows that enrollment in ethnic-studies classes can improve student attendance, academic performance, and acquisition of high school credits for students of color who join these courses (Cabrera et al., 2014; Dee & Penner, 2017).

THREE STEPS YOU CAN TAKE

Now that we've explored considerations and strategies for providing access, support, and challenge to MLs, we would like to suggest three steps that you can take in your own classrooms and schools, as well as tools that will guide you in your work. These steps can each be taken individually, but their impact will be even greater if you work with your CRT teams for a collaborative approach.

Step 1: *Provide access.*

Set a Goal to Increase Student Access

Equitable access to the curriculum, advanced coursework, and extracurricular programs and activities is a significant equity issue. In Chapter 2, we asked you to consider possible areas of inequity that may exist for ML students and their families and choose one to explore. Because access is such an important issue, we'd like you to set a goal to increase access in one area in your classroom or school. This could be the same equity issues that you researched in Chapter 2, or it might be a new issue that you wish to tackle.

If you wish to focus on your access in your classroom, you can set a goal specific to making the grade-level content more accessible to all students in your classroom. For example, you might set a goal to strengthen your teaching of academic language to MLs in your content area or to implement routines that support greater access to grade-level texts. Figure 4.11, the Goal Setting for Access Planning Template, is a tool that you can use for this purpose.

Figure 4.11   Goal Setting for Access Planning Template

Equity issue I would like to focus on:		
Rationale (Why is this an important issue in your context?)		
Desired outcome (What do you hope to change or achieve?)		
Timeline	**Action Steps**	**Resources or Support Needed**
(1) Step 1 by _____		
(2) Step 2 by _____		
(3) Step 3 by _____		
(4) Step 4 by _____		

Source: Adapted from Staehr Fenner, 2014.

Step 2: *Provide support.*

Expand Scaffolded Support for MLs

The Scaffolded Lesson Planning Checklist, Figure 4.12, can be a great tool to help you plan for scaffolded lessons.

Figure 4.12   **Scaffolded Lesson Planning Checklist**

1 I know the **strengths and needs** of each ML . . .

in relation to the language demands of the lesson. I have set individual goals to help my MLs progress in their acquisition of language and content.

☐ Yes ☐ No

2 I have analyzed the **language demands** . . .

of the lesson and identified areas that may be challenging for my MLs.

☐ Yes ☐ No

3 I have developed a list of **key vocabulary** . . .

to preteach and determine how I will teach and provide opportunities to practice this vocabulary.

☐ Yes ☐ No

4 I have determined specific aspects of **language use** . . .

that I will focus on during my lesson.

☐ Yes ☐ No

5 I have determined what **background knowledge** to teach . . .

(if any) and how to teach it in a concise manner.

☐ Yes ☐ No

6 I have determined how to effectively **group students** . . .

in order to most effectively support their learning of content and acquisition of English.

☐ Yes ☐ No

7 I have included opportunities for students to practice **key concepts** . . .

in varied ways, using multiple modalities.

☐ Yes ☐ No

8 I have selected **home language resources** . . .

(as appropriate) that can support MLs in learning the new content and academic vocabulary.

☐ Yes ☐ No

9 I have selected or developed **scaffolded materials** . . .

to support MLs of varying language proficiency levels (e.g., graphic organizers, sentence stems and/or sentence frames, and visuals).

☐ Yes ☐ No

10 I have determined how I will assess **student learning** . . .

and how I will scaffold the assessment for MLs of varying language proficiency levels.

☐ Yes ☐ No

Source: Adapted from Staehr Fenner and Snyder, 2017; Staehr Fenner, Snyder, and Monick, 2019.

Review the checklist and consider which steps you feel like you are doing well and in which areas you could improve. The checklist is also a great collaborative tool. You can discuss it with your grade-level or team colleagues as a way to provide consistent scaffolding to MLs across content areas. If you are an administrator, you might consider using the tool as a needs assessment for educators in your school or district. For example, educators might identify those areas of the scaffolding checklist in which they feel they have the greatest need for professional development (PD). You might consider providing mini-PD sessions on specific topics related to the checklist (e.g., strategically grouping students, incorporating multiple modalities into instruction). We also advise that you not focus on all areas of the checklist simultaneously and instead start small, examining one or two areas with a colleague at first and then expanding your lens.

Step 3: *Provide challenge.*

Develop an Interdisciplinary, PBL, or Social Justice Themed Unit

As you look for opportunities to challenge MLs, consider adding an interdisciplinary, PBL, or social justice themed unit to your teaching repertoire. If possible, think of how you might collaborate with colleagues to develop and implement the unit. If you are an administrator, brainstorm how you might be able to showcase the work of educators who are already incorporating interdisciplinary, PBL, or social justice themed lessons into their teaching. Figure 4.13, Interdisciplinary, Project-Based Learning, or Social Justice Themed Unit Planning, is a template that was adapted from a tool created by our colleague Marley Zeno to support educators' PBL work. It has been adapted so it could be used for developing a variety of unit plans. See Appendix C for another planning template that was developed to support CRT units.

Figure 4.13   Interdisciplinary, Project-Based Learning, or Social Justice Themed Unit Planning

Directions: Reflect on the academic and linguistic tasks or text that MLs will need to engage with in this project. Analyze the possible challenges in background knowledge, academic vocabulary, and oral language. Determine supports for MLs in these areas.	
Project or unit title:	
Driving question(s):	
Key learning goal(s):	
Final product:	
Assessments and assessment tools:	

Potential challenges for MLs	Potential supports
Background knowledge needed:	Supports for building background knowledge:
Academic vocabulary needed:	Supports for academic vocabulary:
Oral language skills needed:	Supports for oral language:
Resources:	
Additional materials needed:	Who is responsible developing these additional supports?
Student groups:	

Summary of Key Ideas

- MLs need access to grade-level content and texts.

- Educators of MLs need to foster an academic mindset in their students and explicitly teach academic language.

- MLs may need scaffolded support in order to engage with grade-level content and texts.

- MLs should be challenged to think critically and reflectively through interdisciplinary units, project-based learning, and social justice units and lessons. They may need scaffolded support to effectively engage with these units and materials.

- MLs should have equal access to college preparatory, honors, and advanced placement courses and enrichment programs (e.g., gifted and talented program). It is the responsibility of the school and district to identify and remove barriers that are preventing equitable accesses to these courses and programs.

Chapter 4 Reflection Questions

1. What was your most significant takeaway from this chapter in terms of simultaneously supporting and challenging MLs?

2. What steps will you take to more effectively support MLs' learning in your context?

References

Anderson, J., & La Rocca, W. (2017). *Patterns of power: Inviting young writers into the conventions of language, grades 1-5*. Stenhouse.

Aslan, Y. (2016). The effect of cross-curricular instruction on reading comprehension. *Universal Journal of Educational Research, 4*(8), 1797–1801.

August, D. (2018). Educating English language learners: A review of the latest research. *American Educator, 42*(3), 4.

Bailey, A. L. (Ed.). (2007). *The language demands of school: Putting academic English to the test*. Yale University Press.

Baker, S., Lesaux, N., Jayanthi, M., Dimino, J., Proctor, C. P., Morris, J., Gersten, R., Haymond, K., Kieffer, M. J., Linan-Thompson, S., & Newman-Gonchar, R. (2014). Teaching academic content and literacy to English learners in elementary and middle school. *IES Practice Guide*. NCEE 2014-4012. What Works Clearinghouse.

Banks, J. A. (2007). *Diversity and citizenship education: Global perspectives*. Jossey-Bass.

Boss, S., & Larmer, J. (2018). *Project based teaching: How to create rigorous and engaging learning experiences*. ASCD.

Cabrera, N., Milem, J., Jacquette, O., & Marx, R. (2014). Missing the (student achievement) forest for all the (political) trees: Empiricism and the Mexican American Studies controversy in Tucson. *American Educational Research Journal, 51*(6), 1084–1118.

California Department of Education's English Language Arts/English Language Development Framework. (2015). *Snapshot 7.1. Investigating language, culture, and society: Linguistic autobiographies* (pp. 726–727). http://www.cde.ca.gov/ci/rl/cf/documents/elaeldfwchapter7.pdf

Dee, T., & Penner, E. (2017, February). The causal effects of cultural relevance: Evidence from an ethnic studies curriculum. *American Education Research Journal, 54*(1), 127–166.

Dweck, C. (2015). Carol Dweck revisits the growth mindset. *Education Week, 35*(5), 20–24.

Farber, K. (2016). *Planning a PBL unit*. Innovative Education in Vermont.

Farber, K. (2017). *Real and relevant: A guide for service and project-based learning*. Rowman & Littlefield.

Farrington, C. A. (2013). *Academic mindsets as a critical component of deeper learning*. University of Chicago: Consortium on Chicago School Research.

Fisher, D., & Frey, N. (2015a). Teacher modeling using complex informational texts. *The Reading Teacher, 69*(1), 63–69.

Fisher, D., & Frey, N. (2015b). *Text-dependent questions: Pathways to close and critical reading*. Corwin.

Gibbons, P. (2015). *Scaffolding language, scaffolding learning, second edition: Teaching English language learners in the mainstream classroom*. Heinemann Educational Books.

Hammond, Z. (2015). *Culturally responsive teaching and the brain: Promoting authentic engagement and rigor among culturally and linguistically diverse students*. Corwin.

Jacobs, H. H. (1989). *Interdisciplinary curriculum: Design and implementation*. ASCD.

Kendi, I. X. (2019). *How to be an antiracist*. One World.

Kinloch, V. (2017). "You ain't making me write": Culturally sustaining pedagogies and black youths' performances of resistance (pp. 25–41). In D. Paris & H. S. Alim (Eds.), *Culturally sustaining pedagogies: Teaching and learning for justice in a changing world*. Teachers College Press.

Kleinfeld, J. (1975). Effective teachers of Eskimo and Indian students. *The School Review*, 83(2), 301–344.

Krashen, S. (1977). Some issues relating to the monitor model. In H. D. Brown, C. Yorio, & R. Crymes (Eds.), *On TESOL '77: Teaching and learning English as a second language—Trends in research and practice* (pp. 144–158). TESOL.

Lenz, B., & Larmer, J. (2020). Project-based learning that makes a difference: Individual passion projects are just one type of PBL—Projects students do collaboratively to make a difference in the community also build agency. *Educational Leadership*, 77(6), 66.

McAdoo, M. (2014, December). Mastering English through project-based learning. *New York Teacher*. https://www.uft.org/news/news-stories/mastering-english-through-project-based-learning

Miller, A. (2012). 6 strategies for differentiated instruction in project-based learning. *Edutopia*. https://www.edutopia.org/blog/differentiated-instruction-strategies-pbl-andrew-miller

National Governors Association for Best Practices, Council of Chief State School Officers. (2010). Common Core State Standards for English language arts and literacy in history/social studies, science, and technical subjects. Appendix A: Research supporting key elements of the standards. Glossary of key terms. Retrieved from http://www.corestandards.org/assets/Appendix_A.pdf

Ness, M. (2018). Three steps for think alouds. *ASCD Education Update*, 60(2).

Paris, D., & Alim, H. S. (Eds.). (2017). *Culturally sustaining pedagogies: Teaching and learning for justice in a changing world*. Teachers College Press.

Pblworks.org. (n.d.). *Quadrats to biodiversity*. https://my.pblworks.org/project/quadrats-biodiversity

Shanahan, T. (2013). Letting the text take center stage: How the Common Core State Standards will transform English language arts instruction. *American Educator*, 37(3), 4–11.

Simmons, D. (2019). How to be an antiracist educator. *ACSD Education Upate*, 61(10).

Snipes, J., & Loan, T. (2017). *Growth mindset, performance avoidance, and academic behaviors in Clark County School District* (REL 2017–226). U.S. Department of Education. http://ies.ed.gov/ncee/edlabs

Spires, A. (2014). *The most magnificent thing*. Kids Can Press.

Staehr Fenner, D., & Snyder, S. (2017). *Unlocking English learners' potential: Strategies for making content accessible*. Corwin.

Staehr Fenner, D., Snyder, S., & Monick, K. (2019). *Scaffolded lesson planning checklist*. https://getsupported.net/free-tools/

Teaching Tolerance. (n.d.). *Using photographs to teach social justice: Exposing gender bias*. https://www.tolerance.org/classroom-resources/tolerance-lessons/using-photographs-to-teach-social-justice-exposing-gender

Teaching Tolerance. (2020). *Teaching about race, racism and police violence*. https://www.tolerance.org/moment/racism-and-police-violence

Ward Singer, T. (2018). *EL excellence every day: The flip-to guide for differentiating academic literacy*. Corwin.

WIDA Consortium. (2012). *WIDA's 2012 amplification of the English language development standards, kindergarten–grade 12*. Board of Regents of the University of Wisconsin System.

Wolpert-Gawron, H. (2018, June). PBL with English language learners: A vital need. *PBLWorks*. https://www.pblworks.org/blog/pbl-english-language-learners-vital-need

Zwiers, J., & Soto, I. (2016). *Academic language mastery: Conversational discourse in context*. Corwin.

Placing Students at the Center of the Learning

Scenario: Lian's Science Class

Lian is learning about food chains in her science class. In previous lessons, students have learned and practiced key vocabulary, which they have added to a glossary. Lian's glossary is a bilingual glossary that includes the Mandarin translation of each word along with an English definition, use of the word in a sentence, and a picture.

(Continued)

149

(Continued)

To begin the lesson, the students write down a student-friendly learning objective on a note-taking guide that they will use for the lesson. They write, "I will be able to understand how energy is gained and lost through a food chain in a specific habitat." Then, in pairs, they talk about what they think they will be learning in class and a question that they have about the topic. The teacher explains the food chain game that they are going to play and gives each student a bag with a picture of the plant or animal that they will represent in the game and 15 beans. The teacher shares a list of sentence stems that they can use when playing the game, and she models what the students will do when they come together for a transaction. Wearing the pictures of the animals that they represent, the students engage in a series of transactions in which they gain and lose beans (energy). At the end of the game, the students count their beans and share their tallies with their classmates. In pairs, they discuss the questions How is energy lost? and How is energy gained? Then, they write individual responses to the questions in their note-taking guide. As Lian works, she refers to her glossary and the note-taking guide.

Source: Activity adapted from Teaching Channel. (n.d.). *Using science games to deepen learning* [Video file]. https://www.teachingchannel.org/video/energy-flow-lesson-plan

CHAPTER OVERVIEW

This chapter is framed around the following guiding principle: **"Culturally responsive teaching places students at the center of learning."** In this chapter, we will begin by defining what it means to put students at the center of learning and discuss research that supports student-centered pedagogy. We will then provide specific strategies for learning about your students and their learning preferences and setting a collaborative tone in your classroom. Next, we will explore strategies for engaging multilingual learners (ML) students and families in goal setting and involving MLs in taking part in self- and peer assessment. We will also share strategies for fostering engaging, peer-to-peer interactions and ways to honor ML growth and achievement. We will end the chapter with three steps that you can take in your classroom, school, or district and tools to support you in taking those steps.

UNDERSTANDING STUDENT-CENTERED INSTRUCTION AND ASSESSMENT AND WHY IT IS IMPORTANT

Placing students at the center of the learning, or student-centered instruction, is an instructional approach in which the students in the classroom shape the content, instructional activities, materials, assessment, and/or pace of the learning within a structured learning environment. Student-centered learning involves regular opportunities for pair and group work. It also includes student-friendly learning goals as well as self- and peer assessments that are framed around instructional standards and learning goals.

Application Activity 5a. Reflecting on Your Learning

We'd like you to take a moment to think about your own learning experiences. Can you recall a time when you felt that you had a significant role in setting goals for your learning, selecting the types of activities that would most effectively support your learning, and assessing your learning? What did that experience feel like? What was required on the part of the teacher and the learning environment in order to support you in having such a role?

Description of learning experience:

How you felt:

Role of the teacher:

Learning environment:

Student-centered instruction and assessment is essential to culturally responsive teaching (CRT) because it allows for greater learner choice, which in turn fosters support for diverse learning needs, motivates learners through engaging and autonomy-building activities, and supports language development and understanding of content through peer-to-peer interactions. Student-centered instruction does not mean that all instruction is guided by student preference, but rather there is ample opportunity for student voice and preference within an instructional framework that is based on specific learning outcomes.

Hammond (2015a), in her discussion of brain-based learning, identifies the impact that culture has on how we share and process information. In cultures with strong oral traditions, information is communicated through storytelling, music, and poetry. The sharing of knowledge in this way requires strong interpersonal relationships. Such information is often pragmatic and extremely relevant to day to day life (Marshall & DeCapua, 2013). In contrast, cultures that are centered around written knowledge transfer do not require the same type of relationships, and information is often more abstract and theoretical. Consider the extent to which in U.S. culture, even in personal interactions, we have shifted heavily to the use of emails and texts to share information rather than face to face or even phone conversations. In thinking about how to effectively engage students who come from collectivist cultures and cultures with strong oral traditions, learning that incorporates story, art, movement, and music and other attention-grabbing strategies may be particularly beneficial (Hammond, 2015a). Further, being able to connect learning to students' daily lives and experiences will foster greater interest (Marshall & DeCapua, 2013).

In addition to considering the role of students in learning activities, it is also important to consider how you will engage students in goal setting and assessment. Gottlieb (2016) writes of the importance of peer and self-assessment as a tool for self-regulated learning. Among the many benefits that she cites of self-assessment include the role that it can have in supporting students in taking responsibility for their learning, recognizing the value of students' perspective as a data source, and offering a shared set of expectations between teacher and student.

In this chapter, we will focus on four areas to consider when thinking of how to place ML students at the center of the learning:

1. Creating a classroom climate that allows for student-centered learning and student choice

2. Involving MLs in setting goals for and assessing their learning

3. Developing lessons that offer peer-to-peer and multimodal learning opportunities

4. Showcasing ML work and celebrating progress

As you read more about these four areas, consider how the look-fors in Figure 5.1 may or may not be present in your classroom or school.

Figure 5.1   Look-Fors for Guiding Principle 3: *Culturally responsive teaching places students at the center of learning.*

✓   Students and teachers develop the classroom norms and expectations together.

✓   Teachers are aware of students' learning preferences.

✓   MLs are given choice in their learning.

✓   MLs are given opportunities to speak and write about their lives and the people and events that are important to them.

✓   MLs are involved in goal setting and assessment through the use of student goal sheets, checklists, peer-editing activities, and teacher–student or student–student conferencing.

✓   ML student work is displayed in the classroom and in the school.

✓   Lessons include activities that foster relationship building (e.g., think-pair-share discussions and collaborative tasks).

✓   Lessons include intentional groupings of students to support student learning and allow for groupings that consider language backgrounds.

✓   Group work is thoughtfully planned and structured so that all students have specific roles or ways to meaningfully contribute.

Source: Adapted from Staehr Fenner and Snyder, 2017.

CREATING A CLASSROOM CLIMATE THAT ALLOWS FOR STUDENT-CENTERED LEARNING AND STUDENT CHOICE

Creating a classroom climate that is conducive to student-centered learning requires learning about your students and their learning preferences. It's important to get to know your students beyond who they are academically and to avoid viewing students through a one-dimensional lens that positions you to see students only as what they might be lacking or the hardships that they have experienced. Learn about students' passions, dreams, and what makes them unique.

It is also essential to develop a supportive classroom environment in which students feel comfortable learning from one another, where learning is seen as a process, and where students aren't afraid to make mistakes. Let's begin with an activity for you to reflect on what you know about the students in your class. If you aren't in the classroom, choose a classroom in your building that you feel you know fairly well or a classroom that you've observed.

Application Activity 5b. Knowing My Students

Step 1. In the left-hand column, write the names of your students from memory. For teachers with more than one class, choose a class with the greatest numbers of MLs.

Step 2. In the middle column, write one fact about each student that does not have to do with academics (e.g., Isabel plays the flute. Tae takes care of his brother after school).

Step 3. In the third column, put a check if you have talked with the student about the information that you wrote in the middle column.

Step 4. Compare your list with your class list and answer the reflection questions.

Student's Name	Nonacademic Fact About the Student	Conversation With Student About the Fact? (Yes or No)

Source: Adapted from Anderson (2018).

Reflection Questions

1. Who did you think of first?

2. Who was harder for you to remember?

(Continued)

(Continued)

3. Who did you have a hard time identifying a fact about?

4. Why do you think you know more about some students than others?

5. How could you build in opportunities to learn more about all your students?

Building a Collaborative Community for the MLs in Your Classroom

Remember that as important as it is for you to learn about your students, it is also important for you to share about yourself. The work of community building is a continual process that is supported through shared understandings of the expectations and rules of the classroom. Establishing classroom norms collectively can be a great starting point for building community. We've included some additional ideas for community building here:

- **What's in a Name?** (adapted from Decker, n.d.): Students complete and share the following information about their

Reflection Activity

Take a minute to reflect on what you would expect to see in a collaborative and supportive classroom. What does the room look and feel like? What kind of activities might you see to help teachers and students learn about and from one another? What protocols are in place to support shared norms, respect, curiosity, and cooperation? Write or draw a response to demonstrate your ideas.

name. This can be a great opportunity to practice and learn to correctly pronounce students' names.

- o What's your full name?
- o Were you named after someone? If so, who?
- o What does your name mean (if anything)?
- o Did your parent(s) consider any other names before deciding on the one you have? If so, what?
- o Why did your parent(s) choose your name?

- What is your nickname (if any)? How did you get that nickname?

- What else should we know about your name?

- **Good News–Bad News or Roses and Thorns**: A successfully strategy that Sydney built into her high school ESOL classes was an opening activity where students highlight something that was going well in their life and something that wasn't going well. Depending on the number of students in your class, you can have all students share, ask for volunteers to share, or rotate through different students each class period.

I wish my teacher knew that I have to take care of my three younger sisters every day after school, feed them dinner, and put them to bed. **Sometimes it is hard for me to finish my homework.**

- **What I Wish My Teachers Knew About Me** (Zacarian et al., 2017): This activity can be a great start-of-the-year activity to allow students an opportunity to share something with you that they feel is important. The teacher should model this activity by also telling the class something significant and could also provide a few examples of the types of things students might share.

- **Venn diagram** (adapted from J. Starr): For this activity, two students create a Venn diagram about themselves, their similarities, and differences. This can be a great opportunity to pair students who may not know each other well, and these Venn diagrams can be hung in the room for students to learn about one another. You can give them some sentence stems to get them started (e.g., *I love, I worry about, I have, I don't have, I would like to, I speak, I can*).

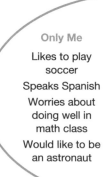

Only Me

Likes to play soccer

Speaks Spanish

Worries about doing well in math class

Would like to be an astronaut

Both of Us

Have an older brother

Loves tacos

Love Ariana Grande's music

Can ice skate

Only My Partner

Likes to draw

Speaks Arabic

Worries about speaking in class

Would like to be a famous chef

- **Exploring learning preferences**: Spending some time having students think about and share their learning preferences can be a helpful tool for educators as they plan their instruction and consider ways to give students choice in their learning. Some student surveys relating to learning preferences are framed around Howard Gardner's (1983) theory of multiple intelligences. There are other examples that ask students to reflect on such questions as whether they prefer working in a group or independently or whether they prefer to work in silence or with noise or music. For some examples of learning preferences surveys for different ages of students, please see Appendix F: Supporting Resources at the end of this book.

- **Incorporate opportunities for students to speak and write about themselves**: Providing ongoing opportunities for students to share their experiences helps build a sense of community and create an atmosphere in which what each student brings to the classroom is appreciated and valued. The authors of the CUNY-NYSIEB guide for educators on *Translanguaging* (Celic & Seltzer, 2013) recommend engaging students in writing identity texts. This strategy developed by Cummins et al. (2005) provides an opportunity for students to create written, spoken, visual, musical, dramatical, or multimodal texts in which students highlight an aspect of their identity. Identity texts can be shared with classmates, other educators, and families.

Figure 5.2 is an excerpt from *Origin Hungry* by Maya Green that was developed based on several family interviews that she conducted. The text is described as "a collection of poetry and essays exploring identity through many lenses: race, gender, relationships, inheritance, and belonging" (Green, 2020). In her preface, she writes, "I collected stories this summer like wild berries off a bush: the sweet of early morning swims in Barbados and tart of Louisiana toil, the name of the plantation where some of your graves still lie; my own South Carolina childhood barely ripe" (p. 9).

When it comes to how teachers can support students in writing identity texts, Green says that, when given the space, students will write about things that are meaningful to them. She explains that her teachers created a classroom community in which students could be vulnerable. They also emphasized the role of storytelling as a tool for social change. According to Green, writing about yourself, your family, and your culture—while incredibly rewarding—can also be challenging at times, and that there is benefit in being able to engage in this type of writing over an extended period of time (M. Green, personal communication, September 24, 2020).

Figure 5.2 Excerpt From *Origin Hungry* by Maya Green

"Freedom Times"

Granmama, tell me the happiest you remember feeling.

I'll say I was a child, ten, twelve.

All the cousins, I'll say five or six, and

my brothers and sisters, we'd run.

Uncle George had a big hill. We used to race up,

race down, our bodies almost remembering

what it was to fly—feet sliding before

ankles, arms spread like wings—

but they forgot last second, and we rolled

down, cloth and skin smeared with earth

and green. And berry juice, dripping down

our chins, blush-red like blood and

it didn't matter. What I looked like,

what I had on. I was a young child.

I was just free . . .

Source: Green, 2020, p. 31.

As you gain a better understanding of your students, you will be better equipped to build in learning opportunities that allow for student choice.

Building in Opportunities for Student Choice

Another characteristic of a classroom climate that is open to student-centered learning and allows for opportunities for students to build on their own learning preferences is student choice. Student choice should be thoughtfully planned and implemented in order to build student autonomy and students' capabilities at making choices that will be most beneficial and engaging to their learning. It is also important that student learning choices be aligned to content and language standards.

If MLs are uncertain about their choices, feel overwhelmed by the number of choices that they have, or if the choice feels in conflict with their learning preferences (e.g., independent vs. collectivist learners), students might select the easiest or most familiar options (Parker et al., 2017). In order to scaffold the process of building in student choice, consider focusing on one area of choice at a time. Consider how you can build student choice in terms of **who** students work with, **what** academic tasks they do to demonstrate learning, **when** they work on certain tasks, and **where** they sit for their work.

Who: Provide opportunities for students to try out what it feels like to work independently, in pairs, or in teacher-selected small groups. Ask students to think about which they prefer and why. What did they notice about their learning opportunities in each of the groups? Be clear on the fact that no one way is better than another, but each person will have different learning preferences. Then, allow students choice on who they work with for some assignments.

What: Consider ways of building choice into assignments. Start by providing only two to three options, with clear modeling of each option. Your options should offer opportunities to demonstrate progress toward or mastery of content and language standards. You can structure the choices so they offer different amounts of support. For example, one option to respond to a reading might be a highly structured task with lots of built-in support (e.g., completing a paragraph frame about key ideas from the text). Another option might provide less structure, such as developing a poster to highlight key ideas from the text. You can also offer a free choice in which students can come up with their own ideas for responding to a text passage. Other ways you might give students choice would be letting them decide which book they want to read on a particular topic or to select which vocabulary words they most need practice with. Parker and colleagues (2017) explain that it is important to discuss with students how to make instructional choices and model the process for students.

When: You can build MLs' autonomy by giving students options for what to work on at a particular time. During a visit to a middle school social studies class, we observed the teacher talk through three different assignments with students that were due at different times in the upcoming weeks. Students were allowed to make choices about what they wanted to work on at that particular time with the understanding that they knew the deadlines for each assignment and had a clear sense of how long certain tasks would take.

Where: Offering students options about where they sit and who they sit with can also be another way of providing students with choice and can support students in recognizing their own learning strengths and needs. For example, students may identify that their learning improves when they are allowed greater movement or when they are seated in a particular area of the classroom (e.g., closer to the word wall or teacher). Flexible seating also allows for teachers to have greater flexibility in assigning students to work with or near other students, thereby offering more varied opportunities for peer-to-peer engagement and interactions (van den Berg et al., 2012).

Syracuse City School District (SCSD) fourth-grade teacher Taryn Michael (personal communication, February 26, 2020) explains how she uses flexible seating in her classroom:

In my classroom, we use flexible seating and choice seating. I believe this supports independence and positive relationships with all students. In the beginning of the school year, you'll notice that it is difficult to introduce these different types of seating. Couches, pillows, and wobble stools are not familiar to (the students), and it is *so* important to teach HOW you use it and WHY it's important to be safe, respectful, and responsible with the seating choices. Many students need examples, reminders, and modeling on how to use the special seats. . . . Also, I think it's important to mention that students do not have assigned seats or name tags. I personally begin the school year with a seat assignment and seating chart, but I slowly wean off the chart and allow the kids to choose where they want to sit. I say, "Choose a responsible seat." . . . They do great with this and generally pick a different seat, and they sit with different students and groups (by their choice) every day. This promotes relationships between all students and gets them all to work with different kids every day. Knowing what I know now and how the group changes every year, I know to slowly integrate the "choice" because the relationship building must happen first! (They also love sitting on a couch!)

As students gain skill and confidence in making choices, you can extend the options for the types of choices that you give them. Figure 5.3, the Tic-Tac-Toe Assessment, is an example of a choice board that you could give students after they complete a story. Students can be asked to finish a certain number of tasks or complete a series of tasks in a row. In this way, while giving students some choice you can also adapt the types of tasks you have students take part in and the scaffolds that you provide so as to meet students' needs and foster students' growth.

Figure 5.3   Tic-Tac-Toe Assessment

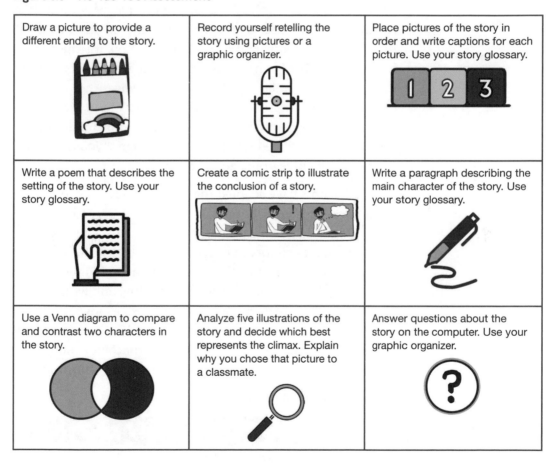

Draw a picture to provide a different ending to the story.	Record yourself retelling the story using pictures or a graphic organizer.	Place pictures of the story in order and write captions for each picture. Use your story glossary.
Write a poem that describes the setting of the story. Use your story glossary.	Create a comic strip to illustrate the conclusion of a story.	Write a paragraph describing the main character of the story. Use your story glossary.
Use a Venn diagram to compare and contrast two characters in the story.	Analyze five illustrations of the story and decide which best represents the climax. Explain why you chose that picture to a classmate.	Answer questions about the story on the computer. Use your graphic organizer.

In this chapter, we have described how to give students choice in their learning. Another critical piece of student-centered learning is the important role that students can have in setting goals for and assessing their own learning. We often find that students are left out of these critical conversations, which are crucial in building their voice in their own learning.

INVOLVE MLs IN SETTING GOALS FOR THEIR LEARNING

In order to incorporate self- and peer assessment into your teaching, an important first step is to support MLs in understanding their strengths and areas for growth more broadly and to set individual learning goals. EL educator Emily Francis explains that she begins each school year by having students review their language assessment scores and set goals for their language development using general descriptors of what students at varying levels of proficiency level can do (Francis, 2019). Because Emily teaches in North Carolina, a state that uses the WIDA ACCESS for ELLs assessment, she provides students with their ACCESS score reports and Can Do Descriptors for their grade level (Francis, 2017). Emily also creates progress reports that she sends home to families in their home languages that are based on these same descriptors. By developing common language that is understood and shared with students and families, everyone can have a shared vision for what progress looks like and what the student learning goals are for the year.

Some educators have adapted the WIDA Can Do Descriptors to develop student-friendly versions. Figure 5.4, Student-Friendly Descriptors for Recounting, is an example of how you might use the Can Do Descriptors to develop student-friendly goals that can support students in thinking about their abilities in each of the four skills (speaking, listening, reading, and writing) and identifying steps that they can take to foster language development. Even if your state does not use WIDA standards, you can adapt your state's English language proficiency framework to ensure it is more student-friendly and share it with students.

Figure 5.4   Student-Friendly Descriptors for Recounting

ELP Level 1	ELP Level 2	ELP Level 3	ELP Level 4	ELP Level 5
I can . . . • Answer *WH* questions (who, what, when, where, how)	I can . . . • Tell the main point from a class conversation	I can . . . • Connect ideas using transition words when talking about science	I can . . . • Summarize the main ideas and key details of information that I hear	I can . . . • Present oral reports that synthesize information from more than one source

Source: Adapted from Board of Regents of the University of Wisconsin System. (2017). WIDA Can Do Descriptors, Key Uses Edition Grades 6–8, p. 4. https://wida.wisc.edu/sites/default/files/resource/CanDo-KeyUses-Gr-6-8.pdf

You should also take steps to involve ML families in setting goals for their children's learning. The Regional Multicultural Magnet School in New London, Connecticut, begins each school year with goal-setting conferences. Held on the two days before classes start for students, the purpose of a goal-setting conference is to help families and students establish both academic and social goals for their child for the school year. Both parents (or guardians) *and* students are expected to participate in the conference. Additionally, parents and students share questions and concerns about the upcoming school year, and the teacher shares behavior expectations, curricular information, and logistics. In order to prepare families for goal-setting conferences, teachers send home questionnaires for both the student and their parent or caregiver, which include questions such as "What are you excited about for this school year?" Teachers also design questions to help them learn about their students' lives, including "What was something fun you did this summer?" or "What is your favorite book you read this summer?"

Fourth- and fifth-grade teacher Susan Hafler from the Regional Multicultural Magnet School says that discussing her students' responses is one of the best parts of goal-setting conferences:

> I learn a lot about my students' lives outside the classroom during goal-setting. I learn who the readers are, about their family, what kids' interests are. It allows me to begin to make personal connections with my kids *and* their parents, which often helps later in the school year when I really need parents' support in addressing social or academic concerns. (S. Hafler, personal communication, February 2020)

We understand that finding the time to host ML family goal-setting meetings could be a challenge. Here are some possible options for building opportunities for goal setting into your relationships with families:

- Look for ways to add goal-setting opportunities at family engagement events. In SCSD, they added goal setting to a regularly occurring family engagement night. Educators and families shared a dinner, and then families had an opportunity to touch base with the EL specialists at each of the schools. To learn more about this event and watch a video, turn to Chapter 7.

- Build goal setting into a classroom and homework assignment. Have students go through a goal-setting exercise in class and then assign them homework to share their goals with their parents or guardians. Ask for parent or guardian feedback. Consider how families who may not have high levels of English or who may not be literate in their home languages can also engage with this activity. (For an example of a template you might use, see Figure 5.14.)

- Prior to parent–teacher conferences, send home a goal-setting document that MLs can complete with their parents or guardians. You can use this as a jumping-off point for your conference.

- Collaborate with other educators (e.g., counselors, general education teachers, EL specialists) to share the responsibility and workload for setting goals with particular students. This is a perfect opportunity to collaborate and reinforce the idea that all teachers must work to foster equitable education for MLs.

Reflection Questions

What steps can you take to involve MLs in setting goals for their learning? What other ideas do you have for engaging MLs in setting goals for their learning?

INCLUDE MLs IN ASSESSING THEIR LEARNING

As you consider strategies for including MLs in self- and peer assessment, consider the steps that you will take to prepare them for developing the skills needed to take part in these types of assessments. Central to engaging students in self-assessment is making sure that they understand the learning goals and the criteria for success. By including student-friendly learning objectives and student-friendly rubrics in your lessons and providing exemplars for what it looks like to successfully meet learning goals and rubric criteria, you can support your students in developing the skills that they need to become more autonomous learners.

SCSD fourth-grade teacher Taryn Michael has a self-assessment station in her classroom. Using a student-friendly rubric, students evaluate themselves on their skills and knowledge in particular areas. For each skill, they determine whether they can't do it yet (Level 1), can do it with help (Level 2), can do it on their own (Level 3), or can teach someone else (Level 4).

For more on how Ms. Michael uses this as a tool for her MLs and their families, please see the video titled *Students Engaging in Self-Assessment*.

Video 5.1

Students Engaging in Self-Assessment

resources.corwin.com/CulturallyResponsiveTeaching

 # Reflection Question

What are some different ways that you have built or you might build self-assessment into your work with students?

Self-Assessment

Gottlieb (2016) describes a variety of ways that MLs can be involved in assessing their learning. She suggests that having students take the lead in preparing for and leading student–teacher conferences can be a strong tool for fostering student responsibility for their learning. In order to prepare for these conferences, MLs need an opportunity to practice the language that they can use to talk about their work and their learning goals. With scaffolded support for discussions, MLs can also build their self-assessment strategies by talking about their work with peers. Figure 5.5, Sentence Stems for Talking About Student Work, provides examples of the types of sentence stems that you can give MLs to support them in reflecting on their work. Prior to peer discussions or student-led conferences, you could have students complete these sentence stems in their journal or on a graphic organizer. These stems can be adapted to be appropriate for students of different ages.

Figure 5.5   Sentence Stems for Talking About Student Work

The learning objective for this task was to . . .

In this work, I wanted to demonstrate . . .

In order to demonstrate . . . , I . . .

Something I think I did well was . . .

Something that was challenging for me was . . .

Something I might do differently next time is . . .

Something I have a question about is . . .

I enjoyed . . .

Self-assessments that include standards-referenced criteria, or criterion-referenced exemplars, can be a useful tool to support student engagement in self-assessment (Gottlieb, 2016). For example, students can use a checklist to identify if they have met certain criteria or rate themselves on whether they were able to meet certain skills. Younger MLs or MLs of lower language proficiency levels might indicate yes or no, select smiley or frowny faces, or provide responses in their home language. You can also use self-assessments to build students' metacognitive understanding of their learning (Gottlieb, 2016).

For example, students can identify different strategies that they use to support their learning. Figure 5.6 and Figure 5.7 provide two different examples of student self-assessments. In Figure 5.6, students can use the self-assessment to measure their understanding of how to tell time using analog and digital clocks. In Figure 5.7, students can identify the extent to which they use different word learning strategies when they encounter an unfamiliar word in a text.

Figure 5.6   Student Self-Assessment Work With Time

1. I know the difference between analog and digital clocks.	Yes	No
2. I can correctly tell time from an analog clock using a.m. and p.m.	Yes	No
3. I can correctly tell time from a digital clock using a.m. and p.m.	Yes	No
4. I can use language for telling time such as *a quarter after, half past, a quarter till, noon*, and *midnight*.	Yes	No
If you answered no to any of the questions, complete this sentence. I would like more help with _____. One thing I could do to practice is _____.		

Figure 5.7   Word Learning Strategies

When I see a word I don't know in a text, I . . .	Often	Sometimes	Never
Say the word aloud to see if I recognize it			
Think about whether the word is a cognate in my home language			
Look for clues around the word that can help me understand the meaning			
Think about the parts that make up the word to help in understanding the meaning			
Look up the word in a dictionary or glossary			
Try to understand the sentence without knowing the meaning of the word			

Peer Assessment

When students understand the criteria for success and are able to effectively self-assess their learning, you can also build peer assessment into your teaching. However, peer assessment might be uncomfortable to some MLs, based on their learning preferences and cultural backgrounds (Gottlieb, 2016). For example, some students from collectivist cultures might be hesitant to appear critical of a peer's work. It is important to frame feedback and assessment as an opportunity for growth and to recognize that all learners continue to develop their skills and knowledge over time. To help students become more effective at giving peer feedback, you can engage students in a critique protocol.

Critique protocols are "structured processes that guide students in giving and receiving high-quality feedback" (Buck Institute for Education, 2017, p. 1). The feedback can be given verbally or in writing, with the goal of having students improve their work and understanding of the content without direct teacher feedback. Students should be taught how to make their feedback kind, helpful, and specific, and should have opportunities to practice doing so. Critiques should focus on one piece of feedback at a time and include specific details or examples. When incorporating the critique protocol into your teaching, include time for the critique process and time for student reflection and revisions. In *Austin's Butterfly: Building Excellence in Student Work* (www.vimeo.com/38247060), Ron Berger provides a model of how you can introduce the idea of a critique protocol to students. Here are two other strategies for implementing the critique protocol:

- **A gallery walk**: Student work is displayed round the room, and students provide feedback to one another in writing on sticky notes. You can specify that feedback be provided related to a specific skill or criterion on a rubric. Students can praise an aspect of the work, ask a question, or offer a suggestion for improvement. Following the gallery walk, students can reflect on the feedback they received and journal about how they want to improve their work (Buck Institute for Education, 2017).

- **A tuning protocol**: Individually or in teams, students present their work to another student or groups of students. The audience asks clarifying questions and provides specific feedback. Students should provide feedback on what they liked about the work and also suggest areas for strengthening the piece of work. As with the gallery walk, the feedback should be specific and focus on one aspect of the work. Students should also provide feedback on the work rather than on the person (e.g., *provide a concrete example from the text to make your argument stronger*).

When building peer assessment into your lessons, provide opportunities throughout the course of a project, not just at the end of the project. By doing so, you will foster the idea of learning as a process and help make the learning process more transparent.

DEVELOP LESSONS THAT OFFER PEER-TO-PEER AND MULTIMODAL LEARNING OPPORTUNITIES

In our work with schools, we frequently conduct classroom observations using an evidence-based tool. We consistently see MLs remaining mostly silent in their content classes. One of our top recommendations to educators is to strengthen the opportunity and quality of ML talk. We believe not only is it important for teachers to increase opportunities for peer-to-peer sharing but also to strengthen the intentional way in which student discussions and collaboration activities are planned and implemented. Hattie's (2012) synthesis of research on the role of teacher versus student talk found that teachers on average talk anywhere from 70 percent to 89 percent of the time. Research from Arreaga-Mayer and Perdomo-Rivera (1996) found that ELs spend less than 2 percent of their day engaged in academic talk. August (2018), in her discussion of research-based instructional practices for supporting ELs' learning, highlights the benefit of peer-to-peer learning. She explains that an important focus of these learning interactions should be peer talk through pair or small-group work that is focused on academic content.

Reflection Questions

What holds you back from incorporating more peer-to-peer activities in your classroom? What are the challenges that you anticipate of building in peer-to-peer learning activities?

Some concerns that we hear from teachers about peer learning activities are about a loss of control, that students will get off task, or that when students speak in their home languages the teacher won't know what is being discussed. Figure 5.8, the Peer Learning Activity Checklist, can help you think through some of the considerations that you should make when designing your peer learning activities, such as how you can make sure your MLs are sufficiently prepared and supported during them.

Figure 5.8   Peer Learning Activity Checklist

Criteria		Yes	No	Follow-Up Steps
	1. Have I developed a peer learning activity that will provide my MLs with • authentic opportunities to speak, • time to strengthen and deepen their responses, and • an engaging discussion prompt or task?			
	2. Have my MLs had sufficient exposure to the content and academic language needed to participate in the activity?			
	3. Have my MLs been taught appropriate nonverbal behavior to support peer learning activities (e.g., looking at people when speaking, nodding understanding)?			

Criteria			Yes	No	Follow-Up Steps
	4.	Do I have a way of monitoring their nonverbal behavior?			
	5.	Have I provided sufficient structure to the activity (including the use of supporting tools) and clear evaluation criteria so as to encourage all of my MLs to participate in the activity?			
	6.	Have I thought about how to intentionally group students?			
	7.	Have I considered assigning roles to students?			
	8.	Have I given sufficient thought to how to structure the classroom or online space so that students can effectively interact and work together?			
	9.	Have I considered how I might use the activity to assess MLs' acquisition and use of academic language and/or understanding of content?			

Source: Adapted from Staehr Fenner and Snyder, 2017, pp. 100–101.

While there are many different types of activities to foster peer-to-peer and multimodal learning, we would like to share some ideas in three areas: games and gaming, storytelling, and oral language activities. In thinking about supporting ML engagement in these different types of activities, it is important to consider scaffolding that MLs might need related to background knowledge or language, as well as how you will model and support all students in having an active role in the activity.

One scaffold is the intentional grouping of students. For example, you might pair MLs who share the same home language, thus bringing in language support that you may not be able to provide. Alternatively, you could create mixed ability or language proficiency pairings in which one student is modeling for the other.

Games and Gaming

Reflection Questions

What's your favorite game to incorporate into your lessons? Or if you aren't currently in the classroom, what's a game that you have experienced or read about? How and why does this game engage learners? What supports do you need to provide so that all students can successfully participate?

Favorite game:

1. What makes it engaging?

2. What supports might you need to provide so all students can successfully participate?

In considering how to incorporate games and gaming into the classroom, there are two different categories of what this might look like. The first category is using games to teach concepts and assess student learning (Aviles, 2018). Ferlazzo and Hull Sypnieski (2012, 2018) recommend the following guidelines when selecting and using games:

- The emphasis should be on the learning.
- After teachers model the games, students should be able to lead the game and create new game materials.
- All students should participate in the game at all times. In other words, students should not be eliminated from the game.

Reflection Questions

Does your favorite game that you described earlier meet these criteria? If not, how might you modify it so that it does?

Louise El Yaafouri (2019) has identified online games that promote student engagement in critical problem-solving skills and at the same time provide scaffolded support that some MLs may need. She shares that simulation games align with culturally responsive teaching pedagogy because of the collaborative natures of these games and devices that are incorporated, such as rhythm, repetition, and story-based learning. In Figure 5.9 we showcase two of her recommended games along with the embedded supports that are provided in each.

Figure 5.9   Scaffolded Online Games to Support Critical Thinking and Community Building

Game, Link, Recommended Grade Level	Description	Embedded Supports
Activate, Grades 6–8	This online game is framed around the topic of civic engagement. Players select a community cause that they must support, then work to raise awareness about the cause, manage their resources, and engage other stakeholders.	Labeled images, guided writing, embedded reading, interactive feedback and support, and repeated practice
Stop Disasters, Grades 6–10 (www.stopdisastersgame.org)	The United Nations Office for Disaster Risk Reduction developed this collaborative game to support learning about natural disaster relief. Players plan cities designed to protect their citizens against natural disasters and manage resources as needed. This game fosters collaboration and problem solving.	Labeled graphics, short definitions, fact sheets for background knowledge, and success reports formulated as a graphic organizer

Source: Adapted from El Yaafouri, L. (2019). 5 free video games that support English language learners [blog post]. https://www.edutopia.org/article/5-free-video-games-support-english-language-learners

A second way to use games in the classroom is to gamify the learning experience through the use of such techniques as awards or badges, gaming themes or narratives, and incorporating a villain that must be defeated by completing certain tasks (Aviles, 2018; Haiken, 2020). In his *Gamification Guide*, Aviles (2016) recommends creating a narrative around your classroom and using these narratives to shape your expectations for students. Similarly, Ramsay (2016) suggests focusing on the key qualities that make games engaging (i.e., competition, challenge, communication, and camaraderie) and consider how you can build those into your lessons.

A low-tech way to incorporate game-based learning in the classroom is to use role play in your lessons. Hovhannisyan (2018) recommends incorporating role-play as a tool to solidify understanding of content that is shared through readings and lecture. He offers the following example:

> You could split your students up into different groups of governments (democracy, monarchy, dictatorship, etc.) and present them with a relevant social issue. Then, ask them to draw from their readings to create a short enactment of how their type of government would respond to that issue. (para. 6)

In order to support MLs of varying language proficiency levels in engaging with this type of activity, it would be important to provide such scaffolds as preteaching and practice with key vocabulary, sentence stems or frames, home language support, graphic organizers to organize key ideas, and opportunities for oral language practice.

Storytelling and Digital Storytelling

As we discussed in Chapter 3, storytelling can be an effective way to build an assets-based perspective of MLs. Storytelling and digital storytelling can be helpful tools for tapping into the cultural backgrounds of MLs who come from or whose parents come from countries that have strong oral traditions. Stories can be true stories from your own life, a story from the life of someone that you know, a story from the news or a current event, a story that took place in history, a fictional story with made-up characters or events, or a story that tells of a hypothetical situation (Liu, 2016). Similar to the identity texts we described on page 159, storytelling can also be a tool for MLs to speak and write about their own experiences.

When thinking about how to include storytelling in your lessons, you will need to be clear on the purpose of the story. Are you using the story to introduce a new topic of learning, to provide an illustration or example of a key idea, or to support students in exploring a social justice issue or to take a critical approach to examining a topic? How does the story relate to your lesson objectives? What is the story's "hook" that is going to catch students' interest? How might you engage students in the story (e.g., using props, music, a relatable situation, student interactions; DeNeen, 2012)? Also consider how you will have students interact with your story. For example, you could have students do any number of these activities:

- Discuss the story in pairs or small groups.
- Work in groups to do a role-play related to the story.
- Provide an ending to the story.
- Do some reflective writing on your story.

Figure 5.10, the Planning for Storytelling in a Lesson template, is a tool that you can use as you make plans to embed storytelling into our lessons.

You can also consider recording and sharing student stories. Green Card Voices is an organization with a mission to share the voices and perspectives of immigrants to the United States. In 2015, Green Card Voices recorded 30 stories of immigrants from Wellstone International High School in Minnesota. These students, who came from 13 different countries, told stories of their family, school experiences, and their dreams. In 2016, Green Card Voices published a book of its stories, and since then, it has published multiple books of immigrant stories. Since 2016, Green Card Voices has expanded its program to work with other schools and districts to support them in encouraging the sharing of immigrant and refugee stories with the goal of building understanding between immigrants, nonimmigrants, and advocates.

Figure 5.10 Planning for Storytelling in a Lesson

Lesson topic:
Learning objectives:
Summary of story (1–2 sentences): Hook: Climax: Purpose:
Scaffolding (e.g., visuals, actions, preteaching vocabulary):
Follow-up activity: • Pair or small-group discussion of takeaway • Role-play or case study • Individual reflection • Providing an ending • Other:

Digital Storytelling

Digital storytelling can be an engaging way to give voice to MLs' experience as well as foster creativity and critical thinking (Alrubail, 2015a, 2015b). It can provide an opportunity for MLs to reflect on and share their stories through the use of such multimedia tools as images, music, audio recordings, and family photos (Alrubail, 2015a, 2015b). Waddell and Clariza (2018) write, "Digital storytelling . . . empowers learners by encouraging them to use prior knowledge and orality as a form of literacy" (p. 230).

In one project, students were shown videos of traditional stories (like a digital comic book) narrated by indigenous elders with illustrations by indigenous artists. These digital stories served as models for students to create their own stories. Students reported that their engagement with digital storytelling "increased their understanding of themselves and their integral relationship with their community. They felt empowered because it taught them to think critically of their personal histories in relation to the existing power structures" (Waddell & Clariza, 2018, p. 231).

Figure 5.11   Digital Storytelling Examples and Supports

Type of Project and Content Area(s)	Project Description	Possible Supports
Photo and sound montage English language arts (ELA)	Students create a PowerPoint presentation that includes a photo and sound montage to respond to a poem or story. The images and sounds can represent key phrases in the poems or themes of the poem or story.	Consider modeling this activity with a single sentence or phrase. You can give students several images and ask them to select which one they feel best represents the phrase and why. Additional scaffolding could include a graphic organizer for organizing ideas, sentence stems to talk about connections between images or sounds and ideas, and pair work.
Autobiography ELA	Students use images, sounds, and text to share an autobiographical event.	Model this activity with your own example. Additional scaffolding could include a graphic organizer for organizing ideas and sentence stems to talk about connections between images or sounds and ideas.
Visual history Social studies	Students create a visual history of the community to represent how it has changed and its members' relationship with various aspects of the community. Students can interview community members as part of this activity.	Consider introducing this activity by having students look at historical pictures of their communities and talk about what they see. Students can work in groups to tell the story of a particular aspect of their community's history (e.g., a changing downtown, employment in a factory). Additional scaffolding could include a graphic organizer for organizing ideas, sentence stems to talk about connections between images or sounds and ideas, and group work.
Docudrama Social studies or science	Students research a time period from the perspective of a person who lived at that time and write a script from the individual's perspective. Students can be asked to include a certain number of historical facts. Students could also do a similar activity from the perspective of a famous scientist and public response to their theory or discovery.	You could model this activity in a low-tech way by having students learn about and role-play different historical figures. Additional scaffolding could include a graphic organizer for organizing ideas, sentence stems to talk about connections between images or sounds and ideas, and group work.

(Continued)

Figure 5.11 (Continued)

Type of Project and Content Area(s)	Project Description	Possible Supports
Model Science or math	Students create a digital product that includes images and narration to provide a model of a particular concept. For example, students might demonstrate a food chain in a particular habitat or develop a real-life problem to model a particular mathematic concept.	Model each of the steps that students would need to take to develop this. Additional scaffolding could include explicit instruction of content vocabulary, a graphic organizer for organizing ideas, sentence stems to talk about connections between images or sounds and ideas, and group work.

Source: Adapted from Hernandez, 2015, and Tech4Learning, n.d.

To engage your students in digital storytelling, have them begin by generating an idea and researching their topic. Next, they should create an outline of their idea, compile the digital media that they will use, and map out their story. Finally, they can create the digital story (Alrubail, 2015a, 2015b). In considering how to support MLs with a digital storytelling project, be sure to provide models of what you are looking for and make sure that students understand the criteria that will be used to evaluate their project. Also, consider what scaffolding they might need to complete the task (e.g., pair work, graphic organizer to organize ideas, academic language support). Also, plan how you will have students share their digital stories and how you will offer feedback to students. Consider how you might provide an opportunity for students to reflect on their process and final product. Figure 5.11, Digital Storytelling Examples and Supports, outlines how you might use digital storytelling in different content areas and strategies for introducing the idea to students and possible supports you might provide.

Oral language Activities

Well-planned oral language activities that support collaborative, academic discussions can be strong tools to foster student-centered learning and culturally responsive teaching. However, without proper structure and support, MLs will be less likely to engage in the oral language tasks if they are not confident in their understanding of the task, their role, or the content and language needed to engage in the task. In our book *Unlocking English Learners' Potential: Making Content Accessible* (Staehr Fenner & Snyder, 2017), we identified four practices that can support ML engagement in academic conversations. These practices were adapted from Zwiers's (Zwiers & Crawford, 2011; Zwiers & Hamerla, 2017) extensive work on academic discussions and account for the specific strengths and needs of MLs when engaging in oral language activities. Figure 5.12, Four Practices to Foster ML Engagement and Participation in Academic Conversations, provides recommended strategies for supporting MLs with each of the four practices.

Figure 5.12 Four Practices to Foster ML Engagement and Participation in Academic Conversations

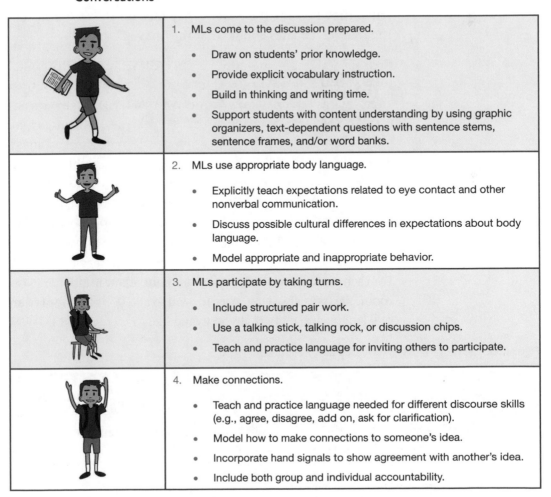

	1. MLs come to the discussion prepared. • Draw on students' prior knowledge. • Provide explicit vocabulary instruction. • Build in thinking and writing time. • Support students with content understanding by using graphic organizers, text-dependent questions with sentence stems, sentence frames, and/or word banks.
	2. MLs use appropriate body language. • Explicitly teach expectations related to eye contact and other nonverbal communication. • Discuss possible cultural differences in expectations about body language. • Model appropriate and inappropriate behavior.
	3. MLs participate by taking turns. • Include structured pair work. • Use a talking stick, talking rock, or discussion chips. • Teach and practice language for inviting others to participate.
	4. Make connections. • Teach and practice language needed for different discourse skills (e.g., agree, disagree, add on, ask for clarification). • Model how to make connections to someone's idea. • Incorporate hand signals to show agreement with another's idea. • Include both group and individual accountability.

Source: Adapted from Staehr Fenner & Snyder, 2017

Dually certified social studies and English as a new language (ENL)[1] high school teacher Megan Brown uses many different types of oral language activities in her sheltered US history class. To see her class engage in a jigsaw activity related to the Trail of Tears, go to the video *Using a Jigsaw Activity With Multilingual Learners*. For this jigsaw activity, Megan intentionally grouped students in order to provide students the support of a peer who shared their same home language as well as to mix student proficiency levels so that the students with higher levels of proficiency were dispersed among the groups. For this activity, students were placed in groups in which they looked at a particular document and image and responded to a question about what they read and saw. Megan explained that her students can invest in the work more fully if they have time to focus on only one piece of the larger puzzle. She said that when they become the expert, they take on the task of teaching their classmates about what they have learned.

Video 5.2

Using a Jigsaw Activity With Multilingual Learners

resources.corwin.com/CulturallyResponsiveTeaching

To explore some different types of oral language activities that you could use in your classroom, read the activity descriptions in Figure 5.13, Oral Language Activities and Resources. In addition to the description of each activity, we have suggested possible scaffolds that MLs might need to effectively engage with the activity and, in some instances, a video in which the strategy is modeled. For each activity, consider how you might adapt it for your classroom. We have also left a space for you to add your own idea of an oral language activity that you would like to use with MLs.

Figure 5.13   Oral Language Activities and Resources

Activity	Description	Considerations for Use in My Classroom
1-3-6 Protocol	In this activity, students are given a discussion question or task that they work on individually. Then, they move to a group of three, where they discuss their responses to the question. Finally, two groups of three combine to form a	

[1]New York State uses the term "ENL teacher" instead of ESOL or ESL teachers.

Activity	Description	Considerations for Use in My Classroom
	group of six. With the group of six, they finalize their answers to the question and present these to the large group. Often, the group of six can also be asked to extend the discussion by prioritizing responses or analyzing the ideas in a deeper way. These three steps can provide MLs opportunities to practice and refine their language and deepen their thinking on the topic. **Possible scaffolding**: modeling, sentence stems, graphic organizers, home language groupings	
Carousel	To set up for this activity, write questions connected to the unit of study on poster paper and around the room. There should be one piece of poster paper per question. Divide students into small groups so that there is one question per group. Give each group of students a different colored marker and assign them a question to start with. Students discuss and write their responses on the poster paper. After two to three minutes, have the groups rotate to another question. You can have each group discuss each of the questions if you have sufficient time. You should encourage the groups to add on to and provide additional evidence to the responses that are written. Debrief each question as a whole class. This activity can also be done in a virtual setting using Google slides and breakout rooms. **Possible scaffolding**: modeling, preteaching vocabulary, word bank, sentence stems, home language translations of questions, home language groupings **Video example**: https://betterlesson.com/strategy/74/resource/3368321	
Debrief Circles (also known as Reel Activity or Parallel Lines)	For this activity, ask students to answer one to two questions independently. Have students count off by twos. They should form two concentric circles, with one student facing another student (e.g., number-ones in the inner circle and number-twos in the outer circle). Have students share their responses to one of the questions with each other. Then, have students in the inner circle move one or two students to the left. Students can then share their responses to the second question. You can have students move multiple times, each time sharing their responses and hearing other students' responses. You can also have students put away their index cards as they gain increasing confidence in speaking about the topic. As a wrap-up to the activity, you can ask students to compare how their responses differed from those of their peers or to share whether their responses changed based on listening to their peers. **Possible scaffolding**: modeling, sentence stems **Video example**: https://vimeo.com/100438366	

(Continued)

Figure 5.13　(Continued)

Activity	Description	Considerations for Use in My Classroom
Gap Activity	A gap activity can be an effective way to support student interactions with content. For this activity, students are paired up. Each student in the pair is given different information. Students must ask each other questions in order to complete a task. For example, one student might have a math word problem to solve. However, the partner's handout has all numbers that are needed to solve the problem. Partner A must ask Partner B questions in order to solve the problem. See Appendix D for an example of a gap activity. **Possible scaffolding**: modeling, question stems, pre-taught vocabulary **Video example**: https://learnenglishteens.britishcouncil.org/exams/speaking-exams/information-gap-activity	
Numbered Heads Together	This activity can be done in a couple of different ways. Student desks should be clustered in groups facing each other. Students can first be given time to work independently on a question or challenge and then come together to discuss collaboratively. Another way of approaching this activity would be to pose a different question for each group of students. They discuss their question, writing responses on a large sheet of poster paper. When time is up, the students move to another question and add on to what the previous group has written. **Possible scaffolding**: modeling, preteaching vocabulary, word bank, sentence stems, home language translations of questions, home language groupings **Video example:** https://www.youtube.com/watch?v=v8uYS48BlUw&feature=emb_title	
World Café	Put students in groups of three or four. Give each group a topic to discuss. One person should be the designated leader. That person should take notes on the discussion. After a set period of time, all students except for the leader should move to another discussion group. They do not have to stay in the same groups. The leader provides highlights of the previous discussion to the new group. A new leader is assigned. The new group discusses the same topic and adds to the notes. Debrief as a large group. **Possible scaffolding**: modeling, preteaching vocabulary, word bank, sentence stems, home language translations of questions, home language groupings **Video example**: https://www.youtube.com/watch?v=YG_6iBcyP7w	

Activity	Description	Considerations for Use in My Classroom
Other ideas:		

Source: Adapted from Staehr Fenner and Snyder, 2017, pp. 103–107.

Next, let's take a look at strategies for showcasing ML work and celebrating their progress.

SHOWCASE MLs' WORK AND CELEBRATE THEIR PROGRESS

A Spotlight on Emir

Our colleague Marley Zeno, a former EL specialist, describes the importance of showcasing ML work (personal communication, February 13, 2020):

> Emir, a third-grade student from Yemen, loved sharing his work. He struggled academically and to retain what he had learned. Any progress was hard-earned, so all of his teachers made sure to celebrate him whenever we could. Even though he could see how far below grade level he was, he stayed motivated and joyful. We knew how crucial it was to maintain that motivation. He once wrote an informational piece on Yemen, describing the food and how schools there were different from schools in America. He asked his classroom teacher to make enough photocopies for everyone to read it—the speech/language pathologist, the principal, the assistant

principal, and me, the EL specialist. Emir and I called the principal and assistant principal together to set up an appointment in their office to share his work. We practiced reading it out loud before the appointment. After he shared with the principal and assistant principal, he told his classroom teacher that he wanted to share his piece with the whole class (this would not have been possible without the warm and supportive classroom environment his teacher fostered). Watching his confidence grow was so powerful. That wouldn't have been possible without his teachers and our administrators making time and space for him to share his success.

Reflection Questions

What lessons can we take from Marley's story about Emir and the need to celebrate ML successes? What is something that you do in your school or district or that you have seen done by other educators to showcase ML work or celebrate their successes?

As we see in the spotlight on Emir, in addition to involving ML students and families in goal setting it is also important to showcase MLs' work and to celebrate their learning and growth. In taking steps to honor ML progress and growth, we are strengthening that assets-based perspective of students that we described in Chapter 3. We are supporting colleagues and the students themselves in recognizing their academic identity and their valuable membership in and contributions to the school community.

We will provide some recommendations for showcasing student work and honoring their success here. In terms of including ML family members and inviting them to take part in family events to share MLs' success, it is important to ask parents and guardians about the best possible times and locations to hold such events. For some families, attending during the school day might be very difficult. You should also consider how you can provide additional support to foster family engagement (e.g., child care, interpreters). For more strategies on fostering family engagement, please see Chapter 7.

Methods for Showcasing MLs' Work

- **Strategic use of bulletin boards**: Consider how you can use the school bulletin boards to showcase ML learning and growth. In the following example, Pennsylvania educator Amanda Tice described how she worked with Lena, a newcomer from Uzbekistan, to complete a class literacy assignment.

Lena's Story

As part of a unit on the Iroquois, the class read Hiawatha the Unifier, a story about uniting the five tribes of the Iroquois. Lena was able to use a translating tool to read the text and supporting handouts in Uzbek. After reading the text students were asked to create a symbolic representation of a hand, demonstrating their knowledge of each of the five tribes with unique picture symbols of each tribe on the hand in each of the five fingers. For example, the Mohawk are known for being the nourishers; therefore, there were a lot of pictures of corn or farm tools for their picture representation on the Mohawk finger. Together, all of the fingers create a hand, which demonstrates that together, all of the tribes are stronger.

Through this lesson, my coteacher and I noticed that Lena really enjoyed drawing. It was nice to see her really engaged with this project and it encouraged us to allow her to incorporate drawing into other activities when applicable. Her final product was truly one of the best that was turned in, and Lena seemed so proud of her work. After putting up her work on the bulletin board, we showed her the display, and she had a big smile on her face. (A. Tice, personal communication, February 17, 2020)

- **Museum exhibit**: Have students work in teams to create museum exhibits related to a specific topic being covered in class. They can create the materials for the exhibit and also develop talking points that they could use if they were a docent for the exhibit. Be sure that your MLs have an opportunity to practice this language with peers or by recording themselves. Then, invite other classes or families to take part in an event in which the students showcase their museum exhibits. For an example of this idea, refer to the Toronto District School Board and the Aga Khan Museum "Finding Home" project that is described in Chapter 3 of this book.

- **Student writing**: There are a variety of ways to showcase ML work through written reflections and other writing tasks. For example, at the beginning of the year you can have MLs write a letter to themselves in which they reflect on the upcoming year and possible challenges or goals for the year. Then at the end of the year, students can read their letter and reflect on their learning that year. Another way to showcase ML work is through a classroom blog. Students can write blog posts on different topics, and you can share the blog with students' families and other classes. Consider how you might incorporate opportunities for MLs' home language into the blog.

- **Family coffeehouse**: Invite families to come to a coffeehouse in which students showcase their work. Components of the coffeehouse might include having students read sections of their work or you can create a showcase of finished pieces. Students can talk about their work and their learning. You'll want to make sure that MLs feel prepared to share and/or discuss their work. A coffeehouse event could be another opportunity to highlight students' cultural background or experiences, if appropriate and if students feel comfortable sharing. As always, select a time and location that is convenient for ML families.

Celebrating MLs' Successes

- **Shout-out board**: A shout-out board can be a place for students and teachers to compliment one another. At the beginning of the year, you should ensure students know the meaning of "shout-out" (since they could take that term literally), explain the type of things that might go onto the shout-out board and periodically leave time for students to write the shout-outs and add to the board. Shout-outs could also be included on an exit ticket, and students can write about things that others did well during the class. This could be an especially good wrap-up to a group activity.

- **Language development celebrations**: Consider having an annual celebration in which you honor MLs' progress in language acquisition. Sydney worked in a district in which each year there was an EL award ceremony that families were invited to. The ceremony included awards for graduating ELs and those who were exiting from the ESOL program. A program such as this could be expanded to include showcasing the work of students pursing a Seal of Biliteracy, students completing heritage language projects, or other significant projects completed by MLs.

- **Written notes**: Writing a short note to students or their parents or guardians can be an easy way to send the message that you are proud of the students and the progress they are making. Keep the notes simple and be specific about what the student did well or where the student has shown growth. Diane notes that it can be very unusual for parents to receive good news from a teacher, so ML parents would most likely appreciate receiving a positive note such as this.

Maria, great job in our class debate on global warming. You supported your ideas so clearly!

Sincerely,

Ms. Brunner

THREE STEPS YOU CAN TAKE

In this chapter, we've explored a lot of different possibilities for creating classroom and school environments that are learner-centered. Now, let's take a look at three steps that you could take as you continue your exploration of General Principle 3: *Culturally responsive teaching places students at the center of the learning.* These next steps can be done individually, but as with many of the activities in this book, they are better done collaboratively in order to increase the opportunity for discussion and reflection on what you learned and planning for follow-up actions.

Step I: *Take steps to involve MLs and their families in goal setting.*

Determine when and how you will support MLs in goal setting. Figure 5.14, the Student Goal-Setting Template, can be adapted for MLs that are not English learners or for different ages of students. For example, it could be modified to focus on goals in certain content areas, goals related to course planning, or goals related to postgraduation plans. Also consider how you can build in an opportunity for celebrating student progress. Ask yourself these goal-setting questions:

1. What steps will you take to involve students in goal setting?
2. How will you involve families in these discussions?
3. What will you do to help students reflect on their progress toward their goals?
4. How will you celebrate their progress?

Figure 5.14 Student Goal-Setting Template

Name:
Grade level:
My language proficiency level is Level _____. By next year, I want to progress to Level _____.
Speaking
My speaking score is _____.
When speaking, I can _____, _____, and _____.
By the end of the year, I want to be able to _____ and _____.
Listening
My listening score is _____.
When listening, I can _____, _____, and _____.
By the end of the year, I want to be able to _____ and _____.

Reading

My reading score is _____ .

When reading, I can _____ , _____ ,
and _____ .

By the end of the year, I want to be able to _____ and
_____ .

Writing

My writing score is _____ .

When writing, I can _____ , _____ ,
and _____ .

By the end of the year, I want to be able to _____ and
_____ .

My nonlanguage goals for the year:

1.

2.

_____   _____
Student signature   Date

_____   _____
Family member signature   Date

_____   _____
Teacher signature   Date

Step 2: *Shadow an ML throughout the day.*

Ivannia Soto (2012), in her book *ELL Shadowing*, describes a process by which "educators within a system can align and become clearer around the specific needs of ELLs within their particular context or setting. . . . The purpose of ELL shadowing is to observe a day in the instructional life of one ELL" (p. 11). While Soto's protocol is targeted toward English language learners, a similar protocol could be used to analyze the experiences of MLs in a particular school. The protocol and observation tools developed by Soto (see Figure 5.15) support educators in analyzing the amount of time a student engages in academic speaking, academic listening, and other tasks such as independent reading or writing. This protocol could also be used to note particular scaffolds or strategies that are used to foster student engagement or learning experiences that build the cultural and linguistic background of the student that you are shadowing.

Having the freedom to spend an entire day observing a single student is an incredible luxury. However, it can also be a powerful tool to identify the priorities for culturally responsive instruction that we discussed in Chapter 2. If you aren't able to shadow a student for an entire day by yourself, consider having a team shadow a student. If you are a preservice teacher, taking part in a day of ML shadowing can provide an excellent opportunity for considering the extent to which what you are learning about in your studies is reflected in the schools.

Figure 5.15 ML Shadowing

Time (5-Minute Intervals)	Activity	Academic Speaking	Academic Listening	Student Not Speaking or Listening	Scaffolds or Strategies to Support Engagement
10:00–10:05	Social studies lecture	N/A	Supposed to be listening	• Independent reading or writing • Off-task	Sentence stems for note-taking

Source: Adapted from Soto, I. (2012). *ELL Shadowing as a Catalyst for Change*. ELL shadowing protocol form, p. 119. Corwin.

Step 3: *Develop a professional learning community (PLC) framed around student-centered learning and assessment.*

Invite a group of interested educators to take part in a CRT PLC. As a group, decide what the focus of your PLC will be. For example, you might do a book study in which you read a book on academic conversations, such as one of Jeff Zwiers's books, and discuss. Another possibility might be to identify CRT priorities in your school using the Culturally Responsive Teaching Checklist (see Appendix B) and setting goals for initiating change. A third PLC option is to take turns presenting activities for supporting MLs' engagement in peer-to-peer and multimodal learning opportunities or tools for engaging MLs in peer and self-assessment. Figure 5.16, the Peer-to-Peer and Multimodal Learning Activities template, is a tool that you can copy and share with others in your PLC group.

Figure 5.16   **Peer-to-Peer and Multimodal Learning Activities**

Activity:	
1. Describe your activity.	2. How would you use the activity to support MLs in engaging in peer-to-peer and/or multimodal learning opportunities?
3. What specific considerations should you make for MLs (e.g., scaffolding, home language opportunities, intentional grouping) when using the activity or strategy for your discipline and/or context?	4. What is a resource that you could share to support others in implementing the activity (e.g., video that models the activity, supporting materials)?

Summary of Key Ideas

- In order to foster student-centered learning, begin by creating a warm and supportive classroom environment.

- Develop lessons that engage students through peer-to-peer learning, gaming, and other multimodal activities.

- Take steps to involve MLs in setting goals for their learning and assessing their progress.

- Showcase ML work and celebrate their progress.

Chapter 5 Reflection Questions

1. Which of the four key ideas resonates most with you? What steps will you take to build your skill in this area?

2. Who might you collaborate with to support the development of culturally responsive lessons that place students at the center of the learning?

References

Alrubail, R. (2015a, February 26). *How to incorporate digital storytelling to empower student voice.* Edutopia.org. https://www.edutopia.org/discussion/how-incorporate-digital-storytelling-empower-student-voice

Alrubail, R. (2015b, September 23). *Empowering ELLs with digital stories.* Tolerance.org. https://www.tolerance.org/magazine/empowering-ells-with-digital-stories

Arreaga-Mayer, C., & Perdomo-Rivera, C. (1996). Ecobehavioral analysis of instruction for at risk language-minority students. *The Elementary School Journal*, 96(3), 245–258.

August, D. (2018, Fall). Educating English learners: A review of the latest research. *American Educator*. https://www.aft.org/ae/fall2018/august

Aviles, C. (2016). *The gamification guide*. http://www.techedupteacher.com/the-gamification-guide/

Aviles, C. (2018, May 10). How to integrate and manage video games in your classroom. *Teched-Up Teacher.com*. http://www.techedupteacher.com/how-to-integrate-and-manage-video-games-in-your-classroom/

Board of Regents of the University of Wisconsin System. (2017). *WIDA Can Do Descriptors, Key Uses Edition Grades 6–8*.

Buck Institute for Education. (2017). *Critique protocols*. http://s3-us-west-2.amazonaws.com/bie-ootg/documents/Critique_Protocols_final.pdf

Celic, C., & Seltzer, K. (2013). *Translanguaging: A CUNY-NYSIEB guide for educators*. The Graduate Center, CUNY.

Cummins, J., Bismilla, V., Chow, P., Cohen, S., Giampapa, F., Leoni, L., Sandhu, P., & Sastri, P. (2005). Affirming identity in multilingual classrooms. *Educational Leadership*, *63*(1), 38–43.

Decker, T. (n.d.). Top 5 ways to get to know your students. *Scholastic*. https://www.scholastic.com/teachers/articles/teaching-content/top-5-ways-get-know-your-students/

DeNeen, J. (2012, November 21). 30 storytelling tips for educators: How to capture your student's attention. *InformEd*. https://www.opencolleges.edu.au/informed/features/30-storytelling-tips-for-educators/

El Yaafouri, L. (2019). *5 free video games that support English language learners* [blog post]. https://www.edutopia.org/article/5-free-video-games-support-english-language-learners

Ferlazzo, L., & Hull Sypnieski, K. (2012). Using games in the ELL classroom, Part 1. *Education Teacher Week*. https://www.edweek.org/tm/articles/2012/09/19/tln_ferlazzo_hull-sypnieski_ell.html

Ferlazzo, L., & Hull Sypnieski, K. (2018). *The ELL teacher's toolbox*. Jossey-Bass.

Francis, E. (2017, August). Grading newcomers: A can do approach [blog post]. *Empowering ELLs*. http://www.empoweringells.com/grading-newcomers/

Francis, E. (2019, August 26). This is us. *Inspiring English Language Learners*. https://inspiringenglishlanguagelearners.weebly.com/blog/this-is-us

Gardner, H. (1983). *Frames of mind: The theory of multiple intelligences*. Basic Books.

Gottlieb, M. (2016). *Assessing English language learners: Bridges to educational equity* (2nd ed.). Corwin.

Green, M. (2020). *Origin hungry*. (Self-published).

Haiken, M. (2020, February 17). 5 ways to gamify your classroom. *ISTE.org*. https://www.iste.org/explore/In-the-classroom/5-ways-to-gamify-your-classroom.

Hammond, Z. (2015a). *Culturally responsive teaching and the brain*. Corwin.

Hammond, Z. (2015b, April 1). Three tips to make any lesson more culturally responsive. *Cult of Pedagogy*. https://www.cultofpedagogy.com/culturally-responsive-teaching-strategies/

Hattie, J. (2012). *Visible learning for teachers: Maximizing impact on learning*. Routledge/Taylor & Francis Group.

Hernandez, M. (2015, August 26). A guide to producing student digital storytellers. *Edsurge.com*. https://www.edsurge.com/news/2015-08-26-a-guide-to-producing-student-digital-storytellers

Hovhannisyan, A. (2018, September 25). How to use game-based learning in the classroom. *Classcraft.* https://www.classcraft.com/blog/features/how-to-use-game-based-learning-in-the-classroom/

Liu, S. (2016, March 24). The power of storytelling in the classroom: 5 ways it can be a great help. *Teach.com.* https://teach.com/great-educational-resources-the-power-of-storytelling/

Marshall, H. W., & DeCapua, A. (2013). *Making the transition to classroom success: Culturally responsive teaching for struggling language learners.* University of Michigan Press.

Parker, F., Novak, J., & Bartell, T. (2017, November 6). To engage students, give them meaningful choices in the classroom. *Phi Delta Kappan.* https://kappanonline.org/engage-students-give-meaningful-choices-classroom/

Ramsay, J. D. (2016, January 27). Using gaming principles to support student learning. *Literacy Worldwide.* https://literacyworldwide.org/blog/literacy-daily/2016/01/27/using-gaming-principles-to-support-student-learning.

Soto, I. (2012). *ELL shadowing as a catalyst for change.* Corwin.

Staehr Fenner, D., & Snyder, S. (2017). *Unlocking English learners' potential: Strategies for making content accessible.* Corwin.

Teaching Channel (Producer). (2017). *Using science games to deepen learning* [Video]. https://www.teachingchannel.org/video/energy-flow-lesson-plan.

Tech4Learning. (n.d.). *Ideas for digital storytelling across the curriculum.* https://www.tech4learning.com/digital-storytelling

van den Berg, Y. H. M., Segers, E., & Cillessen, A. H. N. (2012). Changing peer perceptions and victimization through classroom arrangements: A field experiment. *Journal of Abnormal Child Psychology, 40*(3), 403–412. https://doi.org/10.1007/s10802-011-9567-6

Waddell, M., & Clariza, E. (2018, May). Critical digital pedagogy and cultural sensitivity in the library classroom: Infographics and digital storytelling. *College & Research Libraries News, 79*(5), 228–232.

Zacarian, D., Alvarez-Ortiz, L., & Haynes, J. (2017). *Teaching to strengths: Supporting students living with trauma, violence, and chronic stress.* ASCD.

Zwiers, J., & Crawford, M. (2011). *Academic conversations: Classroom talk that fosters critical thinking and content understandings.* Stenhouse.

Zwiers, J., & Hamerla, S. (2018). *The K–3 guide to academic conversations: Practices, scaffolds, and activities.* Corwin.

Leveraging Students' Linguistic and Cultural Backgrounds

Reflection Question

As you read the following scenario, write a list of the culturally responsive practices that you see included in the lesson. What did you note?

Scenario: Manny's Art Class

Manny enters his art class and his teacher, Ms. Bell, tells the class that they are going to be learning about an artist named Diego Rivera. She asks the class if they have heard of Rivera and what they know about him. Next, she places the students in groups. Because she has enough students for home language groups in Spanish and Arabic, she places these students together. The remaining multilingual learners (MLs) and non-MLs she intentionally groups by personality so as to encourage active discussions.

She presents the students with images of Diego Rivera's paintings and murals and asks them to talk about what they observe. She then asks them to write down a list of words related to what they notice about the paintings or what they think the author is trying to portray. The students in the home language groups can use whichever language they prefer to share their observations.

After the groups share out, Ms. Bell introduces the class to some key vocabulary that the students will be exploring this unit. She introduces the new words through the use of visuals and student-friendly definitions. Students write these words in their student glossaries. The English learners (ELs) in the class also write down a translation and note whether the word is a cognate in their home language (e.g., "mural" is a cognate in English and Spanish).

Next, Ms. Bell reads aloud the story *Diego Rivera: His World and Ours* by Mexican author Duncan Tonatiuh. She asks students to listen for ideas on what inspired Diego Rivera's art. As she reads, she pauses to highlight Spanish words that are embedded in the story (e.g., conquistadores, luchadores) and asks students to define these words if they know the meaning. After the story is finished, the class returns to their small groups to see if there is anything that they want to add to their observation lists based on the story heard.

Now that we have seen an example of how culturally responsive practices can be embedded into a lesson, we would like you to take a minute to reflect on your own classroom or a class you have observed.

Reflection Activity

Directions: Consider a recent lesson that you taught (or observed). Respond to the following questions about the lesson.

Lesson: _____

1. What steps did you or the teacher take in the lesson to connect to students' prior experiences and learning?

2. What opportunities did you or the teacher provide for students to use their home language(s) or a language other than English in the lesson?

3. What resources did you or the teacher use for the lesson?

4. To what extent are these resources representative of the MLs in your classroom?

CHAPTER OVERVIEW

This chapter is framed around the following guiding principle: **"Culturally responsive teaching leverages students' linguistic and cultural backgrounds."** In this chapter, we'll explore why leveraging MLs' linguistic and cultural backgrounds is essential to culturally responsive teaching (CRT) and what it means to do so. We'll take an in-depth look at strategies for leveraging MLs' cultural and linguistic backgrounds, tools for incorporating multicultural resources into the curriculum, and strategies for incorporating translanguaging and home language practices into lessons. We'll conclude the chapter with three steps that you can take in your own classroom or school to incorporate MLs' linguistic and cultural backgrounds.

WHAT IT MEANS TO LEVERAGE STUDENTS' LINGUISTIC AND CULTURAL BACKGROUNDS

In her powerful 2009 TED Talk *What Are the Dangers of a Single Story*, Nigerian author Chimamanda Ngozi Adichie identifies the negative impact that a single story (or having only one

way to understand a person or a group of people) can have on both dominant cultural groups and those in the minority. She shares what it means to read literature in which your own experiences are not represented and the impact that this can have on your ability to tell your own stories. She also gives a warning about having only one perspective on the experiences and realities of a person or a group of people. She jokingly tells of her American college roommate asking to hear some of her "tribal" music and being surprised when Adichie played Mariah Carey for her.

Adichie's talk provides an important reminder that leveraging all students' linguistic and cultural backgrounds benefits not only MLs but also non-MLs. Fundamental to the idea of culturally responsive teaching is the belief that cultural diversity brings strength to a group, and when culturally responsive instruction is implemented effectively, it promotes growth in all students through the opportunities to learn and hear varied perspectives. In thinking about our work with MLs and their families, it is essential to identify situations in which students and families are being viewed through the lens of only a single story (often a deficit story) and reflect on the steps that we can take to widen the lens and explore a multitude of voices and experiences.

In addition to providing a more enriching and engaging environment for all students, exploring students' linguistic and cultural backgrounds also succeeds in fostering MLs' engagement because they see a place for themselves in the curriculum. Ladson-Billings (2001) describes the need for teachers to promote a flexible use of students' local and global culture. This means that teachers must provide opportunities for students to draw on their multiple identities and languages while learning. Furthermore, Hammond (2015), in her discussion of brain-based learning and culture, emphasizes the way in which new understandings must be built through connections to existing funds of knowledge. She explains that in order to "make learning stick," it is essential to determine what students know and make connections between their existing schema and the new information (p. 49).

The use of multicultural resources is a critical step toward fostering a learning environment that recognizes a place for all students. The Cooperative Children's Book Center at the University of Wisconsin–Madison collects data on the children's and young-adult books that they receive each year that are written by and about people of color and from First/Native Nations. While there has been a slight increase in the number of published books that include people of color, authors of color and First/Native Nations authors are still largely underrepresented. As educators, we must seek out literature in which authors of color and Native authors share stories rather than giving preference to white authors who are writing about multicultural characters or individuals. Figure 6.1, Children's Books by and/or About People of Color and First/Native Nations Received by Cooperative Children's Book Center 2002–2018, provides a summary of books they have received since 2002.

Figure 6.1 Children's Books by and/or About People of Color and First/Native Nations Received by Cooperative Children's Book Center 2002–2018

Year	Number of Books Received by CCBC	Africans/ African Americans		American Indians/First Nations		Asian Pacific Islanders/ Asian Pacific Americans		Latino	
		By	About	By	About	By	About	By	About
2018	3,653	202	405	38	55	351	314	197	249
2017	3,700	132	355	38	72	279	312	118	218
2016	3,400	94	287	23	55	217	240	104	169
2015	3,400	108	270	19	42	176	113	60	85
2014	3,500	85	181	20	38	129	112	59	66
2013	3,200	69	94	18	34	90	69	49	58
2012	3,600	69	119	6	22	83	76	58	54
2011	3,400	79	123	12	28	76	91	52	58
2010	3,400	102	156	9	22	60	64	55	66
2009	3,000	83	157	12	33	67	80	60	61
2008	3,000	83	172	9	40	77	98	48	79
2007	3,000	77	150	6	44	56	68	42	59
2006	3,000	87	153	14	41	72	74	42	63
2005	2,800	75	149	4	34	60	64	50	76
2004	2,800	99	143	7	33	61	65	37	61
2003	3,200	79	171	11	95	43	78	41	63
2002	3,150	69	166	6	64	46	91	48	94

Source: Data on books by and about people of color and from First/Native Nations published for children and teens compiled by the Cooperative Children's Book Center, School of Education, University of Wisconsin–Madison. http://ccbc.education .wisc.edu/books/pcstats.asp

Reflection Questions

1. What do you note after analyzing this table?

2. What does it make you think about representation in your classroom library?

Understanding what it means to leverage MLs' cultural and linguistic backgrounds can feel somewhat abstract. You may be asking yourself, *How do I know if I am doing this correctly?* Figure 6.2 shows some look-fors that we will explore further in this chapter.

Figure 6.2   Look-Fors for Guiding Principle 4: *Culturally responsive teaching leverages students' linguistic and cultural backgrounds.*

✓   Teachers use a variety of instructional strategies to assess, activate, and build MLs' background knowledge.

✓   Multicultural materials and resources are incorporated throughout the curriculum and school.

✓   Social justice and anti-racism resources are incorporated throughout the curriculum.

✓   Lessons and units include perspectives of individuals that come from MLs' home cultures (e.g., literature written by nondominant voices).

✓   Lessons include opportunities for MLs to use bilingual resources (e.g., dictionaries, books, or glossaries) and home languages (as appropriate).

✓   Leaders or role models from ML communities are included in the learning (e.g., community members are invited to speak in class).

Source: Adapted from Staehr Fenner and Snyder, 2017.

LEVERAGING MLs' BACKGROUNDS

In this section, we will explore strategies for leveraging MLs' backgrounds through a three-component process.

I. Know your MLs' backgrounds.

2. Seek out opportunities in the curriculum to connect to prior experiences and learning.

3. Activate prior knowledge.

Consider this scenario shared with us at one of our professional development sessions:

> At the beginning of a unit on life in Mesopotamia, an educator remembered that a student of hers, Pablo, had worked on a family farm before immigrating to the US from Guatemala. Privately, she asked him if he would be willing to share a little about his experience and what it meant to be dependent on the land and the weather for daily life. She gave him some questions to guide his thinking on the topic. He was thrilled to be able to talk about the family farm, the farming practices that they used, and the skills that were needed. In addition, the other students in the class were excited to learn more about a classmate of theirs who tended toward the quieter side.

Of course, every topic does not lend itself to this kind of opportunity to highlight MLs' backgrounds and experiences. Nor is there always time for such work. However, this scenario wouldn't have been possible had the teacher not known about her student's background prior to moving to the United States. In leveraging MLs' backgrounds, it is also important to consider the possibility that students might not feel comfortable sharing previous experiences or there may be trauma associated with those experiences.

As we have already explored Component 1 (Know your MLs' backgrounds) in Chapter 3 and Chapter 5, we will focus on Steps 2 and 3.

Component 2: *Seek out opportunities in the curriculum to connect to prior experiences and learning.*

As you begin a new unit of study, spend a little time thinking about connections that students might be able to make to prior experiences and learning. Also consider which students might be able to share their experiences or expertise on a topic to support other students. You can also think about community resources that you could draw on for the unit. The following questions can guide your reflection:

1. What experiences might my students have had that could offer a connection to the new content?

2. What have my students already learned that will help them in understanding the new material and mastering the standards that are aligned to this content?

3. Which students might have background knowledge or skills that could support others in engaging with the new content?

4. What community resources might support student learning?

Component 3: *Activate prior knowledge.*

Once you have identified possible connections to students' prior experiences and learning, there are many interactive and engaging strategies to activate students' prior knowledge that can be used with MLs of varying levels of English proficiency (Staehr Fenner & Snyder, 2017). All of these activities can be aligned to standards-based content.

Carousel brainstorming: Post four to five essential questions on chart paper around the room. These questions should be related to content that you will be introducing and should support students in making connections to prior learning. Have students move in pairs or small groups around the room, responding to each question on the chart paper. Student groups can spend two to three minutes with each question before moving on to another question. For each question, they can read what has already been written about that topic and add to or respond to it.

Image discussion: Give pairs or small groups of students an image related to a topic that you will be studying. You can ask students to respond to guiding questions about the images, or you could have them generate words and phrases related to the image or how they feel in looking at the image. Manny's art lesson at the beginning of this chapter is an example of how image discussions can be used to activate students' background knowledge.

Shared experiences: Shared experiences can be a great strategy for activating prior knowledge. A field trip is one example of a shared experience that would support students in linking prior experiences with new learning.

However, if leaving school grounds isn't feasible, a teacher can also make use of the available resources at the school. For example, a teacher introducing a unit on the five senses to students might take students to a particular location in or around the school (e.g., the cafeteria kitchen, the band room, a grassy spot) and ask them to think about what they see, hear, smell, taste, and feel. She could also ask then ask them to recall a favorite place they have been and write down what they remember about the place using descriptive words associated with the five senses. Virtual field trips are another strategy for creating a shared experience.

Concept sort: For this activity, you will create sets of index cards with images, words, or phrases that relate to key concepts that you will study. Have students work in pairs to sort the cards into categories. Depending on the topic and backgrounds of the students, you can provide the categories, or you can ask students to come up with categories. As an example, in preparation for a unit on the water cycle you might ask students to sort images or words into the categories of liquid, solid, and gas.

To see how educator Megan Brown helps build her students background knowledge before beginning a lesson on the Trail of Tears, watch the video *Activating and Building Background Knowledge*.

Video 6.1

Activating and Building Background Knowledge

resources.corwin.com/CulturallyResponsiveTeaching

Reflection Question

What is a favorite strategy that you have for activating students' prior knowledge?

STRATEGIES FOR INCORPORATING MULTICULTURAL RESOURCES

A second key strategy for leveraging students' cultural and linguistic backgrounds is to incorporate multicultural resources into your curriculum. In reflecting on the use of multicultural resources, it can be easy to rationalize that by including resources for specific events or celebrations, you are successfully leveraging students' home cultures. However, including a book about Day of the Dead or an activity related to Lunar Year is only one small step toward the systematic and intentional integration of multicultural resources into curricula.

Emily Style, in her article "Curriculum as Window and Mirror" (1988), describes the need for "curriculum to function both as window and as mirror, in order to reflect and reveal most accurately both a multicultural world and the student herself or himself" (p. 1). Thus, we want to expose students to educational resources that allow them to learn about the realities of others as well as see reflections of their own experiences. The offering of diverse types of resources and activities built around such resources will support students in developing understanding of and the skills to navigate other cultural perspectives. Look for opportunities to include multicultural resources at every opportunity in your classroom and curriculum.

> "I know there is **strength** in the differences between us. I know there is **comfort** where we overlap."
>
> – Ani DiFranco

To get you started, consider using multicultural resources:

- In the classroom library
- As a read-aloud
- To introduce a unit
- As a mentor text
- Included as images and quotes on the wall
- To provide supplementary materials to scaffold instruction for MLs through the use of home language or modified text
- To initiate discussion related to social justice, anti-racism, cultural understanding

To hear Syracuse City School District (SCSD) educators speak about strategies they use to incorporate multicultural resources into the curriculum, watch the *Incorporating Culture and Multicultural Resources Into the Curriculum* video clip.

Video 6.2

Incorporating Culture and Multicultural Resources Into the Curriculum

resources.corwin.com/CulturallyResponsiveTeaching

Tools for evaluating your classroom libraries and curriculum are provided further on in the chapter. What follows is a description of different types and uses for multicultural resources along with some examples of how they might be incorporated into the curriculum.

Provide a Mirror and a Window

Perhaps one of the most critical purposes of multicultural resources is to provide students with an opportunity to reflect on their own experiences through the content provided (a mirror) and give students an opportunity to learn about and reflect on the experiences of others (a window).

New York City educator Stephanie Reyes developed a thought-provoking mirrors and windows unit plan for use by teachers at her elementary school. As part of this project, students are asked to analyze books in their classroom libraries through the lens of mirrors and windows.

Reyes recommends creating a word wall with key terms that can be used to provide a foundation for the unit. She included short definitions for such terms as diversity, race, ethnicity, and empathy. She explains, "I think the most important place to start is by having common language and giving children the vocabulary that they can use to be able to talk about their identity in a way that other kids can understand" (S. Reyes, personal communications, October 9, 2019).

As part of the word wall, students use the following definitions to understand the concept of mirror and window books.

- "Mirror books reflect your own personal identity."
- "Window books show human experiences different from your own. They help strengthen your sense of empathy. They help you see things from another perspective and learn more about the world." (Reyes, n.d., p. 22)

As part of this unit, students are asked to choose a book and reflect on what they notice about the book and how it makes them feel. Through the use of discussion and graphic organizers, students talk about what a mirror book might contain and what a window book might contain. They also conduct a survey of their classroom library to determine what is included in their library and what is missing. Figure 6.3, Growing Roots and Wings, is the tool that is used for the library survey. The unit plan also incorporates a lesson in which students write letters to authors and publishers, emphasizing the important need for books that are both mirrors and windows.

Figure 6.3 Growing Roots and Wings

Data Collectors: _____		
Book Bin: _____ Total # of Books in Bin: _____		
We Are Looking for Books That . . .	**Tallies**	**Total**

(Continued)

Figure 6.3   (Continued)

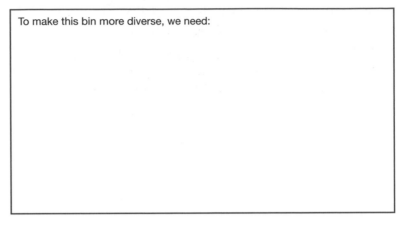

Source: Reyes, S. (n.d.) Diversity in your classroom library mirrors and windows project. *Teachers Pay Teachers*. https://www.teacherspayteachers.com/Product/Diversity-in-your-Classroom-Library-Mirrors-and-Windows-Project-4320636

Figure 6.7, the Student Resource Assessment, is a tool that you can use to take your own classroom resource inventory in order to help you identify possible gaps in students' access to mirrors and windows and your classroom.

Introduce an Alternative Perspective

Similar to the concept of providing a window is the explicit purpose of giving students an alternative lens for understanding the specific content being studied. When planning for a new unit of instruction, consider how you might incorporate alternative or less frequently explored viewpoints as a way to provide another perspective on the topic.

Educator Cindy Yetto described how, in teaching about the Age of Exploration, she uses the picture book *Encounter* (1996) by Jane Yolen, which tells of the story of the arrival of the conquistadors through the lens of the Taino people. After reading the book together, her students are then asked to debate whether or not Columbus deserves a day in his honor (C. Yetto, personal communication, July 19, 2019). Through resources that provide alternative perspectives, you can explore with students the ideas of dominant narratives and learn to recognize how dominant narratives are learned and shared. You can also practice the skill of questioning and looking for less frequently shared stories.

Multicultural resources can also be used to introduce students to the role that MLs have played throughout history. For example, when studying a unit on space exploration you can add a book on Ellen Ochoa, the first Latina astronaut, to your collection. Confer with colleagues who speak other languages to get book recommendations as well.

Reflection Questions

1. What is an alternative perspective or unheard voice that needs to be discussed in your content area?

2. What resources might you add to the curriculum?

Support Social Justice and Anti-Racism Units and Foster Discussions of Culture and Cross-Cultural Understanding

Multicultural resources, including articles, books, podcasts, film, and artwork, can provide rich content for social justice and anti-racism units. They can also support discussions related to culture and cross-cultural understanding. You might be questioning how—with an already packed curriculum—you can fit one more unit into what you have to teach. Some of these resources may  have a natural connection with content that you are already studying, and they will provide an opportunity for students to think about and interact with the content in new and perhaps deeper ways.

You can increase student access to and then showcase books that have social justice and anti-racism themes, which students might select for independent reading. As an example, in the children's chapter book *The Chupacabras of the Río Grande*, while the main characters are engaging in a search for mythical creatures called the chupacabras, they are also learning about protests connected to the building of a border wall on the Texas–Mexico border and family separation resulting from US immigration policy. This book was cowritten by Adam Gidwits, who authored a series of books called the *Unicorn Rescue Society* (2019), and Mexican American author David Bowles. The story also integrates words and short phrases in Spanish.

In Chapter 4, we included a variety of resources for developing social justice units. What follows is a list of three resources related to anti-racism education. We provide additional resources in Appendix F.

- Embracerace.org offers a list of children's books that can be used when talking about race, racism, and resistance. (www.embracerace.org)

- Facing History and Ourselves is an organization that provides resources and lessons ideas framed around understanding historical events as a tool to fight against bigotry and hate. "Responding to #LivingWhileBlack: Confronting Unexamined Bias in Everyday Life" is a list of recommendations for helping educators and their students explore implicit bias and the consequences of implicit bias in our society. (www.facinghistory.org)

- Teaching Tolerance has a series of lesson plans for students in Grades 6–12 specific to anti-racist education. One of the lessons included provides a strategy for integrating an anti-bias framework into discussions of texts. Students analyze texts related to the four anti-bias domains of identify, diversity, justice, and action. All of the lesson plans include considerations for ELs. (www.tolerance.org/learning-plan/antiracist-education)

In order to scaffold social justice or anti-racism units for language learners, you can provide differentiated material that can support MLs of varying language proficiency in exploring a similar theme or topic. For example, if you want to discuss youth activism, there are numerous books, articles, and videos on Malala Yousafzai that would be appropriate for students of varying grade and proficiency levels. You can also look for ways to decrease the linguistic demands of this work by using visual materials to support discussions, providing sentence stems to give students a starting point for sharing their ideas, and using graphic organizers to help students organize their thinking related to a particular topic.

Incorporate Multilingual Resources

An additional use of multicultural resources is the inclusion of multilingual resources. Multilingual resources can serve as both a scaffold for instruction and a model for MLs' language use.

To Scaffold Content

Content that is taught in English can be reinforced for ELs through home language material. Depending on the age and home language literacy level of the students, home language material can be used in small-group work, sent home with students for homework, or shared as a read-aloud. For example, the text *El Ciclo de Vida de la Rana (The Life Cycle of a Frog)* (2005) by Bobbie Kalman and Kathryn Smithyman could be read first in English and then later in Spanish with a group of Spanish-speaking MLs who might need the concepts reinforced. The book could also be a resource for a minilesson on English and Spanish cognates or other cross-linguistic comparisons (sounds, sentence structure, translation exercises [Celic & Seltzer, 2013, p. 45]). As with use of all home language material, it is essential to know your students' home language literacy levels in order to select appropriate materials and lessons.

To Highlight the Role of Language as Part of Culture

There is an increasing number of books with bilingual or bicultural main characters. Including these books into your curriculum not only gives value to the benefit of bilingualism, but these books also serve as a model for students to integrate their home languages into their work. The early-reader *Yasmin* series written by Saadia Faruqi (2019) about a young Pakistani girl living in the United States is an example of how books can incorporate language to emphasize aspects of a culture. In these stories, Urdu words such as baba (father), jaan (life—nickname for loved one), and hijab (headscarf) are integrated into stories. The stories also include talking points, an Urdu–English glossary, and facts about Pakistan. A series such as this can provide a strong model for students to write their own bicultural stories.

An educator once told us about a student of hers who wrote a narrative about his Spanish-speaking grandmother, but when including dialogue, all the language was in English. This teacher asked the student if that is really what his grandmother had said. The student ended up reworking his narrative to include his grandmother's voice in Spanish. He was happier with what he had written, and the other students in the class loved his story. In addition to incorporating multilingual resources into your classroom, you can also include strategies to promote MLs' use of home languages.

STRATEGIES TO SUPPORT TRANSLANGUAGING AND USE OF HOME LANGUAGE IN THE CLASSROOM

You can support your students in using their home language to further their learning and language development through using translanguaging practices. **Translanguaging is the use of more than one language to communicate, as is typical of bilinguals, in order to make full use of their linguistic resources (Creese & Blackledge, 2010; García et al., 2017).** Yip and García (2015) explain that "educators must acknowledge the students' full linguistic repertoire as a resource for learning, and not as a problem" (para. 13).

In Figure 6.4, you can see an example of translanguaging. During the *Syracuse City School District Steps to the Seal Program,* students develop their heritage language literacy skills by completing a personal memoir with their families. In this example, Simon Yeh uses both his heritage language, Karen, and English as an integrated communication system. He employs his full linguistic repertoire to describe his journey from Thailand to Syracuse. To read more about the Steps to the Seal Program, see Chapter 8.

While instructional strategies to support translanguaging vary, we have included a few ideas:

Figure 6.4   **Example of Translanguaging**

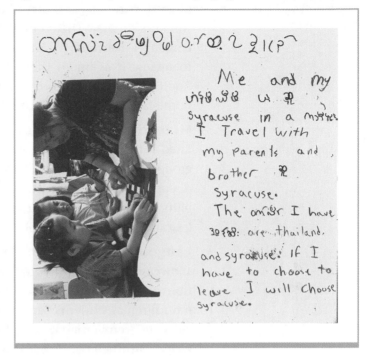

- **Cognate word study** is one strategy to support translanguaging. **Cognates are words in different languages that are derived from the same original word or root**. In addition to having the same meaning, the words look and sound similar. For example, "dictionary" in English is *dictionaire* in French. Some ideas for supporting students in studying cognates include the following:

  o Identifying cognates while reading and adding to a cognate chart

  o Sorting sets of cognates (e.g., family–*familia*) on cards and circling differences in cognates

  o Identifying false cognates (words that look and sound similar but have different meanings)

  o Sorting cognates and false cognates into two different groupings

  o Practicing pronunciation of cognates and identifying intonation and stress differences (Colorín Colorado, 2007)

- **Building of background knowledge** can be accomplished through a translanguaging approach in which students preview the content to be studied in their home language, learn it in English, and then come together to review it again in their home language (Cole, 2019). Additionally, students can annotate English texts with home language translations (Celic & Seltzer, 2013, p. 92).

- **Multilingual discussions** and products can be incorporated into unit plans. For example, you can intentionally group students so that they can engage in translanguaging discussions about content. You can also build in the possibility of authentic, strategic multilingual products into your lessons, such as the example that we shared on page 215.

- **Language portfolios** can be built wherein students can showcase their multilingual work and explore their relationship to their language(s) through self-assessment. Even monolingual students can use them to record experiences with different languages and cultures and list their language learning goals (Celic & Seltzer, 2013, p. 23).

There is also a wide variety of online resources for supporting students' home language use, many of which can be used in distance-learning environments. In Figure 6.5, we provide a few recommendations.

Figure 6.5   Digital Resources and Tools to Support Home Language Use

Digital Resource and Link	Resource Description
Immersive Reader www.onenote.com/learningtools	This tool is available for Microsoft users in Word and One Note. It includes a variety of features, including reading texts aloud, highlighting different parts of speech, and translating texts into other languages.
G Suite for Education https://edu.google.com/	Google Suite includes multiple platforms to support multilingual learners through communication (Google Classroom, Meet, and Chat), text-to speech read-aloud support (Read Aloud), collaboration (Docs, Sheets, Slides, Forms), and translation (Translate).
Glossaries for ELLs/MLs NYS Statewide Language Regional Education Resource Network & NYU Steinhardt https://steinhardt.nyu.edu/metrocenter/language-rbern/education/glossaries-ells-mlls-accommodations	This site provides ELA, math, science, and social studies glossaries in multiple languages for varying grade levels.

Digital Resource and Link	Resource Description
Bilingual Study Notes (science and social studies) NYU Steinhardt www.research.steinhardt.nyu.edu/metrocenter/resources	This site offers a series of bilingual study guides on key science and social studies topics at the elementary levels. Languages include Bengali, French, Haitian, Korean, Chinese (simplified and traditional), and Spanish.
2lingual www.2lingual.com	This is a bilingual search engine. You can choose two different languages, and the results come up next to each other.
PhET University of Colorado Boulder www.phet.colorado.edu/en/simulations/translated	This resource offers science simulations in multiple languages.
SupportEd Practical Strategies and Resources to Teach ELs Online www.getsupported.net/distancelearning/	This is a collection of resources compiled to support English learners through distance learning.

Reflection Question

What is your favorite digital resource for supporting students' home language use?

INVITING FAMILIES AND COMMUNITY MEMBERS INTO THE CLASSROOM

A final recommendation to leverage MLs' cultural and linguistic backgrounds is to look for ways to invite ML families and communities into the learning. It's important to do this in a respectful way that doesn't serve to put families on display.

Which of the following ideas might work in your context or with your content?

Offer opportunities for the families of all students to share something about their background or a skill or interest that they have. If families don't feel comfortable speaking, maybe they can teach your class how to prepare a dish, model a skill, or respond to questions from students through the use of an interpreter.

Explore ways that ML community members are benefitting the community. For example, you could take a field trip to visit a small-business entrepreneur in your area. Have the entrepreneurs talk about how they got started in their business, challenges that they had, and strategies that they used to build their business. You could also look for MLs who are serving in community service roles and have them speak to your class about their job and how they prepared for the position.

Assign students interview projects in which they have to learn more about their families or ML community members. They can record family members speaking in English or their home language and share highlights from the interview with the class. If the interview is in a language other than English, the student who conducted the interview can talk about what the person said and identify some keywords. You can also develop community video projects in which students highlight unique aspects of their communities to share with their classmates.

THREE STEPS YOU CAN TAKE

Now that we've explored a variety of ways to leverage MLs' linguistic and cultural backgrounds, let's take a look at three steps that you can take in your own classrooms and schools and a few tools to help you in your work. As with previous chapters, each of these steps can be done individually, but you can also consider how you might approach these strategies in your CRT teams for a school-based approach.

Step 1: *Evaluate your curricular resources.*

A key step in including resources that are mirrors and windows for students is to evaluate the materials that you are currently using. Use the Assessing Multicultural Resources Tool (Figure 6.6) to review your classroom library, the literature used in your curriculum, or other curricular resources from the perspective of the MLs in your class. For each criterion, decide if there are many examples represented in your library or curriculum, a few examples, or no examples. You can take notes in the table to indicate where you have gaps in resources.

For example, you may find that while you have some resources for Spanish-speaking students, you have few resources for students who speak Thai. In taking part in this resource review, it is also important to reflect on how ML characters or people are portrayed in the resources. Ask yourself whether the books will serve to offer alternative perspectives for students in your classes or reinforce preexisting stereotypes (the "single story").

As you conduct your review, also consider if there are ways that you might make greater use of the multicultural resources that you have. For example, could any of the resources become a new mentor text? After you finish your review, identify areas where you feel you are doing well and those areas where you could improve. Consider what steps you can take to strengthen your use of multicultural resources.

Figure 6.6   Assessing Multicultural Resources Tool

MLs in Your Class:			Students' Home Languages:	
Criteria	**No Examples**	**A Few Examples (1–5)**	**Many Examples (6 or more)**	**Notes**
Characters or people who **look** like MLs				

(Continued)

Figure 6.6   (Continued)

Criteria	No Examples	A Few Examples (1–5)	Many Examples (6 or more)	Notes
Characters or people who come from **similar backgrounds** or who may have similar experiences as MLs				
Resources that provide **role models** from MLs' home cultures				
Resources that **incorporate** students' home language(s)				
Materials that share the **perspectives and voices** of groups that are often underrepresented or marginalized				

Reflection Questions

1. Are there any resources that you have concerns about? For example, did you come across resources that may serve to reinforce stereotypes or portray a certain cultural group from a deficit-based perspective? Which?

2. Did you find a multicultural resource in your collection that gave you a new idea for integrating it into your curriculum? What resource? How will you integrate it?

You can also ask students to evaluate individual resources based on their own experiences in order to have a sense of whether or not students can see themselves in the resource. Figure 6.7, Student Resource Assessment, is a tool that can be adapted based on the grade and proficiency levels of your students.

Figure 6.7   Student Resource Assessment

Criterion		No	Somewhat	Yes
1.	Are the characters in the story **like you or people you know**?			
2.	Does the place in the story remind you of a place that you have **lived or visited**?			
3.	Do **you and your family** talk like the characters in the story?			
4.	Do the **events in the story** remind you of anything that has happened to you or your family?			

Source: Adapted from Cultural Relevance Rubric (p. 198) in Ebe, A. (2010). Culturally relevant texts and reading assessment for English language learners. *Reading Horizons, 50*(3), 193–210.

Once you have evaluated your own classroom, consider how you can extend the use of multicultural resources in your school. Work with your school librarian or media specialist to create a catalog of multicultural resources and include notes on distinguishing features in the book or how the resource might be used. Figure 6.8, Template for Multicultural Resource Library, is an example of a tool that could be shared across the school so that teachers can borrow materials from one another.

Figure 6.8   Template for Multicultural Resource Library

Title, Author, Location	Genre	Lexile Level	Distinguishing Features for MLs
La Vida de un Mariposa by Dona Rice; ESOL resource room	Nonfiction	180 Guided Reading Level E	Spanish translation of *The Life of a Butterfly*
The Name Jar by Yangsook Choi; school library	Fiction Picture book	590	Main character: Korean girl new to US schools; importance of a name
Freedom Soup by Tami Charles; first-grade classroom	Fiction Picture book	410-600	Historical story about the Haitian Revolution as told by a grandmother to her granddaughter; passing down of tradition and history

If you want to conduct a more extensive evaluation of your school's curricular materials through the lens of multiculturalism, the *Culturally Responsive Curriculum Scorecard* (2019) developed by J. Bryan-Gooden and colleagues at the Metropolitan Center for Research on Equity and the Transformation of Schools at New York University can be an excellent tool. The scorecard provides an opportunity for teams of educators and family members to evaluate the curricula at the school from the perspectives of representation, social justice, and teachers' materials (the level of guidance provided to support teachers in implementing culturally responsive lessons).

Step 2: *Explore new multicultural resources.*

A second step that you can take is to explore a new multicultural resource and consider how it might be used in your classroom. You can find new resources through discussions with colleagues or online multicultural book lists. Some examples of multicultural book lists have been saved in Appendix F: Supporting Resources.

Application Activity 6a. Multicultural Resource Sharing

Figure 6.9, the Multicultural Resource Sharing Tool, is a tool that you can use to reflect on a new resource and how you will use it in your classroom. This activity can be completed independently, or this tool could also be used as part of a professional learning community or team discussion. Educators could come to the discussion with one new multicultural resource they had used or were planning to use in their classroom. In addition to the resource-sharing tool, teachers could also share a short description of their lesson plan and any supporting materials that they used. Ideally, all these documents could be accessed through an online document-sharing platform so that teachers could search and access each other's plans.

Figure 6.9   Multicultural Resource Sharing Tool

Title	Author
Type of book (e.g., fiction, nonfiction, picture book, easy reader chapter book, young adult novel)	**Grade level**
Distinguishing features (e.g., theme, author or characters from students' home cultures, mirror or window text, multilingual text, audio version of text)	**Topic, theme, or standard to which it is aligned**

Possible use (check one or more)
☐   Read-aloud
☐   Mentor text and/or skills text
☐   Classroom library
☐   Resource for content topic: _____
☐   Introduce a topic or theme: _____
☐   Support social justice theme: _____
☐   Support anti-racism theme
☐   Initiate discussion of culture or cross-cultural understanding
☐   Home language support
☐   Other _____

Steps for introducing this text to students	Additional notes on using this book

Step 3: *Take steps to build home language, translanguaging resources and opportunities, and family and community resources into your lessons.*

In addition to incorporating more multicultural resources into your lessons, consider how you will leverage MLs' cultural and linguistic backgrounds by incorporating opportunities for students' home language use and/or integrating families and community members into your lessons. Figure 6.10, Lesson Planning for Home Language Use and Family and Community Involvement, is a tool for you to plan for instruction that supports MLs linguistically. Once you have implemented your lesson, be sure to share with colleagues so they can hear about the successes you are having and aspects of the lesson that you might change. For a more comprehensive planning tool, refer to Appendix C: Culturally Responsive Unit Planning Template.

Figure 6.10   Lesson Planning for Home Language Use and Family and Community Involvement

Lesson Topic	MLs' Home Languages	Home Language Resources
Implementation of translanguaging strategies (check those that you will use)		
☐ Cognate word study	☐ Collaborative translation	☐ Background knowledge in building in L1
☐ Academic discussions	☐ Cultural modeling (discussions of translations)	☐ Integrated writing
☐ Other: _____		
Family and Community Resources		

Describe how you will leverage ML family and/or community resources. Examples might include the following:

- Inviting parents or family members to share an aspect of their culture or a skill they have
- Inviting an ML community member to share information on a relevant topic
- Incorporating an interview into the unit
- Incorporating a community exploration or video project into the unit

Summary of Key Ideas

- Look for opportunities in every unit to leverage MLs' cultural and linguistic backgrounds.

- Multicultural resources should be selected to offer a mirrors and windows perspective, explore alternative perspectives, provide opportunities to engage in critical learning about social justice and anti-racism topics, and support home language use.

- MLs benefit from having opportunities to use home language resources and engage in translanguaging practices.

- Seek out opportunities to invite families or community members into your classroom or to support students in learning about and exploring diverse community resources.

Chapter 6 Reflection Questions

1. After reading this chapter, what is your most significant take away related to strategies for leveraging students' linguistic and cultural backgrounds?

2. What is one step that you would like to take to strengthen the use of multicultural resources in your context?

References

Adichie, C. (2009). *What are the dangers of a single story?* [Video file]. www.npr.org/2013/09/20/186303292/what-are-the-dangers-of-a-single-story

Bryan-Gooden, J., Hester, M., & Peoples, L. Q. (2019). *Culturally responsive curriculum scorecard.* Metropolitan Center for Research on Equity and the Transformation of Schools, New York University.

Celic, C., & Seltzer, K. (2013). *Translanguaging: A CUNY-NYSIEB guide for educators.* The Graduate Center, CUNY.

Cole, M. (2019, March). Translanguaging in every classroom. *Language Arts, 96*(4), 244–249.

Colorín Colorado. (2007). *Using cognates to develop comprehension in English.* www.colorincolorado.org/article/using-cognates-develop-comprehension-english

Cooperative Children's Book Center, School of Education, University of Wisconsin–Madison. (2019). Publishing statistics on children's/YA books about people of color and first/native nations and by people of color and first/native nations. http://ccbc.education.wisc.edu/

Creese, A., & Blackledge, A. (2010, February). Translanguaging in the bilingual classroom: A pedagogy for learning and teaching? *The Modern Language Journal, 94*(1), 103–115.

Ebe, A. (2010, September/October). Culturally relevant texts and reading assessments for English language learners. *Reading Horizons, 50*(3), 193–210.

Faruqi, S. (2019). *Yasmin the explorer.* Picture Window Books.

García, O., Johnson, S., & Seltzer, K. (2017). The translanguaging classroom: Leveraging student bilingualism for learning. Caslon.

Hammond, Z. (2015). *Culturally responsive teaching and the brain.* Corwin.

Ladson-Billings, G. (2001). *Crossing over to Canaan.* Jossey-Bass.

Reyes, S. (n.d.). Diversity in your classroom library: Mirrors and windows project. *Teachers Pay Teachers.* https://www.teacherspayteachers.com/Product/Diversity-in-your-Classroom-Library-Mirrors-and-Windows-Project-4320636

Staehr Fenner, D., & Snyder, S. (2017). *Unlocking English learners' potential: Strategies for making content accessible.* Corwin.

Style, E. (1988). Curriculum as window and mirror. *Listening for all voices.* Oak Knoll School Monograph. https://www.nationalseedproject.org/itemid-fix/entry/curriculum-as-window-and-mirror

Tonatiuh, D. (2011). *Diego Rivera: His world and ours.* Abrams Books for Young Readers.

Yip, J., & García, O. (2015, Fall). *Translanguaging: Practice briefs for educators.* www.traue.commons.gc.cuny.edu/volume-iv-issue-1-fall-2015/translanguaging-practice-briefs-for-educators

Uniting Students' Schools, Families, and Communities

Scenario: A Multicultural Celebration at Lian's School

Lian is excited to attend and perform at a multicultural celebration at her school tomorrow night. It's an annual event, and there is always lots of delicious food from around the world, such as tamales, beignets, pierogies, fish stew, tabbouleh, and other food that she hasn't tried before. Also, many of her friends will be wearing traditional clothing from their families' home countries and performing songs and dances. Everyone in the school is invited, and it's the one night that most of the multilingual learner (ML) families attend an event at the school. The festive evening always ends with a DJ playing music and everyone dancing.

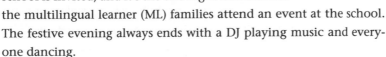

Reflection Questions

1. Have you ever been to an event like the one at Lian's school? If so, what did you like about it? What did you learn from it?

2. What are the benefits of multicultural celebrations such as the one described?

3. What might be the unintended consequences or concerns of holding such celebrations?

A multicultural event can be an effective way to bring together community members and celebrate the cultures that make up that community. However, the unintended consequence of such events is that they can limit the focus on culture to one annual event and in doing so keep culturally responsive teaching (CRT) as something on the periphery rather than a central tenet of the school culture. Such events can also present CRT as celebrations or explorations of only the surface level of culture, such as food, clothing, and music. As explained by Paul Gorski (2008), "Despite overwhelmingly good intentions, most of what passes for intercultural education practice, particularly in the US, accentuates rather than undermines existing social and political hierarchies" (p. 516).

Gardner (2019a) shares several possible alternatives to hosting an international night, including inviting immigrant parents or community members to speak in classes about their background and culture or a particular topic (e.g., a Vietnamese refugee could speak to students who are learning about the Vietnam War, etc.). Another suggestion she provides is to ask immigrant parents or community members for information teachers may need for their instruction, urging educators to resist Googling for lesson plans when teaching about different backgrounds or cultures when they may have firsthand sources of that information through ML families. Whenever inviting families to speak about their experiences or give their perspective on a particular topic, it is essential that family members feel their participation is optional and they only need share what they feel comfortable sharing. The use of an interpreter might be needed to make sure this idea is appropriately conveyed and that families don't feel any pressure to participate.

In addition to bringing ML families to the school, another idea is to visit places ML students and their families may spend their time outside of school, such as places of worship, stores, and community centers.

Reflection Questions

1. Why does ML family and community engagement matter to ML student achievement?

2. How does encouraging family and community engagement support culturally responsive teaching?

3. What strategies do you use or do you plan to use to support ML family and community engagement?

CHAPTER OVERVIEW

This chapter is framed around our final guiding principle: **"Culturally responsive teaching unites students' schools, families, and communities."** In this chapter, we shift from a focus on instructional strategies and resources for CRT to a focus on building partnerships with families and communities in support of MLs. We begin by exploring what family engagement is and why it is important for our work with MLs. Next, we discuss five strategies related to fostering ML family engagement and collaborating with ML communities:

 1. Create a welcoming environment for ML families.

 2. Build relationships with ML families.

 3. Communicate effectively with ML families.

 4. Overcome barriers to ML family engagement.

 5. Empower ML families.

After a discussion of these five strategies, we offer three steps that you can take in your work to unite ML students, schools, families, and communities. We end the chapter with a summary of key ideas from the chapter and chapter reflection questions.

DEFINING FAMILY ENGAGEMENT

To ensure we are all on the same page when it comes to our concept of family engagement, let's begin by examining what we mean by this term. **Family engagement is ongoing, meaningful interaction between schools and families that is characterized by two-way communication. Its focus is on supporting student learning** (Garcia et al., 2016).

In the past, in the field of education, we often referred to this concept as "parent involvement" rather than "family engagement." We use the term "family" instead of "parent" to recognize that MLs may live with and have strong relationships with family members instead of or in addition to parents. These family members may play a crucial role in the student's education and should be included by schools and communities (Staehr Fenner, 2014). The use of the word "engagement" rather than "involvement" indicates an active partnership and shared responsibility between families and educators.

ML family engagement can take many forms, and it's essential to use a strengths-based approach to recognize the many ways that ML families are already engaged in their child's education (Garcia et al., 2016). For example, ML families often have strong beliefs in the value of education, and education may be seen as a priority in their family (Noel et al., 2016; Sibley & Dearing, 2014; Tobin et al., 2013). Families may model respect for teachers and engage in rich dialogues with their children about the events of the school day. It's essential that we build on the practices that are already in place as a means of further engaging ML families and fostering warm and respectful relationships (Office of the Education Ombudsman, 2012; Noel et al., 2016; Sibley & Dearing, 2014; Tobin et al., 2013).

The Importance of ML Family Engagement and Federal Law

There are many reasons that family engagement is crucial to all students, MLs and non-MLs. Research indicates effective family engagement is associated with many positive student outcomes, including increased high school graduation rates, higher grades and test scores, a higher level of English language proficiency, improved social skills, and increased enrollment in postsecondary education (Ferguson, 2008; Henderson & Mapp, 2002; Lindholm-Leary, 2015; National Academies of Sciences, Engineering, and Medicine [NASEM], 2017). Family and school partnerships can also help remove language, cultural, and social barriers that might stand in the way of student achievement.

In addition, the 2015 Every Student Succeeds Act (ESSA) mandates family engagement as an essential element for improving student outcomes for all students. School districts are required to ask for and respond to recommendations from families, as well as share with families how they can support their children's education and acquisition of English. In order to facilitate this outreach, educators should receive training and support related to effective tools and strategies for communicating and partnering with ML families. This support to teachers is critical, as effective teacher engagement practices at the classroom level can foster family involvement at the school level (Calzada et al., 2015).

Section 3115(c)(3)(A) of ESSA requires districts to use Title III funds to "provide and implement other effective activities and strategies that enhance or supplement language instruction educational programs for English learners which shall include parent, family and community engagement activities." Further, districts must conduct effective outreach to parents of ELs (English learners), including holding regular meetings in order to seek and respond to parent recommendations [ESEA Section 1112(e)(3)]. In envisioning how to include parents and families in our schools, Gardner (2019b) advocates for holding separate events for ML families (e.g., ML family graduation information) as well as ensuring ML families are included equitably in all schoolwide events (e.g., schoolwide family math night).

Counterstories in ML Family and Community Engagement

When we examine ML family and community engagement on a deeper level, we must also examine the role of **counterstories, which are unofficial stories that serve to challenge the narrative of those in power (Chapman, 2007).** Critical theory holds that all relationships are structured around power, and within these relationships certain groups have privilege while others do not. Mainstream practices (which include classroom practices) often reinforce oppressive systems that are organized around class, race, and gender (DeCuir-Gunby et al., 2013). These mainstream practices do not always create space for the experiences and knowledge of marginalized populations. Therefore, counterstories told by people who belong to marginalized groups, such as MLs, offer valuable data for teachers who work with students from these communities. Counterstories serve to challenge the status quo, confront exclusion, highlight widely held unjust beliefs, and call for a reallocation of power within relationships (Delgado, 2013).

In terms of counterstories related to MLs' family and community engagement, Staehr Fenner (2014) notes that ML families often participate and are very actively engaged in their children's education in ways that may be less obvious or visible to some educators. For example, even though they may not be able to attend in-school events on a regular basis, they may ensure their children complete their homework and encourage them to study (Staehr Fenner, 2014). Simpson Baird (2015) shares that the focus on parent engagement as a means to improve student achievement has resulted in an implicit definition of what engagement looks like for all parents instead of an inductive understanding of what actually occurs in ML families. Her review of 31 research studies found that ML parent engagement is centered around three key relationships: (1) between families and schools, (2) between parents and children, and (3) among families. These three types of relationships exist along a continuum from school-directed to parent-led. In addition, the relationships present a counterstory to the standard practices that define parent engagement and instead reveal that ML parents' involvement is characterized by dynamic processes. This research underscores the need for educators to more deeply examine their beliefs as to what ML family engagement looks like, challenging what we believe to be "standard practices."

Choi (2017) writes that for immigrant and nonwhite families such as hers, the absence of genuine, two-way communication from school to family can be especially harmful. The author holds that collaboration between teachers and parents exists only to further ensure the teachers' success and make their jobs easier by having parents support discipline issues. Further, she contends that school rules clash with ML families' cultural norms, which serves to propagate institutional racism. **We feel that it is always crucial to listen to and acknowledge counterstories, especially those from ML parents that may make white educators feel uncomfortable, in order to have a deeper understanding of ML families' experiences so that we can further support them and actively challenge the mainstream narrative.**

Community Schools and Partnerships

In addition to shifting from focusing on parent involvement to family engagement, our field has also been more purposefully inclusive of the role of community in fostering support for MLs. When families, schools, and communities work together, student learning is improved and schools, families, and communities are strengthened (Stefanaski et al., 2016). School and community partnerships will vary by location, but some examples of collaborative efforts might include before- and after-school tutoring or enrichment programs, food pantries or food giveaways at schools, programs to provide dental or medical services in the school, housing or legal services, and partnerships in which high school students can earn college credit by attending local community colleges or universities.

One way to empower ML families is to connect them to community services and community organizations that can offer services that families may not know about. Collaborating with community organizations is also an effective way to increase the impact you can have. Some possible organizations to consider include the following:

- Local hospitals
- Community support groups
- Charitable organizations
- Academic enrichment programs
- Community colleges and universities
- Local landlords who are supportive of ML families
- Park districts
- Community activists
- District community liaisons

Zacarian and Soto (2020) highlight three key requirements of school–community partnerships (p. 116). According to these authors, each district or school needs to do the following:

1. Identify a need and/or an asset that would benefit from a community partner.
2. Identify local resources that will address the needs/assets.
3. Take steps to create partnerships that are mutually beneficial and as enduring as they are transformative.

In Application Activity 7a. Identifying Potential Community Partners, we would like you to operationalize this idea and identify the particular assets and needs of MLs and their families in your context that could be supported through community partnerships. Then, consider individuals or organizations that could be a potential partner and who the point of contact might be for each organization. This will lay the groundwork to take steps to create these mutually beneficial partnerships. In thinking about assets and needs, you should consider not just basic needs but also enrichment opportunities. For example, in Sydney's home community a local PTA partnered with a community theater organization to offer scholarships to ML students to take part in a summer theater camp.

Application Activity 7a. Identifying Potential Community Partners

ML Families' Assets and Needs	Potential Partner(s)	Point of Contact

As in previous chapters, we are sharing a list of look-fors related to this chapter's guiding principle. The look-fors in Figure 7.1 can be helpful in making the principle more concrete but are not comprehensive. We have compiled the complete list of look-fors in the Culturally Responsive School Checklist that is provided in Appendix B.

Figure 7.1   Look-Fors for Guiding Principle 5: *Culturally responsive teaching unites students' schools, families, and communities.*

✓   The school visually demonstrates a commitment to multicultural families and students (e.g., flags from students' home countries, signs posted in multiple languages, student work displayed on walls).

✓   Information and resources that are shared with families are provided in the home languages of ML families.

✓   Interpreters are provided at all school events.

✓   Educators use a variety of tools to communicate with ML families (e.g., emails, phone calls, texts in home languages, flyers in home languages).

✓   School administration looks for ways to remove barriers that might prevent ML families from participating (e.g., timing of events, child care, transportation).

✓   ML family members are actively involved with school committees or organizations that are open to parents (e.g., PTA).

Source: Adapted from Staehr Fenner and Snyder, 2017.

FIVE STRATEGIES TO FOSTER ML FAMILY ENGAGEMENT AND COMMUNITY COLLABORATION

Now that we have explored what ML family engagement is and why it is so important, let's dive into the five strategies for fostering ML family engagement and collaborating with ML communities. We also note that this is not an exhaustive list of strategies, and we encourage you to further explore any additional strategies you may be using.

Create a Welcoming Environment for ML Families

One strategy for uniting schools, families, and communities is to consider your first interactions with ML families and the type of environment into which you welcome them. Consider what it might be like to walk into your school as someone who is new to the school, the district, and even the country. Consider how new families are greeted and how key information is shared.

Reflection Questions

What is the experience like for new families enrolling in your school or district? How do you know?

There are several ways that we can ensure that we are inclusive of ML families at the time of enrollment. In districts with large numbers of MLs, we recommend having a welcome center geared toward ML families. If your district's ML population size does not lend itself to having a separate welcome center, there are many ways you can support families upon enrollment. One suggestion is for schools to maintain a list of multilingual student ambassadors who can give tours in home languages and serve as buddies for new students. You could also identify potential community volunteers such as college students for this activity if appropriate.

For all districts, the school enrollment process should be easily accessible all year long because new students arrive throughout the school year. It is challenging for any student to start at a new school midway through the school year, and this challenge is amplified if families are navigating an unfamiliar educational system in a language other than their home language. We want students to begin to build their academic identity during the enrollment process so that students see themselves as a member of the school community and have an opportunity to discuss goals for their learning (DeCapua et al., 2009). Key information about the school and district should also be shared at the time of enrollment in families' home languages (Breiseth et al., 2011). It is best if essential information is shared both orally and in writing, as well as by someone with whom families feel comfortable so that they can ask questions.

Breiseth and colleagues (2011) recommend sharing the following key information with families:

- Tools for understanding and navigating the school system
- Free and reduced-cost breakfast and lunch options

- School or city transportation options
- How information about inclement weather and school closings or delays is shared
- How information is communicated by administration and classroom teachers
- The school calendar (including teacher workdays, holidays, conferences, field trips)
- Instructional and other types of supports that are available to students and families

Reflection Questions

How is essential school and district information shared with new families in your district? What can be done to improve the process?

ML Welcome Centers

When new ML families register their children in a district, their first stop is usually at the local school. We have found that information shared at schools can vary widely from school to school, and sometimes inconsistent information is shared across schools or not provided. For districts with a large enough ML population, we recommend establishing welcome centers or refining existing centers to ensure they are truly welcoming for ML families. Depending on the size of the district and access to public transportation, one or more satellite welcome centers may provide services tailored to ML families in certain geographic locations. A district's welcome center can set the tone for how ML families feel about their place within the district, so it is essential to give thought to several aspects of a welcome center. In our experience as educators who worked in welcome centers and also through our work with SupportEd in helping districts establish and enhance their own welcome centers, we recommend that welcome centers provide the services—many of which are also federally mandated—detailed in Figure 7.2, Welcome Center Services and Descriptions.

Figure 7.2   Welcome Center Services and Descriptions

Service	Description
Home language survey	Given to all students; determines the language(s) spoken in the home and whether the child should be assessed for English language proficiency
Family interview	Gathers more information on children's previous schooling, interests, and backgrounds
English language proficiency assessment	Identifies whether a child is an English learner and is eligible for English for Speakers of Other Languages (ESOL) services
Notification letter	Provides parents information, including the child's identification as an EL, information on the ESOL program and instructional methods, and exit requirements for the program
Health services and immunizations	Partners with local health services to provide physicals and vaccinations required for school enrollment
Tests in math and other content areas	Offered for students without transcripts or with unclear transcripts to demonstrate course knowledge for credit in home language as appropriate
Home language tests	Provides secondary credit in home language (world language) upon passing and determines proficiency for elementary dual language programs (if applicable); provides valuable information about home language literacy for content teachers and ESOL specialists
Evaluation of foreign transcripts	Awards credit for courses studied in students' home countries (if applicable)
Interpreters	Assist families with providing information verbally in the home language
Community liaisons	Connect families with community resources, including ESOL classes for adults and public transportation options

Community liaisons connect families with resources and services available within the school district and larger community. For example, community liaisons can provide information about how to navigate the school system, how to obtain free and reduced-price meals through the school district, and districtwide ML family/parent orientation sessions. They can serve as a bridge to the community by sharing information in parents' home languages about recreation and library programs, health insurance, child care programs, public transportation in the community, adult education programs, job training, and employment.

Build Relationships With ML Families

The second strategy for uniting schools, families, and communities is to build relations with ML families. In order to build an effective relationship with ML families, it is important to begin with an assets-based perspective by recognizing that ML families may be engaged in numerous ways that are not apparent or perhaps in line with how we traditionally think of parent engagement. When families are not meeting your expectations for engagement, start from a place of empathy and consider what else may be going on in their lives. It is also important to recognize that ML families may come from cultures where parents are not expected or encouraged to work in partnerships with teachers or take part in school events.

You can learn more about ML families and build relationships with families by taking part in community events in which families participate, such as sporting events or community festivals, by organizing a community walk, and by conducting home visits.

Community Walks

A community walk is a student- or parent-led tour that helps break down barriers between schools and communities, enabling educators to learn about students' communities on the students' and/or parents' terms (Safir, 2017). We need to learn more from people with intimate knowledge of both the wonderful but sometimes hidden resources of the community and also the issues communities might be facing. Touring the neighborhood will help teachers and staff members appreciate the life and soul of the community where they teach, develop deeper relationships with families, identify community resources to tap, and enrich instruction using what they learn about families' cultures and backgrounds. Teachers can learn more about the realities of the physical environments in which their students live. For example, the neighborhood may have neglected parks, not enough stop signs and crosswalks, and a lack of recreational places for teenagers and young adults. Teachers can also use this opportunity to learn about the pride that many shop owners feel for their businesses and community. In terms of timing, a community walk in the first week that teachers and staff members return to school can ground educators in a deeper sense of students' communities, which will permeate the rest of the school year.

Home Visits: Proceed With Caution

Home visits can be an excellent opportunity to learn more about your ML families and build relationships with them (Ernst-Slavit & Mason, n.d.; Staehr Fenner, 2014). One study by Johns Hopkins University of 12 elementary schools in Washington, DC (Sheldon & Jung, 2015), that contained 23 percent English learners found that students whose families received home visits had a significant reduction in absences. These students were also more likely to achieve or exceed grade-level reading comprehension than students whose families did not receive a home visit, after controlling for prior differences in attendance and reading comprehension.

However, for some families a home visit may feel intrusive or something to be fearful of. It's important that you clearly communicate the purpose of the proposed home visit and emphasize to families, using an interpreter as needed, that it is completely optional. **Family visits also don't have to happen in the home. In order to be respectful of families, you can offer a choice of locations in the community where you might meet, such as at a library or religious center the family attends.** If a family agrees to hosting a home visit, before arranging it have your initial contact be by someone who speaks the family's home language and can fully share the purpose of the home visit.

In their article on the *Colorín Colorado* website, Ernst-Slavit and Mason (n.d.) recommend that educators visit families early in the school year before there are any issues or concerns with the student. This will set the tone for the school year. As you prepare for a home visit, be sure to set a purpose for the visit, such as sharing resources or collaborating to set academic goals. It's essential to schedule in advance and communicate details of the visit in the family's home language. It's also important to take someone who can interpret for you if you do not speak the family's home language. Before you go, be sure to learn the names of the family members that you will be meeting with and also perhaps learn a few words in the home language as a way to show respect for their culture. As you prepare for the home visit, think of a positive story that you want to share about the student. Figure 7.3, Planning for an ML Home Visit, can help you prepare for a positive home visit experience that will help you build your relationship with an ML family.

Figure 7.3   Planning for an ML Home Visit

Student's name:
Parent(s)' or guardian(s)' name(s):
Goal of home visit:
Staff who will make initial contact:
Location of home visit:
Need for an interpreter ❑   Yes ❑   No If yes, language: _____
Positive story to share about student:
Resources to share with family:

Source: Adapted from Staehr Fenner, 2014, p. 123.

Communicate Effectively With ML Families

A third strategy for uniting schools, families, and communities is to consider and strengthen how you communicate with ML families. Often when thinking about communicating with ML families, we think only about how we can reach families with important information. However, it is also necessary that families feel that they can communicate effectively with their children's teachers and schools. When you share information with families, consider the following questions:

❑ Do all families have access to this information?

❑ Will all families be able to understand the information that is shared?

❑ Do families have a way of letting us know if they do not understand?

❑ What can we do to make the information more accessible and easier to understand for all families?

Parent and guardian interviews or surveys at the school level could be one way of determining the best ways of communicating with families. In addition, we also recommend less formal methods, such as one-on-one conversations with parents or guardians using interpreters as needed and also speaking with students to ask how their parents or guardians feel most comfortable communicating (e.g., in person, by phone, by text, using an app). It is also important to recognize that you may need to be flexible and use a variety of different types of communication strategies in order to foster stronger communication with ML families. Figure 7.4, Considerations When Communicating With ML Families, provides some considerations for using different communication tools or strategies with ML families.

Figure 7.4   Considerations When Communicating With ML Families

Communication Tool or Strategy	Consideration
Texting apps with translated services	Talking Points and Remind are two free apps that teachers can use to send messages to families. Both offer the option to translate messages. As with all virtual translation services, it is important to recognize that the translation may not be entirely accurate. Talking Points also allows recipients to respond in their home languages. Remind doesn't allow for responses, but it does allow teachers to send PDFs, photos, and voice clips. Certain language groups might be more likely to use different apps (e.g., WhatsApp), so we recommend asking parents and students which texting apps they're already using and begin with those.
Social media	While social media can be an effective tool for spreading the word to ML families, it should not be depended on as not all families might use or regularly access social media sites. If you are using social media as a communication tool, provide translations of the messages that you share.

Communication Tool or Strategy	Consideration
Translated materials or notes	Translated materials and notes can be sent home in students' homework folders. It is important to have reliable translations of materials, and it is also important to recognize that students' parents or guardians might have a range of literacy skills in their home language.
Bilingual staff or family liaison	Bilingual staff or a family liaison can be invaluable for fostering parent communication and outreach. However, it's important that bilingual staff are not called away from teaching or student support to interpret.
Face-to-face options	Face-to-face options can be a great way to communicate with ML families. Possible opportunities might be during drop-off or pickup, at community events, or at school events. Consider if you will need to secure an interpreter for these interactions.

Caroline Espinoza-Navarrete and Aimee Ackley at Thomas O'Brien Academy of Science and Technology (TOAST) in Albany, New York, created a generic family invitation form that can be completed and used for all types of events that occur at the school. Family members become familiar with the form during their time at the school. The form is translated into families' home languages so teachers have less need for ongoing translation services (see Figure 7.5, TOAST Generic Family Invitation Form).

Figure 7.5   TOAST Generic Family Invitation Form

You are invited to come to TOAST school:

Day of the Week		Month			Date	Time
1) Sunday 5) Thursday		1) January 5) May 9) September				
2) Monday 6) Friday		2) February 6) June 10) October				
3) Tuesday 7) Saturday		3) March 7) July 11) November				
4) Wednesday		4) April 8) August 12) December				

A Musical Concert	Open House	An Athletic Event
A Play	Parent Workshop	Dinner

(Continued)

Figure 7.5   (Continued)

A Dance Performance		Peace Parade		A Movie	
Ice Cream Social		Field Day		Scholastic Book Fair	
Multicultural Event		Academic Event		Fun Event With Your Child	
Science Fair		Art Show		Kindergarten Moving Up Ceremony	
Father's Breakfast		Parent Meeting (PTA)		Graduation for _____ Grade	

This event is free	The school will provide food for this event.		This event has limited spaces.	
This event costs	Please bring food to share (Pot Luck).		For questions, please contact _____	

Please return this form to your child's teacher.

☐ I plan to attend this event.

☐ I need an interpreter.

Name:_____

Phone number:_____

Email address:_____

Source: Created by Caroline Espinoza-Navarrete and Aimee Ackley (Generic Parent Invitation -English), Thomas O'Brien Academy of Science & Technology, Albany, New York.

Overcome Barriers to ML Family Engagement

A fourth strategy for uniting schools, families, and communities is to overcome barriers to family involvement. To identify possible barriers, you can brainstorm general barriers as a team as well as barriers related to a particular event. If possible, you can also survey families to identify supports that they may need in order to take part in school events and activities.

For Application Activity 7b, consider possible barriers we have listed to ML family engagement in your context. Then, for each barrier consider possible solutions.

There is also space to add your own barrier and solutions. An example of language as a possible barrier has been completed for you. As we mentioned in the previous section on communicating effectively with ML families, there are several possible solutions to language barriers, such as using bilingual parent liaisons and staff, having translated materials, and having parent volunteers who communicate information.

Application Activity 7b. Brainstorming Possible Barriers to ML Family Engagement and Possible Solutions

Possible Barriers	Possible Solutions
Language	• Parent liaisons • Bilingual staff • Translated materials • Home language phone tree/volunteers
Transportation	
Time	
Childcare	
Understanding of school system and role of parent	
Fear	
Other _____	

Now that you have had an opportunity to brainstorm barriers and solutions to family engagement, we would like to share some of the solutions we have seen used in schools. While filming the video for this book, we had the great privilege of attending a family night that was held in the Syracuse City School District. Families of ELs or former English learners in the district were invited to take part in an evening event in which they were able to meet and talk with their children's English as a new language (ENL) or former ENL teachers. The event was publicized through adult ESOL classes and the schools. It was held in the Refugee Assistance Program Center, which was a familiar location for many families. The event began with a dinner and was followed by a welcome by one of the district ENL coaches. Next, families moved into classrooms by language groups. The ENL teachers from throughout the district circulated among the classrooms to meet with parents. To see the agenda for the evening, go to the Three Steps You Can Take section at the end of the chapter.

To learn more about the event, view the video *Building Relationships With Multilingual Families Through Family Engagement Events*.

 Video 7.1

Building Relationships With Multilingual Families Through Family Engagement Events

resources.corwin.com/CulturallyResponsiveTeaching

Figure 7.6, Possible Barriers to ML Family Engagement and Possible Solutions, provides some other examples of strategies that districts are using to overcome barriers to family engagement. While some of these solutions may be beyond your control, there are possible solutions that you can explore with school and district administrators.

To respond to the barrier of transportation, some schools provide district busses to take families from their apartment complexes to the schools for certain school events such as Back-to-School Night or school concerts. Other transportation

Figure 7.6   Possible Barriers to ML Family Engagement and Possible Solutions

Possible Barriers	Possible Solutions
Language	• Parent/guardian liaisons • Bilingual staff • Translated materials • Home language phone tree/volunteers
Transportation	• Rides to school events • Ride-sharing resource • Information about public transportation • Meeting with families in their community
Time	• Flexibility in scheduling conferences and events • Parent/guardian survey
Child care	• Provide child care for conferences and school events
Understanding of school system and role of parent (or guardian)	• ML meetings to provide information about school system and education • School tours • Community volunteers to share information in home language
Fear	• Demonstrate support for ML families (regardless of status) • Adult education programs • Family support groups

Source: SupportEd, 2018.

solutions include ride-sharing resources, information about public transportation, and meeting with families in their communities rather than at the schools, which might be less accessible.

Possible solutions to barriers of time include having flexibility in scheduling conferences and events and conducting a parent/guardian survey to find out about possible time constraints for families. An easy solution to child care issues is to provide child care for conferences and school events. Explore the possibility of middle school, high school, or college students needing service hours who would be willing to volunteer their time.

Possible solutions to strengthening families' understanding of the school system include having ML family meetings to provide information about the school and the education system, along with sharing strategies that families can use to support their children's academic success. School or community volunteers can also be recruited to provide this information in families' home languages.

To respond to the potential fear that families might feel, it is important that schools demonstrate commitment to ML families regardless of their immigrant status. To demonstrate this support, use inclusive language and be transparent about offering resources and support for undocumented students. Families should have access to these resources without having to share their status. However, by being open about your commitment to undocumented students, students are more likely to ask you for help when they need it. Additionally, when programs such as adult education programs or family support groups are conducted in schools, families will become increasingly more comfortable and familiar with school settings.

Empower ML Families

In addition to removing barriers to ML family engagement, it is also important to use strategies to empower ML families. Fostering ML family engagement and empowering ML families has benefits beyond academic outcomes for students. Empowering ML families benefits the school, ML parents and guardians, and the community. In order to support ML families in this way, we can apply a scaffolded advocacy framework (Staehr Fenner, 2014). In Chapter 4, we explored the concept of scaffolded instruction, temporary instructional supports that allow MLs to effectively engage with academic content and foster language acquisition. In a similar vein, **scaffolded advocacy entails providing the "just-right" amount of advocacy for MLs, with the goal of MLs and their families successfully advocating for themselves.** As families become more familiar with the US educational system and learn advocacy skills, they will require fewer advocacy efforts from others to obtain an equitable education for their children (Staehr Fenner, 2014). Educators can use scaffolded advocacy as they strive to empower ML families and in doing so will support ML parents and guardians in being better positioned to advocate for themselves and their children in the future.

To reflect more on scaffolded advocacy and the benefit of empowering ML families, please complete Application Activity 7c. For this activity, we'd like you to read the following quote and answer the reflection questions.

Application Activity 7c. Reflecting on Parent Quote

"Before I wanted to help in the classrooms, but I felt ashamed or embarrassed and felt like I would not be of value or that I did not have anything to offer. I thought to myself, how can I help? But then [after training to be a volunteer] what I learned is that I am valuable and I have a lot to offer and even though I did not go to school very much (four months of first grade and I did not go beyond that), I learned that there is a lot I can do to help and I am glad to be a volunteer here. Even when my kids no longer go here, I still plan to help [the school]. I think what we should really change is our roots of where we come from. As Latino families, we often think of well, you leave the child at school and let the teacher do all the work. But what we are learning here is this school is about collaboration and what we want is for our children to be

(Continued)

(Continued)

more successful than we were. We can do that by talking to them and telling them the importance of education, and that is important, but also as ourselves, we need to make the effort and we need to be an example for them that you can do something if you try hard" (NASEM, 2017, p. 279).

Reflection Questions

1. What does this quote suggest about possible barriers to ML family engagement?

2. What does it suggest about how to foster ML family engagement?

3. What are some opportunities that your school provides for families to take on leadership roles in your school? How might you support ML families in taking on these roles?

There are several different ways to support ML family empowerment (see Application Activity 7d). One strategy is to institute adult education programs in schools for parents of MLs that support the parents in learning new skills and also help raise their comfort level with being in the schools. Sydney taught adult ESOL classes in an elementary school as part of a family literacy program and found that when parents were used to coming to the school for English classes they were more likely to participate in other school events. Diane worked in a rural district where there was no adult ESOL class for her elementary students' parents and guardians, so she partnered with the local community college to begin a class for them, which was held at the elementary school. Word spread to their colleagues and other family members who also wanted to learn English, and the local sweet potato and cucumber processing facility provided transportation to those employees who sought English instruction. Just as with Sydney's experience, those parents who took part felt more comfortable coming to the school to meet with teachers and attend events.

Syracuse City School District (SCSD) hosts an educational program called Parent University, which has the goals of giving support to families so "they may achieve personal academic and non-academic goals; providing parents and families with the necessary resources to support their children's emotional growth and development; and increasing the number of parents who feel positively connected to their child's school" (SCSD, n.d., para. 2). Some of the topics covered during Parent University include CPR, learning with an iPad, and building a strong credit history. To learn more about Parent University and other strategies used by SCSD to foster ML family engagement, watch the video *Building Relationships With Parents Through Parent University and Nationality Workers*.

Video 7.2

Building Relationships With Parents Through Parent University and Nationality Workers

resources.corwin.com/CulturallyResponsiveTeaching

Other strategies for empowering ML families are to institute district- and school-level parent advisory committees for MLs, take steps to ensure that committees and school support teams include parents of MLs, and offer volunteer opportunities for ML families.

Gardner (2019b) recommends hosting an ML parent panel in which three to six parents (or guardians) share information about schools in their home country and other relevant information. This could be an opportunity to have families share with the community what they have found challenging about navigating the school system and what has helped them with these challenges. Gardner also recommends inviting ML parents to provide input on the rules and values that are practiced at school and explore differences that might exist between home and school practice. In addition, she recommends having ML families provide input on the ML curriculum. For example, as you are reviewing your curriculum to ensure that it provides both windows and mirrors for students, include ML families in these critical discussions. **One example of a district that actively engages its ML parents is Manassas City Public Schools (MCPS) in Virginia. MCPS formed an ESOL advisory committee that is made up of parents, community members, staff, and students. The committee meets three times a year to provide guidance and recommendations on the ESOL program and the Title III grant. Interpreters are present at each meeting to ensure parents can meaningfully participate and share their perspectives.**

In her blog post "Yes, We Could!! The Story of How Latino Parents Revived Our School's PTA," Fulton County Schools, Georgia's bilingual community liaison Ingrid Montenegro (2018) describes steps that their school took to revive a parent teacher association (PTA) by reaching out to parents and providing the type of scaffolded support parents needed to become involved in the PTA. To respond to parent concerns about not knowing what to do and not having enough time, Montenegro writes,

> I promised that I would stay and work side by side with them. I told them that together we would learn everything we needed to make our organization work and grow. I started by offering leadership and protocol classes with the help of a Latino community leader. Little by little, with successes and failures, the pioneer Latino parents started organizing their first fundraising events and leading their own board meetings. (2018, para. 6)

Reflection Questions

1. What are community organizations that you might collaborate with in support of ML families?

2. How might you collaborate with them?

Application Activity 7d.
Family Empowerment Scenarios

To apply the concept of ML family empowerment, let's take a look at three scenarios. Select the elementary, middle school, or high school scenario from the ones that follow. Then, answer the reflection questions.

ELEMENTARY SCHOOL

While your elementary school has an active parent volunteer community, you've noticed that there are no ML parents or guardians involved in volunteering. You've sent out information to ML parents in their home languages to encourage them to volunteer, but still, no ML parents have expressed a desire to volunteer at school. You would like to collaborate with your school's volunteer coordinator and administrators to ensure ML parents are included as volunteers and take on meaningful volunteer roles.

MIDDLE SCHOOL

Your middle school PTA president and administrators are complaining that despite there being a significant number of MLs in the school, none of the ML parents have joined the PTA or attend PTA meetings. PTA meetings are held on the first Wednesday of the month at 9:00 a.m. They feel that families of MLs are not interested in supporting

(Continued)

(Continued)

the school. You would like to brainstorm some ideas with the PTA president and your school administrators to increase ML family attendance and engagement.

HIGH SCHOOL

Your high school has a robust program for parents (or guardians) of junior and senior students to provide them information about high school graduation and options after high school. These monthly meetings are held during weekday evenings, and the school's guidance counselors are tasked with planning the content of the meetings and doing the parent and guardian outreach. While many fluent English-speaking parents attend the meetings, you notice that your MLs aren't represented. You'd like to work with the counselors and school administration to increase ML family engagement in the graduation, college, and career information program.

Reflection Questions

1. What steps might you take to strengthen ML family engagement related to the scenario you selected?

2. Who might you collaborate with?

3. What resources might you need?

THREE STEPS YOU CAN TAKE

Now that we've explored five strategies for uniting students' schools, families, and communities, we would like to suggest three steps that you can take in your own schools and communities, as well as tools that will guide you in your work.

Step 1: *Determine family engagement priorities.*

An important first step to increasing ML family engagement is to determine your ML family engagement priorities. To help you prioritize your areas of focus, individually or as a team complete Figure 7.7, Determining ML Family Engagement Scale, which is divided into mindsets and actions. For each area, indicate your evidence for choosing the rating you did. Then, answer the questions that follow. In order to determine your evidence, we also suggest you ask your families information captured in this tool and additional information you'd like to obtain through a focus group, survey, and/or through a conversation with them, using interpreters as needed. Many times, we make assumptions about what ML families want and need from their schools and communities, but it can be rare to ask families themselves.

Figure 7.7   Determining ML Family Engagement Scalew

Area of ML Family Engagement	Scale: 1 (Lowest) to 5 (Highest)					My/Our Evidence
My/Our Mindsets						
1. Our school (or district)* values its ML families' home languages and cultures.	1	2	3	4	5	
2. Our school staff has an assets-based perspective when working with ML families and has high expectations of families.	1	2	3	4	5	
3. Our school demonstrates a commitment to all ML families regardless of immigration status.	1	2	3	4	5	

*Please substitute "district" for "school" when appropriate.

(Continued)

Figure 7.7 (Continued)

Area of ML Family Engagement	Scale: 1 (Lowest) to 5 (Highest)					My/Our Evidence
My/Our Actions						
4. Our school provides a welcoming environment for ML families through visual artifacts (e.g., flags, maps, student work) and the inclusion of materials and resources in families' home languages.	1	2	3	4	5	
5. Our school supports educators in learning about ML families' backgrounds, communities, and home language in order to foster understanding of ML families' perspectives.	1	2	3	4	5	
6. Our ML families participate in their children's education as much as our non-ML families.	1	2	3	4	5	
7. Our school conducts home visits with its ML families if families are comfortable with them or uses other creative strategies to build relationships with families.	1	2	3	4	5	
8. Our school offers flexibly scheduled and flexibly located events that are specific to the needs of ML families; we also work to increase opportunities for ML families to take part in whole-school events.	1	2	3	4	5	
9. Our school communicates information well to ML families and makes use of interpreters and translated materials to effectively share information with families.	1	2	3	4	5	
10. ML families are aware of ways to communicate with their children's teachers and school and reach out when they have a question or issue to discuss.	1	2	3	4	5	
11. Our school has an appropriate rate of ML family volunteers in classrooms and for events, based on percentage of ML families enrolled in the school.	1	2	3	4	5	

Area of ML Family Engagement	Scale: 1 (Lowest) to 5 (Highest)					My/Our Evidence
12. Our school partners with local organizations to support ML families who may need support for basic needs (e.g., health care, food pantries, housing services) or to provide other types of services.	1	2	3	4	5	
13. Our school advocates for its ML families who have not yet developed their own voice in the school context.	1	2	3	4	5	
14. Our school develops ML family leadership so that families can serve as their own advocates.	1	2	3	4	5	
15. Our school has a plan to increase ML family engagement and advocacy.	1	2	3	4	5	

Source: Adapted from Staehr Fenner, 2014; Breiseth et al., 2011.

Reflection Questions

1. In what areas do you feel that your school or district is taking appropriate actions to support ML family engagement?

2. In what areas do you feel that your school or district most needs to improve?

3. Which one area would you like to focus on to increase ML family engagement?

4. What will be your first step?

Step 2: *Host a community walk.*

Lauren Markham, Community School Manager of Oakland International High School (OIHS) in California, noted that OIHS coined the term "community walks" (personal communication, November 25, 2019). OIHS is a public school for newcomers in the rapidly gentrifying city of Oakland. At OIHS, teachers are divided into groups and led through a professional development experience by students, families, and community members over the course of one Friday in the fall. Students plan for the event, set up classrooms, and meet with teachers to present salient information about their communities. After the field trips, teachers take part in restorative justice circles aligned with different community groups (e.g., Afghan, Burmese) to process their experience. Figure 7.8 is the template that OIHS students use to plan their community walk.

Figure 7.8   Community Walk Student Planning Template

Community Walk Name: _____

What is a community walk? *A community walk helps teachers learn more about students' communities and cultures. It's like a field trip—where the teachers are the students and the students/parents are the teachers! What important things do we want our teachers to learn about our communities?*

What are our community's assets (strengths)? Name 3.

1. _____

2. _____

3. _____

What are our community's challenges? Name 3.

1. _____

2. _____

3. _____

What's the Plan?

Time	Activity	What Do You Want Teachers to See and Learn?
8:30–9:00	Teachers meet to frame the day, prepare for walks, set intentions.	
9:00–10:00	Student Teach-In: You teach a class to your teachers about your community's history, backgrounds, strengths, and challenges. You can have teachers read books, watch videos, listen to stories, and ask questions. (You are in charge—they have to listen to you and do what you say!)	
10:00–11:15	Field Trip # 1: Visit a place where we can learn about the histories, strengths, challenges, and/or resources of your community.	
11:15–12:30	Field Trip # 2: Visit a place where we can learn about the histories, strengths, challenges, and/or resources of your community.	
12:30–1:30	FOOD! Let's share a delicious meal together! OIHS will pay. This can be at a home or at a restaurant. Where should we go?	

Source: OIHS, 2020.

Figure 7.9 is a sample agenda filled in for a community walk in a Salvadoran neighborhood. You will notice how this agenda includes a push toward providing a deeper understanding of the political situation in El Salvador along with social justice for Salvadoran immigrants.

Figure 7.9   Sample Agenda for Salvadoran Community Walk

El Salvador Community Walk Schedule	
Time	**Activity**
8:30–9:00	Teachers meet in cafeteria: framing of day, preparation for walks, and intention setting.
9:00–10:15	Student Teach-In
10:15–10:30	Break
10:30–11:15	Skype with Jose Cabezas, Reuters photojournalist based in El Salvador, about current political situation and migration root causes.
11:15–12:00	Leave for Immigrant Legal Defense
12:00–1:00	Visit Immigrant Legal Defense, an organization dedicated to promoting justice through the provision of legal representation to underserved immigrant communities.
1:15–2:00	Lunch @ Los Olivos Restaurant

Source: Adapted from OIHS, 2020.

Step 3: *Host an ML Family Night Event with parent–teacher conferences.*

Plan an event to help connect ML families with their children's teachers. An event like this can be used to build relationships with ML families, engage students and families in goal setting, and respond to families' questions and concerns. We have provided an example of the agenda used by SCSD, Figure 7.10, Syracuse City School District Parent Meet-and-Greet Agenda. We have also included a tool—Figure 7.11, Family Night Event Planning—to support your initial planning efforts.

Figure 7.10   Syracuse City School District Parent Meet-and-Greet Agenda

OFFICE OF ENL, WORLD LANGUAGES, AND BILINGUAL EDUCATION

PARENT MEET-AND-GREET

AGENDA

5:00–5:45	Dinner Is Served
5:45–6:00	Welcome Address
6:00–7:00	Conferences*

See conference schedule below.

Time	Room 3	Room 6	Room 7	Room 8
	Languages & School Names			
	Somali/Swahili	Karen/Burmese	Nepali/French	Arabic/Tigrinya
6:00–6:15	Henninger, Brighton Academy, Huntington, Blodgett, Bellevue, Lemoyne, Seymour	Corcoran, Ed Smith, HW, Delaware, McKinley, Dr. King	PSLA, Grand, Roberts, Franklin, Salem Hyde, Webster	Nottingham, Frazer, Lincoln, Dr. Weeks, Porter, Latin
6:15–6:30	Corcoran, Ed Smith, HW, Delaware, McKinley, Dr. King	Nottingham, Frazer, Lincoln, Dr. Weeks, Porter, Latin	Henninger, Brighton Academy, Huntington, Blodgett, Bellevue, Lemoyne, Seymour	PSLA, Grand, Roberts, Franklin, Salem Hyde, Webster
6:30–6:45	Nottingham, Frazer, Lincoln, Dr. Weeks, Porter, Latin	PSLA, Grand, Roberts, Franklin, Salem Hyde, Webster	Corcoran, Ed Smith, HW, Delaware, McKinley, Dr. King	Henninger, Brighton Academy, Huntington, Blodgett, Bellevue, Lemoyne, Seymour
6:45–7:00	PSLA, Grand, Roberts, Franklin, Salem Hyde, Webster	Henninger, Brighton Academy, Huntington, Blodgett, Bellevue, Lemoyne, Seymour	Nottingham, Frazer, Lincoln, Dr. Weeks, Porter, Latin	Corcoran, Ed Smith, HW, Delaware, McKinley, Dr. King

Figure 7.11 ML Family Night Event Planning Tool

Title of event:
Date and time:
Location:
Purpose:
Participants:

Possible barriers to ML family attendance with solutions:

Barrier 1:   Solution:

Barrier 2:   Solution:

Barrier 3:   Solution:

Agenda (key activities for event):

Task	Description	Person or People Responsible
Reserve space and date		
Invite teachers, staff, and interpreters		
Plan publicity and disseminate		
Provide food and drink		
Remove possible barriers for families		
Share additional resources with ML families		
Invite community organizations		
Other: _____		

Summary of Key Ideas

- Create a welcoming environment for ML families through the inclusion of flags, maps, student work, and materials and resources in families' home language.

- Build relationships with ML families through such strategies as community walks and home visits.

- Communicate with ML families through a variety of ways and share different ways that ML families can communicate effectively with the school and their children's teachers.

- Use strategies to remove possible barriers to ML family engagement by addressing barriers of language, transportation, child care, and others.

- Empower ML families by supporting their involvement in school organizations and committees and by sharing volunteer opportunities.

Chapter 7 Reflection Questions

1. What is a new strategy for strengthening ML family engagement that you would like to try?

2. What steps might you take to identify barriers to ML family engagement in your context?

References

Breiseth, L., Robertson, K., & Lafond, S. (2011). *A guide for engaging ELL families: Twenty strategies for school leaders*. https://www.colorincolorado.org/sites/default/files/Engaging_ELL_Families_FINAL.pdf

Calzada, E., Huang, K., Hernandez, M., Soriano, E., Acra, C. F., Dawson-McClure, S., Kamboukos, D., & Brotman, L. (2015). Family and teacher characteristics as predictors of parent involvement in education during early childhood among Afro-Caribbean and Latino immigrant families. *Urban Education*, *50*(7), 870–896.

Chapman, T. K. (2007). Interrogating classroom relationships and events: Using portraiture and critical race theory in education research. *Educational Researcher*, *36*(3), 156–162. https://doi.org/10.3102/0013189X07301437vChapman

Choi, J. (2017). Why I'm not involved: Parental involvement from a parent's perspective. *Phi Delta Kappan*, *99*(3), 46–49.

DeCapua, A., Smathers, W., & Tang, L. (2009). *Meeting the needs of students with limited or interrupted schooling*. University of Michigan Press ELT.

DeCuir-Gunby, J. T., Walker-DeVose, D. C., Lynn, M., & Dixon, A. D. (2013). Expanding the counterstory: The potential for critical race mixed methods studies in education. In *Handbook of critical race theory in education* (pp. 248–259). Routledge.

Delgado, R. (2013). Storytelling for oppositionists and others. In R. Delgado & J. Stefancic (Eds.), *Critical race theory: The cutting edge* (3rd ed.). Temple University Press.

Ernst-Slavit, G., & Mason, M. (n.d.). *Making your first ELL home visit: A guide for classroom teachers*. https://www.colorincolorado.org/article/making-your-first-ell-home-visit-guide-classroom-teachers

Ferguson, C. (2008). *The school–family connection: Looking at the larger picture—A review of current literature*. National Center for Family and Community Connections With Schools.

Garcia, M. E., Frunzi, K., Dean, C. B., Flores, N., &. Miller, K. B. (2016). *Toolkit of resources for engaging families and the community as partners in education: Part 2—Building a cultural bridge* (REL 2016–2151). U.S. Department of Education, Institute of Education Sciences, National Center for Education Evaluation and Regional Assistance, Regional Educational Laboratory Pacific.

Gardner, L. (2019a). *10 possible alternatives to international night*. https://www.immigrants refugeesandschools.org/post/10-possible-alternatives-to-international-night

Gardner, L. (2019b). *Separate or together: Unpacking the "EL family event" vs. "all-school family event" debate*. https://www.immigrantsrefugeesandschools.org/post/separate-or-together-unpacking-the-el-family-event-vs-all-school-family-event-debate

Gorski, P. (2008). Good intentions are not enough: A decolonizing intercultural education. *Intercultural Education*, *19*(6), 515–525.

Henderson, A. T., & Mapp, K. L. (2002). *A new wave of evidence: The impact of school, family, and community connections on student achievement*. National Center for Family and Community Connections With Schools.

Lindholm-Leary, K. J. (2015). *Sobrato family foundation early academic and literacy project after five full years of implementation: Final research report*. Sobrato Family Foundation.

Montenegro, B. (2018). *Yes, we could!! The story of how Latino parents revived our school's PTA*. https://getsupported.net/latino-parents-revived-our-schools-pta/

National Academies of Sciences, Engineering, and Medicine. (2017). *Promoting the educational success of children and youth learning English: Promising futures, Box 7.5*. National Academies Press. https://doi.org/10.17226/24677

Noel, A., Stark, P., & Redford, J. (2016). *Parent and family involvement in education, from the National Household Education Surveys Program of 2012: First look.* NCES 2013-029-REV. http://nces.ed.gov/pubs2013/2013028rev.pdf

Office of the Education Ombudsman. (2012). *Engaged parents, successful students: An overview of local and national parent engagement efforts.* http://www.roadmapproject.org/wp-content/uploads/2012/11/Final-Report_Engaged-ParentsSuccessful-Students-Report-9-12-12.pdf

Safir, S. (2017). Community walks create bonds of understanding. *Edutopia.* https://www.edutopia.org/blog/community-walks-create-bonds-understanding-shane-safir

Sheldon, S. B., & Jung, S. B. (2015). The family engagement partnership: Student outcome evaluation. *Johns Hopkins University School of Education.* http://www.pthvp.org/wp-content/uploads/2016/09/JHU-STUDY_FINAL-REPORT.pdf

Sibley, E., & Dearing, E. (2014). Family educational involvement and child achievement in early elementary school for American-born and immigrant families. *Psychology in the Schools, 51*(8), 814–831.

Simpson Baird, A. (2015). Beyond the greatest hits: A counterstory of English learner parent involvement. *School Community Journal, 25*(2), 153–175.

Staehr Fenner, D. (2014). *Advocating for English learners: A guide for educators.* Corwin.

Stefanaski, A., Valli, L., & Jacobson, R. (2016). Beyond involvement and engagement: The role of the family in school–community partnerships. *School Community Journal, 26(2)*, 135–160.

SupportEd. (2018). *Possible barriers to EL family engagement and solutions.* https://getsupported.net/wp-content/uploads/Barriers_and_Solutions_Tool.pdf

Syracuse City School District. (n.d.). *Parent university.* http://www.syracusecityschools.com/ParentUniversity

Tobin, J., Adair, J. K., & Arzubiaga, A. (2013). *Children crossing borders: Immigrant parent and teacher perspectives on preschool for children of immigrants.* Russell Sage Foundation.

Zacarian, D., & Soto, I. (2020). *Responsive schooling for culturally and linguistically diverse students.* W. W. Norton & Co.

CHAPTER EIGHT

Putting It All Together

CHAPTER OVERVIEW

In our final chapter, we will explore advocacy tools and strategies that you can use as you work to implement our five principles in your context. We'll begin the chapter by introducing the National Education Association's (NEA) five-step framework for EL (English learner) advocacy and reflect on how it can be applied to strengthening culturally responsive teaching for MLs (multilingual learners) and their families. As we explore the advocacy framework, we'll apply it to a specific case study. Then, we will share several examples of innovative programs that are being used in various school districts that help to foster a districtwide climate that is supportive of MLs. We'll conclude the chapter by sharing some final thoughts on the urgent need for culturally responsive teaching (CRT) work and highlighting key themes that are found throughout this book.

USING ADVOCACY TOOLS AND STRATEGIES TO SUPPORT YOUR CRT WORK

In their advocacy guidance document *All In! How Educators Can Advocate for English Language Learners* (2015), the National Education Association offers a five-step approach for planning and carrying out advocacy work. We have used and shared this framework extensively, and as a result, we have slightly modified the language and order of these steps from their original form. For each of these five steps, we will explore how it can be applied to your CRT work with MLs and their families, offer recommendations and reflection questions to guide your work, and explore what the step might look like in practice. The five steps are as follows:

 Step 1. Isolate the issue.

 Step 2. Know students' and families' rights and relevant research.

 Step 3. Develop your allies.

 Step 4. Identify your outlets for change.

 Step 5. Organize and educate others. (adapted from NEA, 2015)

Depending on your advocacy issue, these steps may not necessarily progress in this specific order. Also, as you work to bring CRT practices into your context, you'll find that you might cycle through this process multiple times in varied ways. As we mentioned in Chapter 7, we support a scaffolded advocacy approach to provide MLs and their families the tools they need to advocate for themselves, and this collaboration is imperative to the five-step process (Staehr Fenner, 2014).

As we use the terms "advocate" and "ally" throughout this chapter, we should examine what those terms mean to us and consider how we might serve as both advocates and allies when engaging with MLs and their families.

Ally: A person or group that provides assistance and support in an ongoing effort, activity, or struggle (Merriam Webster, n.d.b)

Advocate: One who supports or promotes the interests of a cause or group (Merriam Webster, n.d.a)

Application Activity 8a. Reflecting on Being an Advocate or an Ally

Describe a time when you acted as an advocate or as an ally. What did you do? What motivated you to take action?

Step I: *Isolate the issue.*

Step 1 is the critical step in which you make sure that your advocacy efforts are correctly focused so as to address the issue or concern that you wish to respond to. There are many advocacy issues to choose from, but narrowing your focus and choosing one issue in which you have the opportunity to make a change is key (Staehr Fenner, 2014).  During this step, your job is to gather information from the concerned stakeholders in order to determine what advocacy efforts are needed and which internal and external factors may be at play. It is also important to reflect on whether the issue is being framed through a deficit perspective and how you can reframe that perspective to consider the students' and families' assets as you speak with others about the issue. Once you have taken steps to clarify the issue and have reflected on your findings, determine your ML advocacy goal. Figure 8.1, Isolating the Issue Tool, can help you think through the process that you might use for Step 1 of the Advocacy Goal-Setting Template (Appendix A).

Figure 8.1   Isolating the Issue Tool

Describe the issue		
List the stakeholders		
Share possible internal and external factors		
Information-gathering steps to clarify the issue with stakeholders and a corresponding timeline for each step	*Steps*	*Timeline*
Note findings from information gathering steps		
Reframe the deficit perspective		
Summarize advocacy goal(s)		

Let's explore what Step 1 might look like with a specific ML advocacy scenario that we will carry through all five steps in this chapter to contextualize our work.

Scenario

In a midsized school district, administration and kindergarten teachers are upset that some ML families don't preregister their kindergarten students for school before school begins each September. Preregistration for kindergarten takes place at the district central office and includes a short assessment of students' language and skills (e.g., identification of colors, numbers, letters). Following the preregistration period, schools hold a Kindergarten Preview Day during which students can be introduced to the school and kindergarten teachers. To publicize the kindergarten preregistration, elementary schools in the district send home information with all current students and share dates with the local media and on school social media channels such as the district Facebook page. However, at the beginning of each school year there are always many new kindergarten students who "turn up" that haven't been preregistered or assessed, and the result is a somewhat chaotic start to the school year. Amanda, an ESOL teacher, and Tony, a kindergarten teacher at one of the schools, have teamed up to take on this issue. Figure 8.2 is an example of their completed Isolating the Issue Tool.

Figure 8.2   Isolating the Issue Tool: Kindergarten Registration Scenario

Describe the issue	ML families not preregistering their children for kindergarten; new kindergarten students unable to come to the Kindergarten Preview Day so are not assessed prior to the beginning of the year	
List the stakeholders	Kindergarten teachers, ESOL teachers, early childhood assessment specialists, district and school administrators, ML families and students, students new to the district, local media	
Share possible internal and external factors	Language barriers, publicity of registration events, unfamiliarity with the district office, family work schedules, transportation, child care, limited family outreach to ML families	
Information-gathering steps to clarify the issue with stakeholders and a corresponding timeline for each step	*Steps*	*Timeline*
	1. Discuss goals for kindergarten preregistration with kindergarten teachers, assessment specialists, and administrators.	December
	2. Through survey, focus groups, and one-on-one conversations with leaders in ML family communities and former parents of ML kindergartners, explore possible challenges to kindergarten preregistration.	January

Note findings from information gathering steps	• Teachers and administrators wish to substantially decrease the number of families registering their children at the start of the school year.
	• ML family surveys, focus groups, and discussions revealed that possible barriers for kindergarten preregistration include the lack of publicity of these events in their home languages, the lack of familiarity with the system for preregistration, and the timing and location of preregistration opportunities.
Reframe the deficit perspective	Rather than assuming ML families are choosing to overlook the times for kindergarten registration, consider how educators can use kindergarten preregistration events to begin to build or strengthen relationships with ML families.
Summarize advocacy goal(s)	• Increase number of families completing kindergarten preregistration prior to the start of the school year by 25 percent through increased outreach in ML communities and holding registration events at locations and times that are convenient to families.
	• Expand preregistration events to include opportunities to share key information with ML families, learn about families, and build relationships with ML families—all in their preferred languages.

Step 2: *Know students' and families' rights and relevant research.*

In order to strengthen your case for the need and urgency around ML advocacy, it is essential to know the rights of ML students and families. In addition, we suggest you refer to relevant research in your advocacy efforts. In this way, you can draw from rights and research to back up your advocacy issue so that it is not one lone voice advocating for MLs and their families. The US Department of Education, Office of Civil Rights (2015a, 2015b) offers a series of fact sheets and memos related to the rights of ELs and families who speak a language other than English in the home.

Here are some examples of these rights that can be helpful in your advocacy work for MLs:

- Students, regardless of their language proficiency level, "are entitled to an equal opportunity to participate in all programs, including prekindergarten, magnet, gifted and talented, career and technical education, arts, and athletics programs; Advanced Placement (AP) and International Baccalaureate (IB) courses; clubs; and honor societies" (US Department of Education, 2015a, para. 11).

- Schools must communicate in a language that families can understand. They must share all information about programs, services, and activities that are shared with parents and guardians who are proficient in English (US Department of Education, 2015b, para. 2).

- Schools must respond to a parent's or guardian's request for language assistance, even if the student is proficient in English. This assistance must be provided free of charge by trained staff or competent outside resources (US Department of Education, 2015b).

Returning to our kindergarten preregistration scenario and considering students' and families' rights, Amanda and Tony know that ML families have a right to receive notification about the registration events in their home language, as well as to have an interpreter at the events. Families also have a right to have all registration materials translated into their home languages. Also, in seeking to provide equitable access to all programs, the district must look for ways to remove barriers that may prevent families from participating in preregistration and taking part in the Kindergarten Preview Day.

Reflection Question

What are the rights of ML families in your context that you can cite as you advocate for them?

Step 3: *Develop your allies.*

During Step 3, it is important to foster relationships with others who can support you in your advocacy work. While it may be easier to begin with natural allies who share your viewpoints, you may also wish to consider collaborating with potential allies, even if they have differing views from you. For this step, we have substituted the original NEA wording of "identify" your allies into "develop" your allies, as this language focuses on the importance of building and maintaining relationships with potential allies through sharing ideas. We may face considerable resistance from colleagues and administrators when it comes to equitable ML education. As educators of MLs, it's imperative to have strategies up our sleeves to lead and advocate for students. Many educators aren't trained in working with MLs so may not be aware of issues facing ML students and may be caught off guard by ML advocates suggesting new procedures or initiatives, including CRT. One strategy for developing allies to support us in our advocacy work is the use of talking points.

Talking Points

Talking points are prepared, succinct statements that lend support to an argument (Merriam Webster, n.d.c). Talking points can be "freestanding" to support one side of an issue, and they can also be created as retorts to an opposing argument. Talking points are typically used in such areas as politics and marketing, which are prone to heavy debates. If you've ever watched a political debate, you've definitely witnessed talking points in action. Yet in education, we don't use this strategy often enough. Figure 8.3 outlines the basics of talking points as a tool to advocate for MLs.

Figure 8.3   The What and Why of Talking Points for MLs

Element of Talking Points	Description
What they are	• Succinct statements designed to persuade or inform and effective tools for preparing for conversations that might be difficult

(Continued)

(Continued)

Element of Talking Points	Description
	• Emphasize a win–win situation for both stakeholders • Present a different way of thinking, drawing from a tool used in fields outside of education
Why use them	• Help prepare you for potentially uncomfortable discussions related to ML advocacy • Facilitate more effective interaction and engagement with teachers and administrators • Showcase your ML expertise

How to Create Your Own Talking Points to Advocate for MLs We recommend five steps in developing your own talking points in service of MLs and their families:

1. After you choose the issue you'd like to advocate for, draft your key, succinct message.

2. Revise your message, emphasizing a "win–win" solution for ML students, families, and colleagues. Ensure that your talking points underscore how students, as well as teachers and/or administrators, will benefit from your suggestion. Also make sure that your solution does not involve extra work for your colleagues.

3. Anticipate your colleagues' pushback. Brainstorm a few statements you think you'll hear from those who may oppose your idea.

4. Add talking points to address the potential pushback, aligning your pushback talking points to what points you imagine the "naysayers" will make.

5. Rehearse and role-play with a colleague, if possible. In this way, you can come to a potentially uncomfortable conversation as prepared as you can be to advocate for MLs.

Scenario reflection: Amanda and Tony decide that they will first approach their principal and the kindergarten team to share what they have learned from ML families, as well as ideas that they have for improving the kindergarten registration process. They have a strong relationship with both the principal and the team, yet they're surprised by a couple of the remarks that are made as they share their ideas. One member of the team says that she doesn't understand why they should be making special accommodations to reach out to ML families. She feels that the focus should be on engaging *all* families of soon-to-be kindergartners. She feels that the families that choose not to take part in the preregistration process are less invested in their child's education than those who do take part.

Reflection Questions

1. How might Amanda and Tony respond to the concerns that ML families don't need specific considerations in relation to kindergarten preregistration?

2. What else might they do to build a team of allies to support them in their advocacy work?

In responding to the questions and concerns of the team, Amanda and Tony used talking points to discuss the benefit of working to remove barriers that ML families shared in regard to taking part in the kindergarten preregistration. They also shifted the conversations from a deficit view of ML families to an assets-based view, which included the possible benefit of using the preregistration process as a starting point for building strong relationships with families, ultimately benefiting students. Figure 8.4 identifies talking point steps with our scenario example aligned to each step.

Figure 8.4   Talking Point Steps With Scenario Examples for Each Step

Steps	Scenario Examples for Each Step
1. Draft your key, succinct message.	"We need to remove barriers that prevent ML families from preregistering their children for kindergarten."
2. Revise your message, ensuring a win–win.	"If we remove the barriers that prevent ML families from preregistering, we'll have fewer students that haven't registered at the beginning of the year, and we'll have more information about our incoming students, including their strengths and needs."
3. Anticipate pushback.	"We don't have time or resources to develop new procedures. The time and resources we'd use won't be worth it." "The families won't be interested."
4. Add talking points to address pushback.	"We are happy to take the lead in developing a series of ML family preregistration events. By offering these events, we can begin to build school and ML family partnerships that will have long-term benefits for student learning. The ML families we've spoken to indicated they would be interested in these events."
5. Rehearse and role-play.	Amanda and Tony rehearsed the potential dialogue they might have when proposing their idea. They felt very confident and prepared for the discussion that ensued.

Step 4: *Identify your outlets for change.*

Step 4 asks you to examine what specifically you can do at different levels (e.g., classroom, school, district, community) related to your advocacy goals and to reflect on how you will know when you have met your goal. The challenge of creating a culturally responsive and equitable school climate for MLs can feel like a herculean undertaking. It can be helpful to identify both short-term and long-term goals, a timeline for these goals, and the specific support and resources you might need for each. It is also important to consider how you will measure your progress and success in meeting these goals. What tools will you use? Figure 8.5, which breaks down the second part of the Advocacy Goal-Setting Template (Appendix A), can help you think through the steps that you'll take.

After reviewing the worksheet, take a look at Figure 8.6, the Goal-Setting Worksheet for Kindergarten Preregistration Planning that Amanda and Tony completed to help them set goals for their advocacy work.

Figure 8.5   Setting Short-Term and Long-Term Goal Worksheet

Short-term goal by _____ : (date)			
Long-term goal by _____: (date)			
Steps and Timeline	**Advocacy Actions**	**Support and Resources Needed**	**Measurement of Success**
Step 1 by: _____			
Step 2 by: _____			
Step 3 by: _____			
Step 4 by: _____			
Step 5 by: _____			

Figure 8.6   Goal-Setting Worksheet for Kindergarten Preregistration Planning

Short-term goal: To host a series of three kindergarten preregistration events at convenient locations throughout the community at varied times during the day so as to meet the needs of ML families. Each event will include home language interpreters, language and literacy assessments, support for filling out registration documentation, and the sharing of essential district information in families' home languages.

Long-term goals:

- Increase number of families preregistering their children for kindergarten before the start of the new school year by 25 percent.
- Build relationships with ML families.

(Continued)

Figure 8.6 (Continued)

Steps and Timeline	Advocacy Actions	Support and Resources Needed	Measurement of Success
Step 1 by: December	Identify dates, times, and locations of events.	ML community leaders to help identify possible locations; administrative support in selecting dates	Locations, times, and dates secured
Step 2 by: January	Develop a plan for family outreach.	PTA leadership and ML community leaders to provide guidance in outreach; funding for translating publicity materials	A developed plan to include social media and local media publicity in neighborhood businesses, PTA

Step 5: *Organize and educate others.*

Step 5 is the work that you can do to expand your advocacy efforts, widen your ally group, and increase your impact. We suggest that you undertake the following:

- Use talking points to expand your allies.

- Seek out opportunities to build on existing programs and infrastructures (e.g., rather than only having a separate back-to-school night for ML families, look for ways to increase ML engagement and support during the current back-to-school night).

- Look for ways to collaborate with others in the community who may also be supporting or interested in supporting ML families (e.g., ML leaders in the community, immigrant advocacy groups, adult education programs).

- Take time to reflect on progress and celebrate your successes!

In organizing and educating others, you are bound to face some individuals in your school and/or the wider community who do not feel the same way you do about MLs. It's important to first establish yourself as a leader who supports MLs so that if you're faced with a situation in which there is conflict, you are better prepared to deal with it. Figure 8.7, Steps for Establishing Leadership and Successfully Dealing With Conflicts, outlines some steps you can take to be seen as a leader and mitigate conflicts with others.

Figure 8.7   Steps for Establishing Leadership and Successfully Dealing With Conflicts

Step for Establishing Leadership and Successfully Dealing With Conflicts	Consideration
1. Model a consistent, positive message about MLs.	Demonstrate your leadership by maintaining yourself as an empathetic ally for MLs and their families who has a consistent message about their strengths, potential, and contributions to the school and community. Others will look to you as an expert on ML assets and education.
2. Develop your relational skills.	Reflect on how you develop relationships with others. Think about how you develop others' trust, provide feedback, motivate and persuade others, support others, and demonstrate your empathy toward them.
3. Learn how politics work in your context.	Develop an understanding of who the key players are in your context (e.g., school or district). Get to know these players, determine what their roles are, what motivates them, and build relationships with them.
4. Recognize and acknowledge other colleagues' expertise aloud.	When you point out something positive a colleague is doing (e.g., how your principal is voicing a commitment to MLs this year), you'll start to build their trust or continue to build the trust you've already established.
5. Approach conflicts related to MLs thoughtfully.	Take a minute to think about the situation, who you are interacting with, and the possible ramifications of your actions on MLs and their families. Keep in mind that many teachers and administrators haven't received coursework or training on educating MLs and are trying their best.
6. Try to first listen and understand others' perspectives, even if you may not agree with them on their approach.	Try to put yourself in someone else's shoes to understand where they may be coming from in terms of MLs. This openness to understanding others' frustrations will provide you a greater depth of understanding of their perspective. Your listening to them will also help strengthen their trust with you.
7. Consider what might be happening on a systematic level to promote others' thinking around this issue.	Reflect on what is happening beyond this person at the systems level to cause your colleague to have this perspective of MLs. For example, assessment, scheduling, and income inequality may play a role in this person's perspective. Dig deeper.
8. Suggest some potential solutions and/or strategies to them to support MLs.	After you've listened to their frustration, know when to gently shift the narrative to what can be done collaboratively to support MLs and/or their families in this situation. By offering your support, you can help them see the potential for a focus on MLs' strengths and potential.

(Continued)

Figure 8.7   (Continued)

Step for Establishing Leadership and Successfully Dealing With Conflicts	Consideration
9. Follow up on your support and solutions for MLs.	To demonstrate your commitment to MLs and their families, check in with a colleague who you've supported to see how your suggestions are working. Revisit regularly and revise your approach as needed. This action furthers your commitment to MLs, their families, and your colleague(s).
10. Find outlets to share ML achievement.	Share positive stories of ML and family assets with your school or district, such as instances in which former MLs become school valedictorians, honor roll students, and/or graduates. Invite successful MLs to the school in person or by video to share reasons for their success. Investigate multiple ways to share your message, such as in assemblies, newspapers, and on social media (with students' and parents' permission).

Source: Adapted from Riggio & Tan, 2014; Staehr Fenner, 2014, 2017; also in Calderón et al., 2020.

In their work to reimagine what kindergarten preregistration might look like, Amanda and Tony shared their new plan with other stakeholders in the community that served ML families, such as an immigrants' right group, a housing and community services nonprofit, and an adult education and job placement program run by a local organization. These organizations attended the preregistration events and shared information about their programs and services. Staff from the local library also attended and led a story time and craft for families. Following the last preregistration event, Amanda, Tony, and their team met at a local restaurant to debrief and celebrate their efforts. They discussed what worked well and what changes they would like to make for the next year. They also discussed how to expand the number of stakeholders who were involved and ways of providing more leadership opportunities to members of ML community groups.

Building Equity Literacy Through Your Advocacy Efforts

As you integrate advocacy tools and strategies into your CRT work, you can seek to build what Gorski (2017) identifies as the four equity-based abilities that educators need in their work for equity:

1. The ability to recognize even the subtlest forms of inequity, such as subtle ways in which students' home languages might be denigrated in a school environment.

2. The ability to respond in the immediate term to inequity, such as by skillfully challenging colleagues or students who denigrate students' home languages.

3. The ability to redress inequity in the long term, such as by effectively and equitably attending to the deeper cultural dynamics of the institution that make people believe it is acceptable to denigrate students' home languages.

4. The ability to sustain equity efforts—even in the face of resistance. (Gorski, 2017, p. 225)

Reflection Questions

1. In which of the four abilities described by Gorski do you feel you are the strongest? Explain.

2. In which of the four abilities described by Gorski do you feel you most need to improve? Explain.

EXAMPLES OF INNOVATIVE PROGRAMS

As you reflect on the five advocacy steps and the scenario that we have woven throughout this chapter and think of ways you might bring it all together through advocacy for MLs and their families, we now widen our lens to share six examples of innovative programs that support CRT. These are programs that have been implemented at the district levels in the Syracuse City School District (SCSD), Fairfax County Public Schools, the New York City Department of Education, and the Boston Teachers Union. These examples can provide further inspiration as you determine where you might like to focus your advocacy efforts and how you might take steps to advocate for MLs and their families.

Career Ladder Program
(Syracuse City School District)

The Career Ladder program is a program that provides financial assistance to full-time school district employees who are not currently teachers to further their education. Participants in the program receive tuition reimbursement for college coursework in an area of study that could support them to expand their career options and advance professionally within the district. Participants who complete an application and are accepted can receive up to 12 credit hours per fiscal year at the state university or community college tuition rate. This program has been instrumental in supporting the increase in numbers of qualified bilingual educators in the district. Seymour teacher Jesus Ortiz, who appears in our Chapter 2 video (*What It Means to Value Diversity*), is an example of one educator who took part in the Career Ladder program. Jesus was formerly a paraprofessional and, after completing the program, became a classroom teacher.

Nationality Workers
(Syracuse City School District)

SCSD employees who are hired as "nationality workers"[1] come from the home communities of ML students in the schools and speak the most common languages of ML families, including Arabic, Somali, Swahili, Karen, Burmese, Kinyarwanda, and Tigrinya. They "provide a variety of services to facilitate communication between students, parents, and school personnel. The intent is to bridge the cultural and linguistic gaps between the home and the school (SCSD, 2016, p. 33). In addition to

---

[1]Other districts may use terms such as "parent liaison" or "parent community liaison."

serving as a liaison between schools and ML families, nationality workers also provide professional development related to their culture and experiences that support educators in better understanding the backgrounds of their ML students. Nationality workers also assist in classrooms to support teachers in meeting the needs of English learners (Syracuse.com, 2019). Our Chapter 5 video, *Using a Jigsaw Activity With Multilingual Learners*, demonstrates how nationality workers can be used to support student learning in the classroom. To hear from Razan Shalash, one of SCSD's nationality workers, as well as learn other ways that SCSD is building partnerships with families, please take a look at the video *Partnering With Multilingual Families*.

Video 8.1

Partnering With Multilingual Families

resources.corwin.com/CulturallyResponsiveTeaching

Steps to the Seal (Syracuse City School District)

The Steps to the Seal program is an innovative pathway designed to support students in graduating with the New York State Seal of Biliteracy (NYSSB) on their diploma. The NYSSB recognizes high school graduates who have attained a high level of proficiency in one or more languages in addition to English. The Steps to the Seal program recognizes that students and families need guidance on obtaining the seal much earlier than in high school and offers that guidance to ML students in Grades K–12. Emily Voegler and Erica Daniels, who began the program, wanted their students to recognize their home languages as assets and to value the cultural heritages and backgrounds of ML families as a district. As part of the program, students take part in evening classes in which they study their heritage language and complete multimedia projects that demonstrate language development in the four skills of listening, speaking, reading, and writing. For example, younger students take photos of their families and communities and write about themselves and their experiences. Through the program, parents and guardians of MLs learn about the benefits of NYSSB, how to obtain it, and are encouraged to help develop their children's home language. For more on how the Steps to the Seal program came to be and the impact it has, take a look at the *Steps to the Seal* video in which Erica Daniels and Meredith Green describe the program.

Video 8.2

Steps to the Seal

resources.corwin.com/CulturallyResponsiveTeaching

Cultural Proficiency Framework, Modules, and Cohorts (Fairfax County Public Schools)

In 2013, Fairfax County Public Schools (FCPS), the tenth-largest US school district, located in northern Virginia, reinvigorated its focus on cultural proficiency. The district began by developing a Cultural Proficiency Framework that includes defining key terminology and professional development goals related to cultural proficiency. The district currently offers annual training modules—required for all FCPS employees—that focus on understanding cultural proficiency and the guiding principles of cultural proficiency. In addition, each school within the district has a designated staff member to be the equity lead who is responsible for leading discussions related to equity issues in the school. The district also offers cohorts of educators an opportunity to engage in more intensive cultural proficiency training that takes place over the course of three days. In addition to framing professional development, the Cultural Proficiency Framework is used by district curriculum writers to infuse CRT into their curriculum work.

We spoke with Tu Phillips, the former manager of the FCPS Equity and Cultural Responsiveness (ECR) team who previously led the initiative from its inception. When asked her opinion on what she would expect to see in a school or district that values cultural proficiency, she identified three specific areas. The first was a mindset that views diversity as an opportunity to grow rather than a problem, which means taking an honest look at diversity. Phillips explained, "We see diversity in all its complexity, we're willing to adapt" (T. Phillips, personal communication, April 27, 2020). Second, she emphasized the need for strong relationships among educators and school staff and the willingness by school employees to be real and reflective in their cultural proficiency work. She recognized the importance of not making assumptions about others while at the same time being thoughtful about the internal work that we each need to do. Third, Phillips explained the importance of having skills to be able to speak up about equity issues in nonthreatening ways and be prepared to listen when others share their concerns with us. She described these skills as a balance of knowing when and how to push forward discussions and knowing when to step back. Phillips said, "Start out soft and build relationships" and "be willing to spend time around it." She also emphasized the importance of being open to what others have to say. "None of us gets it right 100 percent of the time when it comes to race, culture, or areas of differences, so we have to be as open to learning and changing as we hope others would be" (T. Phillips, personal communications, April 27, 2020, and July 30, 2020).

Brooklyn District 15 Middle School (New York City Department of Education)

New York City elementary and middle schools are divided into 32 districts. In New York City Schools, middle schools are "unzoned," meaning that parents (or guardians) can indicate which middle schools they would like their child to attend instead of only being able to attend the school for which they are zoned due to where they live. Families are able to rank their choices of schools. In spring 2019, District 15 in Brooklyn began an effort to diversify and desegregate that district's highly segregated middle schools. The plan, created with community and parent input, maintained family rankings but eliminated so-called "screens" such as grades, test scores, and attendance. Instead, they switched to determining students' placement in middle schools through a lottery in which 52 percent of seats were reserved for priority students.[2] Priority students were defined as ELs, those who qualify for free and reduced lunch, and/or those who live in temporary housing. This percentage mirrors the demographics of District 15. This shift to reserving seats for priority students sparked difficult and important conversations between parents, teachers, and students. All of these stakeholders had to confront the coded language around "good schools" and "bad schools" and the reality of resource allocation and historic marginalization. The shift to priority students could be seen in two middle schools. One school went from having 34 percent of sixth graders in the priority groups in 2018 to 56 percent in 2019. Another school went from 83 percent of sixth graders in priority groups in 2018 to 60 percent in 2019 (Marley Zeno, former ENL teacher, personal communication, June 30, 2020).

Episode 5 ("We Know It When We See It") of *The New York Times'* Serial podcast series *Nice White Parents* by Chana Joffe-Walt is a valuable resource to learn more about the desegregation efforts in District 15 and to explore the topic of school desegregation more generally.

Unafraid Educators (Committee of the Boston Teachers Union)

Unafraid Educators is an organizing committee of the Boston Teachers Union that focuses on support for undocumented and immigrant students and families. The group organizes political campaigns, facilitates professional development for educators, provides resources to students and families, and administers a scholarship for undocumented students in Boston. As an example of one of their campaigns, in response to reports that student information was being shared with Immigration Customs and Enforcement (ICE), Unafraid Educators collaborated with the Student Immigrant Movement to protect undocumented students against information sharing that could endanger students' well-being. The organization also widely distributes information for undocumented and immigrant students who are interested in attending college.

CONCLUSION

In Chapter 1, we shared with you our five guiding principles for CRT work and asked you to rank them in their order of importance to you. Now that you have explored the guiding principles in greater depth, we would like you to once again rank them and consider whether your priorities have shifted.

---

[2]See https://d15diversityplan.com/wp-content/uploads/2019/10/191008_D15_DataSummary.pdf for more details.

Application Activity 8b.
Prioritizing the Guiding Principles

Directions: Rank the five guiding principles in order of importance to you. Then, answer the reflection questions that follow.

_____ Culturally responsive teaching is assets-based.

_____ Culturally responsive teaching simultaneously supports and challenges students.

_____ Culturally responsive teaching places students at the center of learning.

_____ Culturally responsive teaching leverages students' linguistic and cultural backgrounds.

_____ CRT unites students' schools, families, and communities.

Reflection Questions

1. Why did you rank them in the order that you did?

2. Have your priorities changed since you began this book? If so, why? If not, why not?

3. Do you have any additional guiding principles related to CRT? If so, what are they?

Our Recommendations

Based on the guiding principles, we would like to offer final recommendations that can guide you in the CRT work that you do both individually and collaboratively.

Individual Recommendations

- Listen to the stories of ML families.
- Examine your interactions with ML students and their families. Reflect on how you might strengthen these interactions and build your relationships with students and families.
- Do the hard work of examining your own bias and privilege.
- Take steps to learn about racist practices and inequities within our education system and steps that are being taken by schools and districts to respond to these practices. Use what you have learned to reflect on your own practices and the extent to which these practices may advantage some students and disadvantage others.

Collaborative Recommendations

- Develop a common language that you can use in your discussions with others. As a team or professional learning community (PLC), begin by reflecting on how you define CRT and other terms that you will use to guide your work.
- Set priorities for your CRT work. Be specific in determining measurable outcomes, steps you will take, and who will be responsible.
- Create a safe space for the work of CRT by building relationships and identifying shared norms for CRT and equity discussions.

Final Thoughts

As we mentioned in the book's introduction, we wrote the final chapter of this book in May and June of 2020, nearly three months after the United States, as well as countries around the world, quickly pivoted to distance learning as a means to continue students' education during the COVID-19 pandemic. During this time, we saw the already prevalent inequities in education become more painfully visible as students' learning became dependent on so many factors, including their access to technology and the internet, families' abilities to support children's education from home, and school districts' and educators' commitment to and creativity in engaging all families and meeting the needs of all types of learners. We sadly saw the differences between individualism and collectivism that we've discussed in this book play out on a national scale to detrimental effects in the personal decision of whether to wear a face mask in public to protect others or not.

We also wrote this final chapter when communities across the United States (and even the world) expressed their outrage at the brutal death of George Floyd on May 25, 2020, at the hands of an abusive Minneapolis police officer and his colleagues who looked on. The death of George Floyd, on top of the tragic deaths of so many other Black Americans, intensified the focus on the deeply rooted racism that is prevalent in our communities. George Floyd's death, and the protests that followed, highlighted the relentless work that we need to do as a nation to address racism and inequity that is embedded in the structures of our society.

These two events—as well as the rise of anti-immigrant sentiment, hate crimes, and actions against immigrants which have been prevalent and growing over the past few years—speak to the urgent need for culturally responsive teaching in schools. Educators have the crucial task of creating school climates that value the school communities that they have committed to educating. If we want to change the system, educators must speak the truth about the inequity and injustice that is prevalent in our society and teach students what it means to advocate for themselves and others. We must specifically teach white students what it means to be an ally to people of color, beginning with their classmates. We must identify and speak out against the inequities that exist within our own classrooms, schools, and districts and commit to working to eliminate these inequities and dismantle racism.

The work of developing a school culture that is centered around the guiding principles of CRT and equity is not an easy path, but we want to thank you for the steps that you have already taken for MLs and their families. We wish you all the best as you continue on your journey.

References

Calderón, M., Dove, M., Staehr Fenner, D., Gottlieb, M., Honigsfeld, A., Singer, T., Slakk, S., Soto, I., & Zacarian, D. (2020). *Breaking down the wall: Essential shifts for English Learners' success*. Corwin.

Gorski, P. (2017). Rethinking the role of "culture" in educational equity: From cultural competence to equity literacy. *Multicultural Perspectives, 18*(4), 221–226.

Merriam-Webster. (n.d.a). Advocate. *In Merriam-Webster.com dictionary*. https://www.merriam-webster.com/dictionary/advocate

Merriam-Webster. (n.d.b). Ally. In *Merriam-Webster.com dictionary*. https://www.merriam-webster.com/dictionary/

Merriam-Webster. (n.d.c). Talking point. In *Merriam-Webster.com dictionary*. https://www.merriam-webster.com/dictionary/talking%20point

National Education Association. (2015). *All in! How educators can advocate for English language learners*. https://www.colorincolorado.org/sites/default/files/ELL_AdvocacyGuide2015.pdf

Riggio, R. E., & Tan, S. J. (Eds.). (2014). *Leader interpersonal and influence skills: The soft skills of leadership*. Routledge.

Staehr Fenner, D. (2014). *Advocating for English learners: A guide for educators*. Corwin.

Staehr Fenner, D. (2017). *SupportEd's top 10 ways to support English learners in 2017*. https://getsupported.net/supporteds-top-10-ways-support-english-learners-2017/

Syracuse City School District. (2016). *2016–2017 English language learner/ multilingual learner education program guidebook*. http://getsupported.net/wp-content/uploads/ENL-Guide-16-17.pdf

Syracuse.com. (2019, Jan. 29). *Language lessons: Multi-literacy program helps students retain native languages*. https://www.syracuse.com/living/2018/12/multi-literacy_program_helps_100_syracuse_students_retain_their_native_languages.html

US Department of Education, Office of Civil Rights. (2015a). *Ensuring English learner students can participate meaningfully and equally in educational programs*. https://www2.ed.gov/about/offices/list/ocr/docs/dcl-factsheet-el-students-201501.pdf

US Department of Education, Office of Civil Rights. (2015b). *Information for limited English proficient (LEP) parents and guardians and for schools and school districts that communicate with them*. https://www2.ed.gov/about/offices/list/ocr/docs/dcl-factsheet-lep-parents-201501.pdf

Appendix A

Advocacy Goal-Setting Template

Directions: Use the following template to set goals and plan your advocacy work related to culturally responsive teaching. In this goal-setting template, you will isolate the issue, plan steps for meeting short- and long-term advocacy goals, and develop talking points that you can use in your advocacy work.

Isolating the Issue

Describe the issue		
List the stakeholders		
Share possible internal and external factors		
Provide information-gathering steps to clarify the issue with stakeholders and a corresponding timeline for each step	*Steps*	*Timeline*
Note findings from information gathering steps		
Reframe the deficit perspective		
Summarize advocacy goal(s)		

Setting Goals

Short-term goal by _____
(date)

Long-term goal by _____
(date)

Steps and Timeline	Advocacy Actions	Support and Resources Needed	Measurement of Success
Step 1 by: _____			
Step 2 by: _____			
Step 3 by: _____			
Step 4 by: _____			
Step 5 by: _____			

Using Talking Points

Identify your key, succinct message.
Revise your message, ensuring a win–win.
Anticipate pushback.
Add talking points to address pushback.

Appendix B

Culturally Responsive School Checklist and Goal Setting

Directions: Individually or with a small group, reflect on the presence of each of these look-fors, grouped by guiding principle, in your context. In cases in which the look-for is not present, brainstorm what you will do to improve how the look-for is incorporated in your classroom or school. Then, based on your responses in the checklist, choose one guiding principle to focus on. List three steps you can take to strengthen that guiding principle in your context.

Look-Fors	Yes	Sometimes	No	To improve on how this look-for is incorporated in my classroom or school, I will . . .
Guiding Principle #1: Culturally responsive teaching is assets-based.				
A. Administrators, teachers, and staff pronounce students' names correctly.				
B. Administrators, teachers, and staff show interest in students' home languages by learning a few words or phrases.				
C. Administrators, teachers, and staff are aware of students' interests outside of the classroom or school setting.				

Look-Fors	Yes	Sometimes	No	To improve on how this look-for is incorporated in my classroom or school, I will . . .
D. The school puts supports in place to help students and their families overcome obstacles that may get in the way of student learning or family participation.				
E. Students' cultural, historic, and linguistic backgrounds are incorporated into instruction.				
Additional look-for:				
Additional look-for:				

Guiding Principle #2: Culturally responsive instruction simultaneously supports and challenges students.

Look-Fors	Yes	Sometimes	No	
F. MLs are taught grade-level content and texts. Instructional texts include a balance of grade-level texts and texts at students' reading and language levels.				
G. Instruction and materials are appropriately scaffolded so MLs are able to access and engage with grade-level content and texts.				
H. MLs have access to and the support needed to be successful in gifted, honors, and/or college preparatory classes.				
I. Instruction includes activities that require students to consider alternative ways of understanding information and push students to challenge the status quo.				

(Continued)

(Continued)

Look-Fors	Yes	Sometimes	No	To improve on how this look-for is incorporated in my classroom or school, I will . . .
J. Instruction includes activities that foster critical thinking and reflection (e.g., open-ended discussion prompts and student monitoring of their learning).				
Additional look-for:				
Additional look-for:				

Guiding Principle #3: Culturally responsive teaching places students at the center of the learning.

	Yes	Sometimes	No	
K. Classroom activities frequently include structured pair and small-group work.				
L. Students and teachers develop the classroom norms and expectations together.				
M. MLs are given choice in their learning.				
N. MLs are given opportunities to speak and write about their lives and people and events that are important to them.				
O. MLs are involved in goal setting and assessment through the use of student goal sheets, checklists, peer-editing activities, and teacher–student or student–student conferencing.				
Additional look-for:				
Additional look-for:				

Look-Fors	Yes	Sometimes	No	To improve on how this look-for is incorporated in my classroom or school, I will . . .
Guiding Principle #4: Culturally responsive teaching leverages students' linguistic and cultural backgrounds.				
P. Multicultural materials and resources are incorporated throughout the curriculum and school.				
Q. Teachers use a variety of instructional strategies to assess, activate, and build MLs' background knowledge.				
R. Lessons and units include perspectives of individuals that come from students' home cultures (e.g., literature written by non-US authors).				
S. Lessons include opportunities for MLs to use bilingual resources (e.g., dictionaries, books, glossaries) and home languages.				
T. Leaders and role models for ML communities are included in the learning (e.g., community members are invited to speak in class).				
Additional look-for:				
Additional look-for:				
Guiding Principle #5: Culturally responsive teaching unites students' schools, families, and communities.				
U. The school visually demonstrates a commitment to multicultural families and students (e.g., flags from students' home countries, signs posted in multiple languages, student work displayed on walls).				

(Continued)

(Continued)

Look-Fors	Yes	Sometimes	No	To improve on how this look-for is incorporated in my classroom or school, I will . . .
V. Interpreters are provided at all school events.				
W. Educators use a variety of tools to communicate with ML families (e.g., emails, phone calls, texts in home languages, flyers in home languages).				
X. School administration looks for ways to remove barriers that might prevent ML families from participating (e.g., timing of events, child care, transportation).				
Y. ML family members are actively involved with school committees or organizations that are open to parents (e.g., PTA).				
Additional look-for:				
Additional look-for:				

Goal Setting

Based on my responses to the checklist, the guiding principle I prioritize to focus on is:

I will take the following three steps to strengthen this guiding principle:

1.

2.

3.

Appendix C

Culturally Responsive Unit Planning Template

I.	Unit topic

2.	Content standard(s) to be addressed; for English learners, also include relevant English language development standard(s)

3.	Assets my MLs bring to the class and how I will make connections to their home languages and cultures, backgrounds, and/or prior learning

Assets:

How I will make connections:

4.	Student-centered learning tasks and assessments

Tasks:

Assessments:

(Continued)

(Continued)

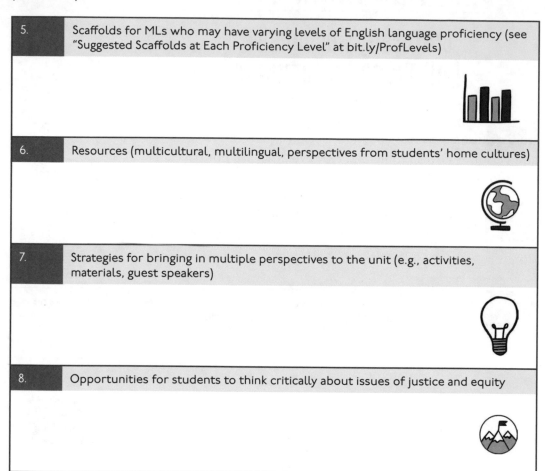

5.	Scaffolds for MLs who may have varying levels of English language proficiency (see "Suggested Scaffolds at Each Proficiency Level" at bit.ly/ProfLevels)
6.	Resources (multicultural, multilingual, perspectives from students' home cultures)
7.	Strategies for bringing in multiple perspectives to the unit (e.g., activities, materials, guest speakers)
8.	Opportunities for students to think critically about issues of justice and equity

Appendix D

Gap Activity

Directions: For this activity, students are put into pairs. One student is Person A, and the second student is Person B. Each student has a problem to solve. Person A solves Problem 1, and Person B solves Problem 2. However, they do not have all the information that they need to solve the problem. Students should take turns asking their partner the questions that they wrote and use that information to solve their problem. First, students should work individually to read their problem. Next, they should complete the questions that they need answers to in order to be able to solve the problem. Question starters are provided. Extra information has been provided to make sure that students are listening carefully to the questions that are asked. This activity can be modified to be used with questions in different content areas.

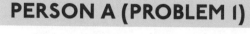

PERSON A (PROBLEM 1)

Source: Photo by Kenny Luo on Unsplash: https://unsplash.com/ @kennyluoping

Problem 1: Akilah wants to buy one book and one magazine at the bookstore. She earned money babysitting. She has no other money.

Question 1: Does she have enough money to buy the book and the magazine?

Solution to Problem 1: _____

Question Starters

How much does _____ cost?

How much do the _____ cost?

How much did . . . How many . . .

Questions for Your Partner	Responses

Problem 2 Information

- Mateo has two adults and three children in his family.
- The fair is open from 4:00 p.m. to 10:00 p.m.
- The family pass is $30.00.
- A child's entrance fee is $6.00.
- There is lots of good food at the fair.
- An adult's entrance fee is $11.00.

PERSON B (PROBLEM 2)

Problem 1 Information

- The book is $10.50.
- The magazine is $4.89.

- A new pencil case is $3.00.
- The bookstore is two miles away.
- Akilah made $15.00 babysitting.

Problem 2: Mateo's family is going to a fair. They can buy a family pass, or they can buy individual (single) tickets. Children's tickets are cheaper than adults' tickets.

Question 2: How much money will Mateo save if he buys the family pass?

Solution to Problem 2: _____

Source: Photo by Brittney Butler on Unsplash: https://unsplash.com/@britjanae

Question Starters

How much does _____ cost?

How much do the _____ cost?

How much did . . .   How many . . .

Questions for Your Partner	Responses

Appendix E

Planning for a New School Year Reflection Tool

Directions: Use this tool to help you reflect on five areas that are crucial for MLs when planning for new school years. You can use it in contexts that provide distance learning exclusively, only face-to-face instruction, or a combination of both practices. Reflect on each of the criteria and jot down your plans to address each. You can then determine which area to prioritize to equitably educate MLs.

Criterion		Our Plans
Social-Emotional Support		
	How will we determine and address MLs' **social-emotional needs**?	
	How will we establish **consistent instructional routines** for MLs during face-to-face, hybrid, or virtual instructional models?	
	How will we implement **culturally responsive** and **antiracist instruction**?	
Formative Assessment		
	How will we assess **MLs' preparedness** to begin instruction in new content?	
	How will we use formative assessment data to **differentiate instruction** of language and content for MLs?	
	How will we use **assessment data** to place students in an appropriate level of English language proficiency (if needed)?	

Criterion	Our Plans
Scaffolding Instruction	
How will we provide **instructional scaffolds** (e.g., modeling, repetition of language, clear directions)?	
How will we provide **materials** that are scaffolded for MLs (e.g., graphic organizers, sentence stems, home language support)?	
How will we intentionally **group MLs** to support their **engagement in activities** (e.g., pair work, home language groups)?	
Collaborating and/or Coteaching	
How will we **collaborate** with our colleagues this fall to support MLs?	
What tools can we use for **coplanning** the instruction and assessment of MLs?	
What will **coteaching** look like this fall to ensure MLs access content and learn language?	
Families and Advocacy	
How can we determine **what multilingual families need** this fall (access to technology, access to school meals, social-emotional support)?	
How can we schedule MLs to provide them the **specific supports** they need (e.g., face-to-face classes, virtual synchronous meetings)?	
How can we advocate for **additional supports** for MLs (access to technology, translated materials, etc.)?	

Appendix F

Supporting Resources

There are so many useful resources to support culturally responsive teaching (CRT). While we can't list them all, we would like to provide you some ideas in one place for where you could look further if you are interested in exploring a particular aspect of CRT. Some of these resources were also specifically mentioned in the chapters. Our reference lists that appear at the end of each chapter are another helpful place to look for further reading.

ANTI-RACISM AND ANTI-BIAS RESOURCES

The Archaeology of the Self is a program designed to encourage understanding of one's own self in order to be a better teacher. The Archaeology of the Self intro video: https://youtu.be/OwC_3cLRJO8

Biewen, J. (host). (2020). *Seeing white* [Audio podcast]. Scene on radio. https://www.sceneonradio.org/seeing-white/

Coates, T. (2015). *Between the world and me*. Spiegel & Grau.

Fleshman, K. (n.d.). *Racy conversations suggested viewing and reading*. http://racyconversations.com/suggested-viewing-and-reading

Glassman, J. (2020). Free resources for supporting antiracist education. *Brainpop*. https://blog.brainpop.com/antiracist-education-free-resources-kids/?fbclid=IwAR3wCx-VLkXbAam TappfjJ-hUHA0kxm6rek-GW94_kz-i3SgqQlpXfxycgU#racism

Harvard Implicit Bias Test. (n.d.). https://implicit.harvard.edu/implicit/iatdetails.html

Joffe-Walt, C. (Host). (2020). Nice white parents [Audio podcast], *Serial*. https://www.nytimes.com/2020/07/23/podcasts/nice-white-parents-serial.html

McIntosh, P. (1988). *White privilege: Unpacking the invisible knapsack.* https://www.racialequitytools.org/resourcefiles/mcintosh.pdf.

Morris, M. (2018). *Pushout: The criminalization of Black girls in schools.* The New Press.

Morris, M. (2019). *Sing a rhythm, dance a blues: Education for the liberation of Black and Brown girls.* The New Press.

MTV Look Different. (n.d.). http://www.lookdifferent.org/what-can-i-do/bias-cleanse

Racial Literacy Project. (n.d.). *Yolanda Sealey-Ruiz.* https://www.yolandasealeyruiz.com/racial-literacy-project

Schwarts, S. (2020). 15 classroom resources for discussing racism, policing, and protest. *Education Week.* https://blogs.edweek.org/teachers/teaching_now/2020/06/15_classroom_resources_for_discussing_racism_policing_and_protest.html

Singleton, G. (2014). *Courageous conversations about race: A field guide for achieving equity in schools.* Corwin.

Tatum, B. D. (2017). *Why are all the Black kids sitting together in the cafeteria? And other conversations.* Basic Books.

Teaching Tolerance. (n.d.). *Test yourself for hidden bias.* https://www.tolerance.org/professional-development/test-yourself-for-hidden-bias

Vargas, J. A. (2015). White people. *MTV.* https://www.youtube.com/watch?v=_zjj1PmJcRM

BOOKLISTS FOR K–12 STUDENTS

Children's Library Lady. (n.d.). *Growth mindset resource centre.* https://childrenslibrarylady.com/growth-mindset-book-lists/

Children's Library Lady. (n.d.). *Perseverance book list & resources.* https://childrenslibrarylady.com/perseverance-picture-book-list/

Children's Library Lady. (n.d.). *Thinking skills and problem-solving teaching resources.* https://childrenslibrarylady.com/thinkers-resources/

Compiled by the Cooperative Children's Book Center, University of Wisconsin–Madison. *50 multicultural books every child should know.* https://graveslibrary.wordpress.com/2013/07/22/50-multicultural-books-every-child-should-know/

Embracerace.org. (2020). *Looking for excellent "diverse" books for children? Start here!* https://www.embracerace.org/resources/where-to-find-diverse-childrens-books

Haynes, S. (2020). *Several antiracist books are selling out. Here's what else black booksellers and publishers say you should read.* https://time.com/5846732/books-to-read-about-anti-racism/

Mulvahill, E. (2018). *18 perfect read-alouds for teaching growth mindset.* https://www.weareteachers.com/perfect-read-alouds-for-teaching-growth-mindset/

Self-Sufficient Kids. (n.d.). *10 children's books about being courageous in the face of adversity.* https://selfsufficientkids.com/childrens-books-courageous-adversity/

CULTURALLY RESPONSIVE TEACHING

Delpit, L. (2006). *Other people's children: Cultural conflict in the classroom.* The New Press.

Delpit, L. (2013). *"Multiplication is for white people": Raising expectations for other people's children.* The New Press.

Flores, N., & Chaparro, S. (2018). What counts as language education policy? Developing a materialist anti-racist approach to language activism. *Language Policy, 17,* 365–384.

Gorski, P. (2020). *Critical multicultural pavilion.* http://www.edchange.org/multicultural/

National Education Association. (n.d.). Resources for addressing multicultural and diversity issues in your classroom. http://ftp.arizonaea.org/tools/resources-addressing-multicultural-diversity-issues-in-your-classroom.htm

Nieto, S. (2013). *Finding joy in teaching students of diverse backgrounds: Culturally responsive and socially just practices in U.S. classrooms.* Heinemann.

Nieto, S., & Bode, P. (2018). *Affirming diversity: The sociopolitical context of multicultural education*. Pearson.

Paris, D., & Alim, H. S. (Eds.). (2017). *Culturally sustaining pedagogies: Teaching and learning for justice in a changing world*. Teachers College Press.

Watson, W., Sealey-Ruiz, Y., & Jackson, I. (2014). Daring to care: The role of culturally relevant care in mentoring Black and Latino male high school students. *Race, Ethnicity, and Education, 19*(5), 980–1002. https://doi.org/10.1080/13613324.20 14.911169

EXPLORING CULTURES

Argawal, M. (2017). 10 great films about immigration and migrant experience. *BFI*. https://www.bfi.org.uk/news-opinion/ news-bfi/lists/10-great-films-about-immigration

Bards, A. (2018). *Five best series: Understanding other cultures*. https://avidbards.com/2018/06/17/5-best-series-understanding- other-cultures/

Geert Hofstede's Cultural Dimensions Index. http://resources .corwin.com/sites/default/files/04._figure_2.3_the_individualism- collectivism_continuum.pdf

White, S. (2015). Twelve documentaries that explore different cultures. *Culture trip*. https://theculturetrip.com/asia/articles/ top-12-documentaries-that-will-open-your-mind-to-other- cultures/

INSTRUCTION AND ASSESSMENT RESOURCES

aleksandra143. (2016, May 3). *Digital story, ESL project: My dog Snoopy*. [Video]. YouTube. https://www.youtube.com/ watch?v=0Ye8LXx8PNg

Aviles, C. (2019). The gamification guide. *Teched-up teacher*. http://www.techedupteacher.com/the-gamification-guide/

Boyles, N. (2013). Closing in on close reading. *Educational Leadership, 70*(4), 36–41. http://www.ascd.org/publications/educational-leadership/dec12/vol70/num04/Closing-in-on-Close-Reading.aspx (How to do close reading with elementary students)

Buck Institute for Education. (2017). Critique protocols: Deeper learning competencies. *Project-based teaching strategies guide.* https://padlet-uploads.storage.googleapis.com/246798421/8d2e5e9f0f95934925aded6f0eed3713/Critique_Protocols___Strategy_Guide.pdf

EL Education. (n.d.). *Critique and feedback: Management in the active classroom.* https://eleducation.org/resources/critique-and-feedback

EL Education. (2012). *Austin's butterfly: Building excellence in student work* [Video]. Vimeo. https://vimeo.com/38247060

Gonser, S. (2020, January 10). Connecting math and science to reading and writing. *Edutopia.* https://www.edutopia.org/article/connecting-math-and-science-reading-and-writing?gclid=EAIaIQobChMIv-CX-pPo6AIVjrbICh28IgSnEAMYAyAAEgK2ZvD_BwE

Green Card Voices. (n.d.). Videos. https://www.greencardvoices.com/videos/

Green Card Voices. (2018). *Story stitch: Telling stories, opening minds, becoming neighbors.* Green Card Voices.

International Children's Library. Free resources in multiple languages. http://en.childrenslibrary.org

MacMeekin, M. (n.d.). A visual list of 28 learner-centered instruction methods. *Wabisabi Learning.* https://www.wabisabilearning.com/blog/28-instruction-methods-infographic

Morris, K. (2019, May 27). *13 examples of great classroom blogs.* https://www.theedublogger.com/13-great-class-blogs/

National Writing Project. (2016, March 31). *Literacy, ELL, and digital storytelling: 21st-century skills in action* [Video]. YouTube. https://www.youtube.com/watch?v=HsJ8Cku1NEo

Turner, A. (2016, June 23). *The power of storytelling in teaching* [Video]. YouTube. https://www.youtube.com/watch?v=-FJD68y7LNo

Wilson, D., & Conyers, M. (2017). Helping struggling students build a growth mindset. *Edutopia*. https://www.edutopia.org/article/helping-struggling-students-build-growth-mindset-donna-wilson-marcus-conyers

Zwiers, J. (n.d.). *5th grade language arts: Argument scale—Scaffolding output* [Video]. https://jeffzwiers.org/videos https://jeffzwiers.org/videos

Zwiers, J. (n.d.). *Argument balance scale visual organizer*. https://jeffzwiers.org/tools

LEARNING PREFERENCE SURVEYS

Georgia Department of Education. (n.d.). *Learning style inventory*. https://www.gadoe.org/Curriculum-Instruction-and-Assessment/Special-Education-Services/Documents/IDEAS%202014%20Handouts/LearningStyleInventory.pdf

Lower Cape May Regional. (n.d.). *Learning style inventory*. https://lcmrschooldistrict.com/mckenna/La%20rentree/learningstyleinventory_survey.pdf

PROJECT-BASED LEARNING

PBL Works. (n.d.). *Buck Institute for Education*. https://my.pblworks.org/projects, http://pblu.org/projects

Project-Based Learning. *Edutopia*. https://www.edutopia.org/project-based-learning

SOCIAL JUSTICE

Global Oneness Project. www.globalonenessproject.org

Gonzalez, J. (2016). A collection of resources for teaching social justice. *Cult of pedagogy*. www.cultofpedagogy.com/social-justice-resources

EngageNY. (n.d.). *Grade 8 ELA module 1.* https://www
.engageny.org/resource/grade-8-ela-module-1 (Middle school
ELA module focused on refugee stories)

Kleinrock, L. (n.d.). *Social justice reading list.* https://www
.teachandtransform.org/reading-list

National Education Association (NEA). Social justice lesson
plans are lessons based around the stories of the NEA Human
and Civil Rights Awards Recipients. http://www.nea.org/
grants/63178.htm

PBS News Hour. (2016). *"He named me Malala": Understanding
student activism through film—Lesson plan.* www.pbs.org/news
hour/extra/lessons-plans/he-named-me-malala-understanding-
student-activism-through-film-lesson-plan

Teaching Tolerance. (n.d.). *Defining activism for grades 6–12.*
https://www.tolerance.org/classroom-resources/tolerance-
lessons/defining-activism

Teaching Tolerance (n.d.). *Using photographs to teach social justice.*
https://www.tolerance.org/classroom-resources/tolerance-lessons/
using-photographs-to-teach-social-justice-exposing-gender

Using Their Words provides a series of social justice themed units
for elementary. http://www.usingtheirwords.org/sje-units/

Index

A SAGE Publishing Company

Helping educators make the greatest impact

CORWIN HAS ONE MISSION: to enhance education through intentional professional learning.

We build long-term relationships with our authors, educators, clients, and associations who partner with us to develop and continuously improve the best evidence-based practices that establish and support lifelong learning.

Solutions YOU WANT | Experts YOU TRUST | Results YOU NEED

EVENTS

>>> **INSTITUTES**

Corwin Institutes provide large regional events where educators collaborate with peers and learn from industry experts. Prepare to be recharged and motivated!

corwin.com/institutes

ON-SITE PD

>>> **ON-SITE PROFESSIONAL LEARNING**

Corwin on-site PD is delivered through high-energy keynotes, practical workshops, and custom coaching services designed to support knowledge development and implementation.

corwin.com/pd

>>> **PROFESSIONAL DEVELOPMENT RESOURCE CENTER**

The PD Resource Center provides school and district PD facilitators with the tools and resources needed to deliver effective PD.

corwin.com/pdrc

ONLINE

>>> **ADVANCE**

Designed for K–12 teachers, Advance offers a range of online learning options that can qualify for graduate-level credit and apply toward license renewal.

corwin.com/advance

Contact a PD Advisor at (800) 831-6640 or visit www.corwin.com for more information